TERRORISM, CIVIL WAR, AND REVOLUTION

Revolution and International Politics, 3rd Edition

Peter Calvert

continuum

NEW YORK • LONDON

2010

The Continuum International Publishing Group
80 Maiden Lane, New York, NY 10038
The Tower Building, 11 York Road, London SE1 7NX

www.continuumbooks.com

Library of Congress Cataloging-in-Publication Data
Calvert, Peter.
Terrorism, civil war, and revolution : revolution and international politics / Peter Calvert. – 3rd ed.
    p. cm.
Rev. ed. of: Revolution and international politics : London : Pinter, 1996.
Includes bibliographical references and index.
ISBN-13: 978-1-4411-6784-2 (hardcover : alk. paper)
ISBN-10: 1-4411-6784-6 (hardcover : alk. paper)
ISBN-13: 978-1-4411-5364-7 (pbk. : alk. paper)
ISBN-10: 1-4411-5364-0 (pbk. : alk. paper) 1. Revolutions. 2. International relations. I. Title.

JC491.C235 2010
327.1–dc22

ISBN: 978-1-4411-6784-2 (HB)
        978-1-4411-5364-7 (PB)

Typeset by Newgen Imaging Systems Pvt Ltd, Chennai, India
Printed in the United States of America by Sheridan Books, Inc

Terrorism, Civil War, and Revolution

Contents

Preface

My original intention, to revise and update the second edition of my *Revolution and International Politics* (1996), changed because although the fear of revolution—of regime change through force—had declined after 1989, a fear of terrorism had instead taken over the domestic and international agenda after "9/11," with some strange consequences. Britain had lived, after all, with some level of terrorism for much of the preceding 40 years, and during that time the terrorists had received little in the way of discouragement from the United States. Yet despite a long series of atrocities and two separate assassination attempts on British prime ministers the basic structure of democratic politics and the rule of law remained intact.

On the other hand, "9/11" was seen in Britain, as in the United States, not just as the atrocity it was, but as an existential threat to our way of life, which it was not. The response was to some extent irrational. It began logically enough when a US-led coalition intervened in Afghanistan to try to close down al-Qaeda by removing their presumed backers, the Taliban. Before this was finished, however, the United States and the United Kingdom embarked on a war to overthrow the political regime of Iraq. Yet Iraq, before this intervention, was the only Arab country where al-Qaeda had no significant support—the only place they could operate was in the one area Saddam Hussein did not control. Soon Iraq had relapsed into civil war and the coalition forces were facing a major insurgency there. Meanwhile the leaders of al-Qaeda escaped and the Taliban regrouped in the borderlands between Afghanistan and Pakistan. Though at a high cost, a degree of peace has been achieved in Iraq; the whole of the Middle East has been destabilized. A dangerously unpredictable regime in Iran has been given a new lease of life. Afghanistan remains an ongoing nightmare.

Terrorism, civil war, and revolution, though in some ways related, present very different problems to the policy-maker, and require quite different strategies. Terrorism is unlikely to bring about regime change in either the United States or Britain. The reaction to terrorism, though, may constitute a greater threat to the way of life of Western political democracies.

CHAPTER ONE

Challenges to the State

Terrorism

Since "9/11" an exaggerated fear of *terrorism* and its possible effects has displaced communism as the specter stalking Europe, but more particularly the United States. Unfortunately, terrorism is an essentially contested concept; that is to say, a concept on which *by definition* there cannot be agreement. In fact one of the reasons why the concept of terrorism is so controversial is because it is often used by states to delegitimize its opponents, domestic or foreign, and at the same time offer a justification for the state's own use of terror against them.

In ancient Greek mythology, terror (Phobos) and dread (Deimos) were the names given to the two horses who drew the chariot of Ares (Mars), the god of war. *Terror*, as the distinction shows, is different from but linked to dread, or as we might prefer to say, fear. Terror is the systematic use of fear to achieve political ends, and fear, as the first modern political theorist pointed out, is an essential instrument of government. ". . . since some men love as they please but fear when the prince pleases, a wise prince should rely on what he controls, not on what he cannot control" (Machiavelli 1950, 98). At its widest it means any action which is intended to create fear or terror, but more particularly inflicting death or serious bodily harm on members of the public in order to achieve a political result. This includes the actions of governments. And the paradox is that today the use of terror is inextricably linked to the idea of using force to make people better, not worse. It is used in this sense by governments, when a minority finds that the people are unwilling to do as they are told, as both by the Jacobins in the French Revolution, and the Bolsheviks in Russia following the revolution of 1917. The French Revolutionary Terror was in fact a method of legitimating a minority government and justifying its continued existence. It was used in particular to enable Paris to colonize the provinces, by sending out revolutionary zealots to create a new centralized order.

The Terror of the French Revolution, moreover, is of crucial importance to the later development not only of the concept of terrorism but of the concept of revolution. The French Revolution has been, and probably still is, seen as the prototype of a great social revolution. It was seen as such by its contemporaries, and so by later theorists of revolution, notably by Karl Marx. But Marx and Engels ridiculed those who saw terror as a means of starting a revolution. And as a Marxist, Lenin also rejected terror or terrorism as a method of starting revolutions, though as a Russian he did see it as have a role in its actual execution. Once open resistance had begun, he made a deliberate decision to use force, not for the restraint or punishment of individual offenders, but simply to instill fear and hence obedience into the majority of the population.

Terror used in this way can be of two kinds: selective and indiscriminate. The use of force by government in the nineteenth century, however wholesale, was normally still selective, in that it was directed toward specific target groups and capable of being regulated in intensity according to the perceived needs of the situation. Yet it was widely accepted by those who wished to believe in governmental stability that only rebels against society made use of force to compel political obedience. When governments used indiscriminate force, as in Russia in 1905, it was taken as a sign not of strength but of weakness. Even then, despite the belief of the Bolsheviks that 1905 was in some sense a rehearsal for 1917, it was not a revolution in that it did not overthrow the government, nor did it bring about significant social or political change. Kalyvas argues that the longer a civil conflict continues, the more likely that indiscriminate violence will be superseded by selective violence (Kalyvas 2006) and this applies also to the use of terror by governments.

Terrorism, on the other hand, is the term given by governments to opponents who use violence against them. However, this too is an essentially contested concept. Ever since Aquinas, political philosophers have been prepared, in certain circumstances, to justify rebellion against a tyrant. The principal characteristic of a tyrant is that he rules solely in his own interest or those of a small clique. His actions are therefore unpredictable and hence they inspire fear. Classically, tyranny was seen as the opposite of freedom. The saying "One man's terrorist is another man's freedom fighter" has been repeated so often that its origins seem to have been lost. However, while accepting that confusion between the two is inevitable, this does not mean that we are exempted from having to make a moral judgment on individual terrorists or acts of terror. A lot depends on how the terrorist (or freedom fighter, or government) seeks to generate terror and whether it is selective or indiscriminate.

Richard English argues that terrorism is, at least for its proponents, a "subspecies of warfare" which is concerned with "the exerting and implementing of power, and the attempted redressing of power relations" (English

2009, 24). This is consistent with the view of Hannah Arendt that the difference between violent and nonviolent action was "that the former is exclusively bent on the destruction of the old and the latter chiefly concerned with the establishment of something new" (Arendt 1969). Terrorists like to think of themselves as soldiers in a higher cause, but they are not able to take on the armed forces of a modern government on equal terms, and so easily justify to themselves and others attacks on agents of government as acts of war. But all too often they come to believe that anything is allowable, since in a situation of necessarily imperfect knowledge, all who do not support them must be their enemies. Killing prominent people other than politicians (businessmen and the like) and setting off bombs in public places in Latin America in the 1970s were not in themselves intended to destroy the incumbent government, but to make it impossible for it to function effectively since its citizens had lost confidence in it. Violence thus became a mere tool in the process of psychological warfare.

Thus, though we must always distinguish between "terror" as a *technique* and "terrorism" as *a belief in the value of terror,* the two are in fact closely related, and as in Ireland, or Israel, the historical myths that the use of terror in earlier times had an ultimately desirable outcome in the form of national independence have led to the diffusion of the techniques of terror to such unlikely recipients as Hindus in India and both Hindus and Buddhists in Sri Lanka. Terror has ceased to be a feature only of the consolidation stage of revolutions, and has become associated with the actual gaining of power. At the same time it has continued to be used in the actual processes of government. In fact, it seems to have been assumed that its use by governments faced with revolutionary challenges is not only normal but also natural. In turn, the security apparatus has become entangled with government in what has become known as the "national security state." Today even a relatively weak government has a staggering potential for the use of violence and destruction, and it is not necessary for it to choose to use it, but only to fail to restrain those whose professional duty is to use it, especially the armed forces and the police. There are many degrees of selective terror, but the fact that it is all carefully directed and calculated does not make its impact any the less.

Fortunately, living in a state of constant fear is very exhausting. Hence the economy of force is like the credit of a bank, effective only until there is a run on the reserves and it becomes clear that there are not enough of them left. This is as true of terrorist movements as it is of anyone else. Terrorists cannot afford to assume that everyone else will accept their assurances that their actions are discriminate. The emphasis in Islam on the importance of the community of believers has enabled some Islamists to believe that if they kill non-Muslims (or even other Muslims) it does not matter as they themselves will be martyrs in a greater cause and those lives are therefore expendable. The true horror of "9/11" was that the instigators were prepared to use hundreds of aircraft passengers simply as ballast for their guided missiles. So, initially there was very little support even from other Muslims for the atrocity. However, horror can be a bad guide to action. The decision by the Bush administration to launch a "war on terror," compounded by the unfortunate slip of the tongue by which it was designated a "crusade," has undercut Western efforts to counter al-Qaeda and its allies ever since.

Insurgency

An *insurgency* in Politics and International Relations is any kind of armed uprising against an incumbent government. In Sociology, insurgency has been used much more generally to define dissension within any kind of organization over the way in which the organization is being directed. In the political sense, however, we normally mean by insurgency a form of armed insurrection, usually seen as being typical of poor, underdeveloped, rural areas (Desai and Eckstein 1990).

> An insurgency is an organized, armed political struggle whose goal may be the seizure of power through revolutionary takeover and replacement of the existing government. In some cases, however, an insurgency's goals may be more limited. For example, the insurgency may intend to break away from government control and establish an autonomous state within traditional ethnic or religious territorial bounds. The insurgency may also only intend to extract limited political concessions unattainable through less violent means. (United States, Department of the Army 1990, 2: 2–0)

Although many countries in the developing world are now heavily urbanized, the forces that gave rise to insurgencies in premodern times appear still to operate today, and among these are the pressures of population growth impacting on limited resources (Goldstone 1991, Foran 1997, Goodwin and Skocpol 1989). Long-running insurgencies have continued in Afghanistan, Algeria, Colombia, India, Iraq, Israel, Nepal, Philippines, Sri Lanka, Sudan, Thailand, among others. Few have a realistic expectation of achieving power, even where they seek secession from an existing state. However, a successful insurgency, involving the use of force, must necessarily result in a revolution; this may not just be a change of government but a change of regime.

The important thing we have to remember, however, is that those who take part in an insurgency do not all do so for the same reasons, but what they have in common is their weakness (Cramer 2006).

Kashmir: The Indian state of Jammu and Kashmir has been an arena of violence since 1989, when an insurgency composed primarily of disaffected local Kashmiri Muslims was effectively co-opted by Islamist militants to wage a jihad, or holy war, against secular India. The roots of the conflict, however, go back to 1947 and the partition of India, when Kashmir was expected to become part of Pakistan. However, its Hindu ruler hesitated, and while he did so, militant elements from Pakistan entered the territory in an effort to force his hand. Support from India was only available on condition that he decided in favor of accession to India, and Indian forces quickly cleared most of the disputed territory of insurgents. The UN Security Council then appealed to both countries to withdraw their forces and allow a referendum to take place to determine the future of the territory, but in the event this never happened. The territory remained divided along a long and inconvenient "line of control," and two further wars between India and Pakistan, in 1965 and 1999, have failed to bring a resolution.

Swat: In the last few years, ostensibly in reaction to US intervention in Afghanistan, militant groups have been attacking and killing civilians as well as the Pakistani security forces in the province of Swat, some 8 miles to the north of the capital Islamabad. Much of the province by the end of 2008 was effectively under militant control despite the presence of 20,000 Pakistani troops, and in some 60 villages, the militants had set up a de facto "parallel government" with Islamic courts imposing Sharia law. Meanwhile more than 800,000 civilians, according to some sources, had left the valley. Local opponents of the militants have been harshly critical of Pakistani civil society for its lack of concern for their plight as well as critical of the military and provincial government for their ineffective measures for controlling the tide of militancy. In fact, in February 2009 a pact aimed at ending violence in Swat, which effectively handed the militants control, had raised fears of a gradual Taliban takeover of more areas of the country. After pressure from the United States, at the beginning of May, the Pakistani government launched a fresh offensive, which was seen as a test of the government's commitment to face up to a growing Taliban insurgency and comes after it was accused of "abdicating" to the militants (ITV News, May 12, 2009).

The amount of violence associated with insurgency varies considerably. According to Weinstein, based on a comparative study of insurgencies in Uganda, Mozambique, and Peru, patterns of insurgent violence vary principally with the amount of difficulty the insurgent movement has encountered in getting its campaign launched. The most important factor is whether or not they have access to material resources. Where resources are abundant, groups try to gain control of them as quickly as possible, cutting short the long process of building up mass support. They are, therefore, much more likely to resort to terror as a technique (Weinstein 2006, 327–8).

In short, the factors that lead to the outbreak of an insurgency are not necessarily those that may enable it to continue to develop, either into civil war, or into a revolution (Collier, Hoeffler, and Sambanis 2005).

Civil War

Civil war is a state of conflict between organized groups seeking to gain or to retain control of a state. Its characteristics are that it involves rival centers of power, one of which seeks to supplant the other, and the sustained use of large-scale conventional forces. To be a civil war, moreover, the conflict must take place within the boundaries of a recognized state—the Irish Civil War of 1922–3 did not spread to the North (Kissane 2007, 3). The Spanish Civil War remains a major example (Durgan 2007).

Insurgencies, where external powers recognize the opposition as belligerents (whether or not they regard them as legitimate), become civil wars. There has been a sharp increase in the duration and number of civil wars in the world since 1945 and no significant decrease since the end of the Cold War. However, Mary Kaldor has noted that the post-Cold War Era has been characterized by a number of conflicts in which the opposition does not seem to have sought to control the state, which have nevertheless involved very high levels of violence often accompanied by massive violations of human rights (Kaldor 2001). Inevitably, casualties are high and there are estimated to have been more than 25 million deaths as a result of civil wars since 1945 (Hironaka 2005, 3). Kaldor argues that the international order needs to be restructured to take account of these changes.

Angola: Angola is an excellent example of how a civil conflict attracts support from outside. As a result, the conflict can easily escalate into a long-running civil war. Following the Portuguese Revolution of 1974, the three national liberation movements in Angola were unable to form a united front and a government that could command general acceptance. With support from the Portuguese Communist Party, as well as from Cuban forces supported by the Soviet Union, the Popular Movement for the Liberation of Angola (MPLA) gained effective control of the government. However, the National Union for the Total Independence of Angola (UNITA), allied with the relatively small but well armed National Front for the Liberation of Angola (FNLA), refused to accept this. Fearing a left-wing government on their borders, the apartheid government in South Africa channeled aid to UNITA, with clandestine support from the United States, which did not long remain a secret. As UNITA control spread across the south of the country, the movement gained support also from the United States and other western powers. It was not until 1991, when the Cuban forces were withdrawn, that a peace treaty was finally signed between the leaders of the two contending organizations, and it was not until 2002, when Jonas Savimbi, the leader of UNITA, was killed by government forces that the war finally came to an end.

Somalia: The origins of civil war in Somalia go back to the time of the dictator Mohammed Siad Barre, president of Somalia from 1969 to 1991. It was he who took advantage of the support he was receiving from the Soviet Union to launch a military offensive against Ethiopia in 1977, with the objective of annexing the Ogaden plateau region and creating a Greater Somalia. Ethiopia successfully beat off the incursions with the aid of Cuban troops because the Soviets withdrew their support for Barre's regime and backed that of nominally Marxist Ethiopia instead. The United States, aware of the importance of naval bases in the impoverished region, stepped in and poured funds into Somalia. However, Somalia's economy deteriorated as drought took hold in the region and the Ethiopians armed rebel clans again weakened Siad Barre. He assumed authoritarian powers, but gradually lost control over much of the country. In 1991, Mohammad Ali Mahdi assumed power, with General Mohammad Farah Aidid holding virtual control of the capital Mogadishu. The clans fought among one another but the majority of the people starved for want of water and food. An estimated 300,000 people died and 1.5 million were forced to flee and seek refuge in neighboring areas.

In response to the famine and human crisis, the UN sent a humanitarian mission and deployed a peacekeeping force in 1992. The heavily armed militias provoked clashes with UN troops and US troops initiated operations to capture Aidid and his lieutenants. But this went badly wrong, culminating in the murder of 18 US soldiers whose mutilated bodies were then paraded through the capital, Mogadishu—the incident which formed the basis for the movie *Black Hawk Down*. President Clinton ordered the withdrawal of US forces and the UN peacekeeping operation collapsed. Its remaining forces were forced to withdraw in 1995.

Since then, international efforts to construct a functioning government have continued. However, between 1998 and 2006 a number of areas formally withdrew from central government and little attention was paid to the nominal government of the country as a whole by the remainder. An unexpected result has been the recurrence of piracy in the Indian Ocean, making use of bases along the long Somali coastline, to raid and demand ransoms from the owners of cargo ships entering or leaving the Arabian Gulf (Burnett 2003, see also Chalk 1998).

Sri Lanka: Tamil insurgency in the North and East of Sri Lanka originated after independence, when the government of Prime Minister S.W.R.D Bandaraniake made Sinhala the sole official language and refused to accord equality to Tamil. Tamils make up about a fifth of the population of Sri Lanka, and those in the North (the so-called Sri Lankan Tamils) are the descendants of people who have lived there for centuries; at a stroke, they were placed at a serious disadvantage in relation to the majority of the population. So it was not inevitable that ethnicity would become the organizing principle of the conflict to come (see also Fearon and Laitin 2003, Goodwin 2008). In 1973, tensions exploded in a series of attacks on Tamils in the capital and elsewhere, following which the militants led by Vellupillai Prabakharan launched in May 1976 a guerrilla movement, the Liberation Tigers of Tamil Eelam (LTTE), popularly known as the "Tamil Tigers," dedicated to the goal of an independent state for Tamils.

In succeeding years, the conflict between the Tigers and government forces evolved into a state of civil war, neither side being able to defeat the other. The Tigers made at least three important tactical innovations which were greatly to enhance the bitterness of the conflict. All of them carried suicide capsules to prevent them falling into the hands of government forces, they made extensive use of women and children, and some even turned themselves into human bombs by detonating explosives concealed in their clothes. Victims of suicide bombers included Rajiv Gandhi, the prime minister of India, who had deployed an Indian Peace-Keeping Force (IPKF) in the island which he was soon requested to withdraw.

In 2002, with Norwegian mediation, the government agreed a ceasefire with the Tigers; this was supposed to lead to peace talks, but the Tigers withdrew from the talks in April 2003, despite the evident desire of Prime Minister Wickremasinghe to keep them going and the fact that in the meanwhile they effectively controlled some $15,000^2$ km of territory in the North and East. As a result the Winckramesinghe government was defeated in the elections in April 2004 and subsequently Mahinda Rajapaksa was elected president on a hard-line policy of no compromises. When the ceasefire broke down in 2006, the government forces launched an all-out attack on the Tigers. In May 2009, the last area under their control was cleared and their leader and some of his closest associates were killed.

Lebanon: Lebanon, which became independent under the auspices of the United Nations, was initially regarded as a success story. Unfortunately, its complex constitutional structure, the product of a sincere attempt to ensure democratic representation of both its large Maronite Christian and Muslim communities, did not protect it from the effects of various external powers to deny control of it to others. As a result, it was in a state of civil war from 1975 to 1990. The savagery of this conflict may be gauged from the fact that in 1992 it was estimated that 144,240 people had been killed; 197,506 wounded; 17,415 missing, presumed dead, since the war began. The casualty toll, largely civilian, featured for the first time the large-scale use of car bombs; 3,641 devices killing 4,386 people. Anything from 130,000 to 250,000 civilians died as a result of the fighting and more than a million were wounded. Beirut, previously the richest and most sophisticated city in the Middle East, was largely reduced to a rubble (*Time*, Monday, March 23, 1992).

The civil war was compounded by the intervention of both Syria and Israel (Dawisha 1980). Establishment of the State of Israel resulted in the displacement to Lebanon of over 100,000 refugees, making up some 10 percent of its increased population. After 1970, when it was evicted from Jordan, the Palestine Liberation Organization (PLO) established itself in Beirut and, supported by Syria, soon asserted a policy of waging war on Israel using Lebanon as a base. This, and the effect of Israeli reprisals, alienated the Christian community in the South of Lebanon and in 1975 open conflict broke out between the PLO and the Christian Phalange. With the situation wholly out of control of the national government, the president called in Syrian troops for support and in 1976 an Arab League summit in Riyadh, Saudi Arabia, brokered a peace agreement which authorized Syria to keep 40,000 troops in Lebanon to maintain order. This left the PLO largely in control of West Beirut and Southern Lebanon and Christians in control of East Beirut and Mount Lebanon.

In March 1978, following repeated PLO attacks, Israeli forces crossed the frontier and occupied most of Lebanon south of the Litani River. The UN Security Council called on them to withdraw and established the UN Interim Force in Lebanon (UNIFIL) as a peacekeeping force. Israeli force withdrew shortly afterwards, leaving behind, however, a so-called security zone some 19 km wide along the frontier, controlled by the South Lebanon Army, made up of both Christian and Shi'a Islamic militias. However, PLO attacks on Israel did not stop, and in June 1982 Israel again invaded Lebanon. Ostensibly, the purpose of Operation Peace in Gallilee was simply to establish an expanded buffer zone; in practice, Ariel Sharon, the main proponent of the invasion, ordered Israeli troops to advance as far as the southern suburbs of Beirut itself. The US government vetoed a Security Council resolution ordering Israel to withdraw. Intense fighting followed as Beirut was besieged from all sides. In it more than 20,000 people died, mainly civilians. Finally, in August 1982 a UN multinational force was landed to oversee the PLO withdrawal from Lebanon and the restoration of peace. On Sharon's initiative, however, Israeli forces allowed Phalangists to enter the PLO camps at Sabra and Shatila, where they proceeded to massacre many hundreds of refugees. The withdrawal of the multinational force was halted, therefore, and talks resumed, while a series of bomb attacks on the United States and other foreign interests resulted in the death of 63 at the US Embassy. Despite this, there was an agreement on May 17, 1983 by which both Israel and Syria were supposed to evacuate their forces. However, Syria refused to accept the agreement, and Israeli defense forces remained in the southern zone until 1990 (O'Ballance 1998, Picard 2002).

In October 1983, truck-bomb explosions cost the lives of 241 US service-men and 58 French servicemen. President Ronald Reagan reacted by with-drawing all US forces from the country. Several more years of conflict followed until the acting prime minister, the Christian General Michel Aoun, was decisively defeated, leading to a peace agreement, mediated by the Arab League, which left Lebanon effectively under the occupation of Syria (*Time*, Monday, March 23, 1992).

Some of the most savage conflicts in recent years, as in Liberia and Sierra Leone, have been in very poor countries, and Cramer argues that this results from entirely rational motives; given the scarcity of resources, violence seems to offer the only way out (Cramer 2006). Kalyvas argues that, paradoxically, the level of violence in civil wars is driven rather by the fact that there are invariably a large number of noncombatants who seek to avoid being drawn in, but at the same time are ready to take advantage of the situation to advance their own interests (Kalyvas 2006, see also Kalyvas 2001). Greed, therefore, cannot certainly be ruled out as a cause of civil wars (Collier and Hoeffler 2001).

The Fear of Revolution

"International politics" is here seen as comprising not only the formal relations between states, the main focus of the subdiscipline commonly known as "International Relations," but also all interactions across formally constituted state boundaries. It is the peculiar characteristic of revolution, as that term is commonly used today, that it not only affects the politics of individual states, but seeks to change those of others, and even to call into question the very nature of state boundaries and of the international system of which they have for so long been an essential part. Revolution is shaped by international politics (Skocpol 1979, Walt 1992) but it also tends in turn to reshape the international order (Falk 1969, Armstrong 1993, Halliday 1999, Katz 2000). Hence its importance.

Theorists of revolution tend to place the state at the center of their analysis. A revolution, after all, is at the least a contest between government and opposition for control of the state, so it would be surprising if they did not. Theda Skocpol, who defines the state as "a set of administrative, policing, and military organizations headed and more or less well coordinated by, an executive authority" (Skocpol 1979, 29), regards it as having a significant degree of autonomy within the social system over which it presides. Despite this, however, she sees the outcomes of revolution as being significantly, if not predominantly, influenced by the prevailing nature of the international system. This, in the present age, has two components: the international system of states and the world capitalist system. Each of these, in turn, she regards as in some degree independent of the other.

But what is revolution and why does it matter? Despite the intense interest that the subject has attracted in both scholarly and popular literature over the past 50 years, it remains curiously elusive. It is, indeed, also an "essentially contested concept," one on which agreement is, *by definition*, impossible. Yet, as Freeman argues (Freeman 1983), despite the deficiencies of leading theories of revolution, it remains a proper subject of social science research.

In a study of the concept of revolution (Calvert 1970a, see also Meisel 1934, Hatto 1949, Stone 1966, Goldstone 1980) the present author traced the history of the concept from its origin in the times of the Italian Renaissance. Then it meant a sudden **seizure** of state power or the forcible overthrow of a ruler. Today, this would be termed a coup, and that is the term that will be used here. But it is from these origins that the root meaning of the term "revolution" comes, and for this reason the idea of violence, real or threatened, is inseparable from it. Since the French Revolution of 1789, which had such a dramatic effect on the rest of the world (Klaits and Haltzel 1994), the word "revolution" has more specifically come to mean a major change in the political and socioeconomic structure of an individual state, brought about by the spontaneous efforts of its citizens, though these efforts may be aided from outside and may in turn act to bring about similar changes in other countries (see *inter alia* Johnson 1964, Moore 1969, Eisenstadt 1978, Skocpol 1979, Billington 1980, Smith 1983, Arjomand 1988, Dunn 1989, Greene 1990, Halliday 2006).

In short, revolution occurs when the use of force results in significant political change. There is no great mystery about revolution. It is not an immense driving force, a "locomotive" of history, and the basis for understanding it is to be found, not in the realms of speculation about the human condition, but in the day-to-day world of power politics and coalition-building. It is, quite simply, the politics of violence. In this book, therefore, I propose to make use of a broad definition of revolution which will comprehend a wide range of phenomena. What these have in common is the forcible overthrow of a government or regime.

For many social scientists, such an overthrow is not a revolution unless it is attended or followed directly by far-reaching social or economic transformation of the country concerned. Certainly, those who think of themselves as revolutionaries, and are members of revolutionary movements, have such goals in mind. For the student of politics, however, and more particularly for the practitioner of international relations, for whom this book is intended, the problem is that in the modern world there are still very many movements and individuals claiming the proud title of revolutionary, which are only so in an aspirational sense. Many of these will justify their seizure of power by the fact that they are revolutionaries, that they intend, that is to say, to carry out such profound transformations that their seizure of power is justified. Yet very few such transformations take place even now; there are very many failed revolutions (DeFronzo 2007, 18–22). The result is that the observer of revolution is presented with a unique conceptual problem: how is s/he to know what to study when, in effect, a revolution is defined not by its origins or events, but by its consequences?

The only possible approach which promises success, therefore, is to adopt a broad definition. The practitioner, even more than the scholar, will find it prudent to treat all such seizures of power or depositions of rulers as revolutions, until proved otherwise. But this approach has also positive benefits. It draws our attention to the great similarities that all such movements have with one another. It emphasizes the close relationship between, for example, social revolution on the one hand, and preemptive military coups on the other. It enables us to study problems on a small scale, such as diplomatic recognition and armed intervention, which in the scale of a major social transformation can lead, and have in the past led, to huge conflicts of global proportions. And which, as the Chinese and French resumptions of nuclear testing have made all too clear, cannot safely be permitted to do so in the future without running the risk of the total annihilation of humanity—an extreme form of what Marx termed "the common ruin of the contending parties."

The Analysis of Revolution

The original purpose of this book, therefore, was to explore the nature and possibility of revolution in the context of international politics, and, by doing so, to cast new light on the nature of international politics itself. With the passage of time, it has become more and more important to investigate the reasons for the extraordinary prevalence and duration of violence in the world which achieves nothing but which too often seems incapable of resolution. The continuing importance of the role of the state in international politics is nowhere more apparent than in the way governments use their power to maintain their control over them. Conversely, international aid and assistance is the most important factor determining the outcome of an insurgency.

What the student of international relations needs above all is to be able to assess the probability of any given kind of upheaval or sociopolitical change in a given area, and, next to that, to have a better idea of how to react to such changes when they occur. This investigation has shown how difficult it is to reach down into the human mind and to try to say which leaders will arise and what sort of support they will gather, but it also makes clear that once leaders and their movements have actually emerged, understanding what is likely to happen next can be at the least immensely helped, not only by possessing a record of information about how such movements and events have proceeded in the past, but in relating all such information by use of a comprehensive general theory. This is the task of social science. What then are the principal conclusions we can draw from this investigation?

We can see more clearly, to start with, how revolution has come to be seen as a politically desirable aspiration, and why its would-be practitioners have been so reluctant to accept the lessons of the past. In conjunction with others, they hope to escape from the restraints of "normal" politics, and to act politically without having at the same time to accept political restraints. Revolutionary politics is, however, normal politics in an unusual situation, as revolutionary leaders are leaders first and revolutionaries afterwards. To break the working rules under which the political system operates is a strategy which no referee exists to decree inadmissible. But it has its risks, the chief one of which seems to be the strong tendency for the sociopolitical order to return to its traditional style of operation, trapping the revolutionaries in the process of change that they have helped to set in motion.

If, as Forrest Colburn has argued, revolution is primarily a problem of poor countries (Colburn 1994, see also Henderson and Singer 2000, Foran 2005), then it seems likely to arrest rather than to promote their economic development. However, the evidence is not clear. First, among the 22 examples he cites, 2, Algeria and Iran, stand out for their relative prosperity; by World Bank standards, they are, unlike the others, "upper middle income" countries. Secondly, during the postwar period there have been two other very obvious examples of revolutions in "upper middle income" countries: Libya and Portugal. Had these been included, the thesis that revolutions are essentially a problem of very poor countries might have looked a lot less convincing. Portugal in the 1970s was by Western European standards, but it was noticeably better off than any country in Latin America and any country in Africa except Libya. It has certainly undergone profound social change since 1974. Thirdly, Colburn's thesis is in fact that poverty is *not* the cause of revolution in poor countries. He therefore rejects both modernization theory, for example, Huntington (1968) and Marxism as adequate theoretical explanations. To combine the two, as he sees Barrington Moore doing, is to remove all elements of voluntarism from revolution; in a memorable phrase he says that Moore's actors "get swept into their assigned places by inanimate social forces which act like giant brooms" (p. 12). Nor, though he praises her for her detailed study of revolutions and her novel conclusion that revolution increases both the power and the autonomy of the state, does he accept the arguments of Theda Skocpol. Her work is not wrong, he asserts, but it does not put the emphasis on the right factors.

For Colburn, it is ideas that matter. It has been the spread of an idea that has led to the choice of the revolutionary road in so many different parts of the world. Or, to put it more specifically, in all but one of the cases he discusses, "a fashionable political imagination" (p. 5), by which he means socialism. However, ideas are not the only causes of revolution, and the course of revolution is affected in each case by factors individual to the country concerned. At times, even Colburn seems to regard socialism only as a source of revolutionary rhetoric cloaking personal rule in a "progressive" cloak. The problem is that, significantly, he does not seem to differentiate between different traditions of socialism. Hence, like others on the right today, he seems to think that the collapse of Marxism-Leninism in Eastern Europe represents the failure of "socialism," and that this means that revolution there has run its course.

Nothing, of course, could be farther from the truth. As recent events in Eastern and East-Central Europe have made all too clear, socialism there was indeed mostly a myth and nationalism is still with us and is today as powerful an impulse toward revolution as it was in the nineteenth century. Nor is Iran an isolated exception; religion, too, has proved no less effective as an organizing principle for revolution in Afghanistan and Sudan. It has up to now been checked in Algeria only by the unconstitutional use of military force. Its future impact on former Soviet Central Asia remains one of the great imponderables.

In the meanwhile, both there and in much of the rest of the world, however, the fashionable political imagination has been focused on free-market capitalism (Kumar 1992). Capitalism may or may not be a good thing. However, one thing Marx was surely right about was its potential to disrupt the fundamental social institutions of family, kinship, peer-group, and community. Nowhere has this been more obviously true than in Russia since 1991. In the mid-1990s, with the collapse of communism still reverberating, capitalism in Russia looked all too likely to collapse before it could even be consolidated. A decade later we can see that a form of capitalism did survive, though one still dominated by the structures of the Soviet State. Not surprisingly, therefore, *nomenklatura* capitalism resembles the caricature of capitalism with which the majority of Russians grew up, rather than the actual structures of established capitalist economies.

We can see, secondly, why, although revolutionaries are many, revolutions in the generally accepted sense of the word are few. Most important from the point of view of international relations is the fact that major revolutions are not, it seems, autonomous and insulated from outside forces. Quite the reverse: the course of each of them has been fundamentally affected by external intervention. What constitutes intervention is certainly disputable. Marxist theorists have already called attention to the pressures of the world economy on the internal social order of individual states as a factor in revolution, and following the dependency theorists, some have seen the operation of the capitalist system itself as a sort of "economic intervention." Here, however, I have tried to show that more traditional interpretations of intervention, military and diplomatic, have their own very special role to play. Undoubtedly, both forms of intervention may on occasion be prompted by the desire to safeguard existing investment or trade links. If so, however, the political consequences of doing so cannot be escaped.

For, thirdly, it is in restraining the impulse to intervention that a state finds its best chance of avoiding revolution in a friendly state, and even of securing its long-term objectives at the cost of some minor and temporary inconveniences. Intervention does not stop revolutions, it helps to cause them. It does not even matter much whether or not the threat to a "revolutionary" state is real, what matters is that it is perceived as such. Hence, President Carter's attempt on April 24, 1980 to rescue the US hostages illegally held by the Iranian Revolutionary Guard, although in no way a danger to the survival of the Islamic revolutionary regime, was seen as such purely because of the power of the state mounting the operation. The result was the further radicalization of the revolution at a moment at which its internal contradictions might well have begun to set it on the course to political disintegration.

For a foreign policy-maker to conduct relations with a revolutionary regime bent on making life difficult for him or her, and so getting its own way, is never easy. It requires three things in all states: self-restraint, knowledge of the situation, and a certain amount of luck. But in the case of liberal democratic states a fourth factor must also be present: the support of the electorate. To achieve this for a policy of self-restraint is a very difficult task indeed. It is seldom a popular policy in itself, and it is always possible that populistic demagogues and sensationalist newspapers will force the hand of the government with their strident calls for violent solutions that will solve nothing and make matters worse. Nor can a government reasonably expect its supporters to be as well informed as it is itself. Hence, it is the duty of every citizen to try to understand that with the greater knowledge that is now available to us, compared with what was known in 1793 or 1918, we can indeed be confident that such a strategy is right. Indeed, we can go further and say that it is not only in our self-interests, but also in that of the world community as a whole, to which in the long term our own individual interests are all linked. The principal conclusion of this book, hence, is that citizens should in future expect and demand of their governments a policy of enlightened self-restraint.

In drawing this conclusion I do not, of course, ignore the evidence that in many cases revolutionary movements in individual countries have sought to ensure their survival in the world by propagating their ideas abroad and even by using subversion to try to secure governments friendly to themselves. What I have done is to point out that the actual overthrow of governments is a very different matter. Propaganda in itself cannot harm a government if the internal political and social conditions are not favorable for its reception. Indeed, the free exchange of ideas is a sign of vigorous social health. Appeals to would-be nationalist minorities, even, need not be too much of a problem for the stability of the country as a whole, always provided that the government avoids the temptation of being stampeded into a posture of repression. Even during the French Revolutionary Wars, it was not French ideas but French armies that installed the puppet governments.

Dealing with a revolutionary government, therefore, is something that can be done with safety if the government that is carrying out the negotiation is confident in the support of its own people. It will be much easier for it to keep that support if it is more widely realized that it is in the interests of even revolutionary states to keep to the forms and rules of international diplomacy. To them it may well seem outdated, a system that they did not devise and which they would prefer to destroy rather than to join. At one time this might have been possible. Today, though, the system has extended world-wide and even those nations that once most strongly objected to it as a relic of the past, such as the United States, France, the former Soviet Union, and China, have found that they must accept it, or have no alternative to the consequences of all-out confrontation.

As their cases show very clearly, there is nothing in the international sphere that a revolutionary state wants to have as badly as it wants recognition, and in the present-day world all sides have an interest in being the first to extend it and to gain the "friendship" of the new regime. Wise diplomats, therefore, will not try to drive hard bargains at this point, but instead, by judicious concessions to secure a state of affairs in which the new government sees clearly that it has much more to gain than to lose from negotiation. One need look no further than the history of the IMF loans in the 1970s to realize that as long as the negotiating process can be kept going, even the most powerful countries can be led to find that they are making concessions that they would previously have thought unimaginable, and discovering their interests as better preserved in the process.

For social science teaches above all that all historical analogies have their limitations outside which they are no longer valid. In the twentieth century, nationalism was certainly powerful, but in a form different from that of the nineteenth century; with the ending of decolonization, the forces it has generated must logically be subsiding. The use of internal military repression on a massive scale has certainly brought quiet to some countries for a brief period at a time, but here too populations have changed in their awareness owing to the spread of ideas and information, and the path of peace by ignorance is no longer a viable option, even if it were not in any case morally abhorrent. Most dangerous of all, in a world divided by superpower confrontation and overshadowed by the threat of nuclear extinction for the whole of humanity, would be for any substantial state to think that it could simply opt out of the world. The temptation in such circumstances for one or other of the superpowers to be drawn into a regional confrontation has repeatedly been demonstrated in Cuba, in Ethiopia and in the Gulf War, as well as for two political generations in the Middle East. It would be much better for them, and much safer for the world, if their leaders were to come to realize that neither revolution nor counterrevolution need affect their own vital interests unless they choose to have them do so. What they can change, in short, is both their perception of threat and their degree of confidence in what is really vital.

To study revolution, a framework for its analysis is essential. Much of the uncertainty about the definition of revolution can be eliminated once it is realized that it can be viewed in four different ways (Calvert 1970b).

First, revolution is a **process** by which people become disenchanted with the incumbent government, on which they focus their failure to attain their political demands.

Secondly, it is an **event** in which an existing government is overthrown and a new one established in its place.

Thirdly, it is a **program** of change instituted and carried through by the incoming government.

Lastly, it is a **myth**, describing the sequence of events in terms which serve to legitimize the actions of the incoming government and the program it has instituted.

The common factor here is the **event**, and it is therefore with the event we must begin. The fall of a government is the determining feature without which a revolution cannot be deemed to have taken place. It is not, however, the only feature of interest. Like all other historical events, revolutionary events (as they will here be termed, to distinguish them from the general phenomenon of revolution) are preceded by causes and followed by consequences. And all but the simplest events may be difficult to unravel in terms of their causes precisely because of the element of surprise that so often attends their onset. Yet it is certainly not true that such events are wholly spontaneous. The use of force to bring about political (and by extension social) change is something that, to be successful, demands an element of preparation, and if interesting consequences are to follow, then, after the event, the new government will have to consolidate its own hold on power.

Hence, to follow D.J. Goodspeed (1962), revolutions, coups etc. can be subdivided into three **stages: preparation, action,** and **consolidation**. This division is a meaningful way of looking at a military action, in so far as revolutions are military actions. Revolutions are, of course, in many other respects not military but political actions, but this does not invalidate the approach. After all, to take a parallel from nonviolent politics, one does not go into a general election without preparing for it, or, more accurately, if like the British Labour Party in 1983 one does go into a general election without preparing for it, then one does not win.

There are other parallels between violent and nonviolent politics, as one might expect. The event of the general election (the actual process of choice) is complete when the votes are counted, but the formation of a government is something that necessarily takes some time, and creation of a change in policy is something that one does not expect to be visible overnight. So, too, in revolutions one finds after the event a period of consolidation. This incorporates at least two major elements: actions taken by the government to ensure its **own** immediate survival, and, the introduction of a program of new policy or policies, designed to carry out the **objectives** of the revolutionary movement.

Preparation

First, revolutionaries must have, if they are to be successful, **clear and relevant** strategic objectives; **clear**, because obviously they have to know what they are doing, or in the case of anything going wrong they are in considerable personal danger; **relevant**, because if they do not seek an effective political target and destroy it, they are going to fail in their overall objective, and they are then going to be very much at risk.

Goodspeed gives the very interesting example of Dublin in 1916, where insurgents sought to liberate Ireland by capturing Dublin and by proclaiming the Irish Republic. They believed that this would be the central element in a vast nationwide uprising. Unfortunately, owing to internal doubts and dissensions they cancelled their plans for the nationwide uprising a week or two before the actual attempt. What happened therefore was a rising in Dublin itself. But Dublin was not, although the capital of Ireland, the actual center of power in Ireland, as Goodspeed is at pains to point out, and even holding political power in Dublin itself was not sufficient.

Secondly, in their seizure of Dublin, the revolutionaries made a major strategic blunder in that they failed to seize Dublin Castle which was the symbolic center of power. They believed that the Castle would be impregnable, though in fact such was the scarcity of military manpower in 1916 that only one elderly night-watchman was on duty at the time. Instead, they concentrated on the Post Office which, as the center of communications was very important, but as a military center was negligible.

So revolutionaries need accurate information. If they are going to form strategic objectives they have not only got to be clear about what they are going to do and to embark upon relevant objectives in military and political terms, they have to be accurate in their assessment of the situation. In the October Revolution in Russia in 1917, it was Lenin's awareness of the fact that the government was extremely weak that led him in the end to throw in his support with those who believed in the immediate seizure of power. Whereas many of his supporters were inclined on theoretical grounds to assume that the government was much stronger than it actually was, he correctly recognized that it was not, and therefore was prepared to revise his theoretical notions in the light of the actualities that confronted him.

Similarly, the French government of 1789—widely held to be the strongest in Europe—was in fact very weak, although its downfall resulted more from accident rather than from preplanning. The kind of spontaneous urban insurrection which was characteristic of the French Revolution has therefore never satisfactorily been repeated in any other country. The lack of plan, and the lack of organization, would not be practicable in the modern state that had the lessons of the French Revolution before it. In fact, even in France it has not been duplicated. But it has been duplicated elsewhere, notably in Iran.

To turn to the tactical level, the first objective is the "neutralization" of government, using the correct sense of the word "neutralize" to mean "to render the government ineffective." It is not necessary for a successful outcome to kill all, or perhaps any, of the members of the incumbent government, and in fact members of incumbent governments do show a startling capacity for survival under most circumstances. The reason is that people are politically effective only in as much as they actually play the role that is assigned to them or modify it in a way that will increase its effectiveness. In Russia in 1917, Kerensky and his government, although they held the title of ministers and they were carrying on the functions of ministers, were not in fact actually "connected up" to the rest of Russia in such a way that they could actually be effective rulers. Therefore, their overthrow did not require—or in fact involve—their physical destruction. More people were killed making Eisenstein's movie than died during the taking of the Winter Palace.

The reason why the individuals who comprise the government are not necessarily meaningful in any individual sense, and what matters is their role in relation to the governmental machine, is that the maintenance of the governmental machine involves the support of the police, of the military and (if separate) of the intelligence forces. Hence, major targets of all revolutionary actions include centers of communications, television and radio stations, means of transport, and generally the ways in which government can communicate with the supporting forces. These are precisely the targets which are selected first for attack by the military or by anyone else.

However, the seizure of political power, even in the twentieth "century of revolutions" (cf. Gross 1958) was not a straightforward business, even for the armed forces, who did it more often than anybody else. There is a real difficulty in selecting optimal targets, because, as noted above, a coup or revolution is not simply a military activity; it is also a political one. It is possible, for example, for a hostile force, an opposition, as any foreign power might, to disrupt the functioning of the state by the sabotage of communications. And some revolutionaries have been carried away therefore and come to believe that these kinds of acts of sabotage and sporadic terrorism can actually bring about political changes of major significance. What in practice tends to happen is exactly the reverse. Any attempt to do this kind of thing results in increased support for the government, and governmental leaders, even if first rank communications are disrupted, have at their disposal usually a substantial layer of second rank communications. The sabotage of a major central telephone exchange in the 1930s no doubt would have disrupted telephone communications almost completely. Today, with automatic exchanges, radio relays, and satellites this just is not practicable. Sabotage on this scale is no longer possible in the sophisticated modern state. It may still be meaningful in the more unsophisticated developing states. Where this is so, however, the second rank of communication is normally entirely in military hands anyway. Hence, the military can step in at any time, using their reserve communications systems, disrupt the official communications, outflank the government, and seize political power, should they have the wish to do so. It is an irony that a third level, the internet, originally developed in 1970 to provide the armed forces in the United States with a system of communication which could survive any attack, is now available not only to civilians, but, as the events in the State of Chiapas in Mexico in 1994 showed, also to insurgents. Hence it is just possible that the balance is now moving back again toward the public.

A distinction can be made, moreover, between symbolic and actual values in targets. The government may not hold any real power, like Kerensky's government in 1917, but it is not sufficient for revolutionaries to disregard it. The Winter Palace had to fall. Governments have a symbolic meaning and revolutionaries that seek to seize political power therefore have always had to accept that they cannot simply pretend that the government is not there and hope that it will go away. Nor conversely can they assume that their view of the real centers of political power in a country are shared by the inhabitants at large. Just as symbolic centers of power, there are symbolic gestures that have to be made. There are symbolic roles as well as actual roles that are to be played.

Next comes the question of contingency planning. All standard military theory assumes the existence of contingency planning, that a general can change his mind in the course of military operation. Ever since the Schlieffen Plan went into action in August 1914 and it proved impossible to reverse it once it was actually started, all military strategy has been much more acutely aware of the existence of a need for contingency planning, allowing for tactical changes in the strategic operation (Holsti 1967, 358–61).

But there are very different problems here for the revolutionary. Luttwak (1968), for example, assumes that leaders should not take part in a military coup, that they should be outside exercising a directing role and prepared to go to the radio station in time to make the appropriate broadcast announcing that they have taken over political power. This is all very well as theory but it does not fit the observed facts. It is extremely hard to believe that members of most military forces would be seen gallantly storming the barricades on behalf of a set of leaders who were not actually present. Goodspeed more accurately assesses the highly symbolic importance of leaders' actions in leading their forces. But at the same time he recognizes that to do this is to take them out of communication with the rest of their troops, that if a change of plan has to be made all kinds of disastrous consequences may follow. Unlike regular military operations, a revolution is not a legal activity; therefore, leaders cannot expect that if they are going into this sort of thing this can change their minds in the middle without some risk of disaster. Contingency planning may not be needed in well-planned military coups. Contrary to popular belief, there are far more military coups every year which fail than actually succeed. When newspapers print, for example, that Bolivia is a country which has had 185 military coups in the course of its century-and-a-half of independence, readers would be relieved if it were made clear that most of these military coups were unsuccessful.

First of all, the seizure of political power almost inevitably involves direct physical control of the capital area as such, or at least of the members of the government. It is impossible for a government to look convincing, unless it controls the national capital. It is the center of communications, the diplomatic center, and the focus of symbolic loyalties for the whole nation. There is practically an unwritten rule that unless it holds the capital a government is not properly the government of the country. But this, of course, in itself raises a question: what are the links between the seizure of political power in the capital and command in the provinces? So often we read of military coups that General X has seized the person of the president of the republic and sent him into exile, and now he, the commander in chief of the forces, has assumed political power, and wonder how is it that his authority is then going to pass in the outer provinces? He may have seized power in the capital, but how can this mean that he actually has political power in the country as a whole?

There are two possible answers to this and both seem to be true. First, there is a general assumption in most countries that the orders that have come from the government in the capital are to be followed in default of any others. This is easier to do if orders do not come from the capital very often anyway, for if citizens do not pay very much by way of taxes to the capital and do not get very much in return, then they have no particular incentive one way or another to worry very much about what happens in the capital. Coups, revolutions, and uprisings are accepted almost as a natural state of affairs.

An alternative explanation is that a bargain has already been struck with provincial leaders, who know which government they are going to support. Sometimes provincial leaders are involved in the bargains taking place before the event, but more often they seem to have arrived at while political power is actually being seized. There is a distinct difference here between the prepared military coup and the kind of uprising in which elements of the armed forces seize political power and then wait for provincial centers to agree or disagree with their decision.

The last question is links with the larger international system, with foreign support. All governments exist in an international environment and governments coming to power suddenly are not automatically recognized by the international community. Most countries, all other things being equal, recognize new governments on the grounds that they are effectively in control of the country. But often, there are considerable ideological reservations and recognition may be withheld or withdrawn. The government of General Pinochet in Chile, though fully in control of the state of Chile, was never recognized by the Soviet Union, and Britain withdrew recognition in 1975 because of the torture of a British subject.

Many governments, notably that of the United States from the time of Woodrow Wilson onwards, have tried to use the device of nonrecognition to try and force political bargains on other countries, especially in the case of Mexico and the Caribbean. By 1975, this had become so unpopular with many newly independent countries, that it had been widely denounced as unacceptable. Hence, it was only when there arose a really outrageous case like Chile or Greece under the Colonels that other powers could exercise that capacity for sanctimonious humbug which is so strong in human nature and express their disapproval by nonrecognition rather than by doing anything concrete. The converse can also be the case. The Provisional Government of Nicaragua was recognized by the United States in 1979, and retained that recognition throughout the time when the White House under Ronald Reagan was working hard to try to overthrow it. President Manuel Zelaya of Honduras tried in 2008 to alter the constitution and extend his term for another 4 years by holding a referendum. Troops seized him in his pajamas (he said) in the early hours of Sunday, June 28, 2009 and deported him to Costa Rica. The Army's move came after President Zelaya sacked its chief of the army, Gen Romeo Vasquez, for refusing to help him organize the referendum. Though President Hugo Chávez of Venezuela blamed the Americans for the intervention (despite having no special knowledge of events), it was immediately denounced by the US president, as well as by the Organization of American States (BBC News, "Honduran leader forced into exile," Sunday, June 28, 2009, online). But nothing happened. When Zelaya made a clandestine return to his country he ended up isolated in a small room in the Brazilian embassy listening to very loud pop music courtesy of the armed forces (Maisonnave 2009). This suggests that the foreign linkage is not particularly important in most cases from the point of view of actual survival, and this is because in most cases governments are overthrown by military movements and the military are, of course, already armed and prepared by their own governments.

In the case of a civilian movement, the question of foreign support becomes very much more important, especially in the case of guerrilla war, when there is an ambiguous moment at the moment of introduction of a guerrilla movement to a provincial area in which it probably has to rely on external support of some kind. However, this presents its own dangers, since it lays the movement open to being regarded as a foreign implant, as will be seen in the case of Che Guevara's expedition to Bolivia (Chapter Three).

Governments, on the other hand, have a perfect right to carry on negotiations with any foreign country they wish. If the government of Brazil, for example, feels that it is faced with the prospect of subversion, it is perfectly in order for it to go to the United States, and buy all the helicopters it likes for counterinsurgency work. It is a legitimate function of any established government to do this. It is therefore a recognized feature of the international system that it is "stacked" in favor of the incumbent governments.

Any attempt at negotiation with foreign powers by insurgents necessarily endangers the success of a revolutionary movement. Leakage of information is especially likely in a foreign capital, where people do not have the same interest in security that people at home have. On the other hand, foreign aid and intervention are of very great significance in the later stages of revolution, if a movement is stalled or where the effect of a change of power in an individual country crucially threatens the stability of the structure of contending alliances, and therefore these risks have to be taken.

Action

The reason that the coup, guerrilla warfare, and urban insurrection form the three main forms of revolutionary action stems from the fact, already mentioned above, that the centers of political power are focused on the government and on the national capital. The overthrow of a government can, therefore, be achieved by action on four distinct levels: the executive power holder, the government, the capital, or the province (Calvert 1967, 1970b). It does not, of course, follow that in any given instance any one of these forms is practicable.

The minimal case is that of an attack on the executive power holder, almost invariably in the form of political assassination. Many writers do not like to think of political assassination as a form of "revolution" because it is not a seizure of political power, but it is merely the removal of an incumbent government. But it has been studied (Leiden and Schmitt 1968, Kirkham et al. 1970) in the same context to which it is clearly related. In only one recent example, the attempted assassination of President Reagan in 1981, has an armed attack on a head of state or government had no discernible political motive. Hence, political assassination is meant to have a political outcome and it does tell us something about the strategy of political violence.

All the successful assassinations of American presidents were politically motivated. Each of the assassins appears to have had some kind of strong political motivation. John Wilkes Booth, for example, was pro-southerner and shot Lincoln out of a sense of revenge for the civil war; Garfield was shot by a disappointed office seeker and McKinley was shot down by an acknowledged anarchist who announced he was doing it for anarchist reasons. And it now seems clear that Kennedy was shot by someone who had sympathies with Cuba and who believed, it appears from his actions, that he had some kind of particular political role to play, though no one now knows what it was. Interestingly enough, all these people were shot in public, according to methods prevalent at the time. In fact, in Kennedy's case, the movie *The Manchurian Candidate* (John Frankenheimer 1962), which was originally released at the height of the Cuban Missile Crisis, involved the shooting of a prominent political figure in a public place by very much the same method which Oswald employed. The movie was showing near where Oswald lived and has rarely been shown since the assassination.

It has been well recognized since at least the time of Machiavelli (Machiavelli 1950) that, in the last analysis, it is not possible to defend a head of state or head of government against political assassination if the assassin is not backed by an organized movement, and there is practically no chance therefore of him giving away his intentions in advance. But in practice, self-betrayal is quite common, and the more so because most, if not all, successful assassinations of prominent political figures involve some collaboration within a group.

However, though it is certainly possible to shoot prominent members of governments in this kind of way, there are two problems. The assassin is unlikely to survive. If s/he does, it is unlikely that s/he can make any effective use of this fact because of their minimal political contact. Unless they are part of a wider conspiracy therefore the fact that assassinations are politically motivated actions is of only limited interest and any consequences are likely to be negative. In the latter part of the twentieth century, moreover, key politicians came increasingly to surround themselves with heavy security. However, all security has weaknesses, and its value is limited by the requirement, in a formally democratic age, to mingle with and speak to their supporters: Yitzhak Rabin, the only Israeli prime minister to be assassinated (so far) was killed by a fellow Israeli (November 1995).

There are two main types of coup, the barracks revolt (termed the *cuartelazo* in Latin America) and the *golpe*, or sudden seizure of power by force by some other group. Modern examples of barracks revolts include the unsuccessful attempt of Colonel Hugo Chávez to overthrow the government of Carlos Andrés Pérez in Venezuela in February 1992. Later the same year, while he was still in prison, a second attempt was made by some of his supporters. It, too, was unsuccessful. However, by 1998 public disgust with the government had grown so much that Chávez was elected president on a platform of cleaning up politics and bringing about a Bolivarian Revolution in which more of the country's considerable oil wealth would be distributed to the poor. In April 2002, a third coup overthrew him and installed a free market-oriented president of the Venezuela Chambers of Commerce, Pedro Carmona, who was given the immediate support of the US government. However, his overconfidence led Carmona within a few hours to dissolve both the National Assembly and the Supreme Court thus alienating almost everybody and precipitating a popular uprising in the capital. The presidential guard recaptured the Miraflores Palace without firing a shot and restored Chávez, who looked rather shaken by his experience. The targets of political violence tend to be much less keen on it than its promoters.

The *golpe* is a very quick seizure of power in which the question of political support is not much considered—it is regarded as being neutral. There are no prior bargains. It is also not a regular barracks revolt because it is not carried out by an officer of the hierarchy and is not a straightforward seizure of power by the military, or displacement of government, though it invariably seems to involve a soldier making use of his military connections in order to seize power and hence nowadays is relatively rare.

A good example was the deposition of President Momoh in Sierra Leone on April 30, 1992. A deputation of junior officers had on their own initiative come to Freetown to complain about the conduct of the war against rebels who had spilled across the frontier from the civil war in Liberia. They demanded better pay and improved conditions. Finding that the president was not at State House, they became angry and drove to his private residence, only to find that only a few minutes before he arrived he had been flown out to neighboring Guinea in his personal helicopter. The junior officers thereupon formed a 23-member National Provisional Ruling Council (NPRC) to run the country and appointed the coup leader, 27-year-old Captain Valentine Strasser, its chair and Head of State.

Even more opportunistic was the coup in Guinea in 2008. Following the death of President Lansana Conte, a junior officer, Captain Moussa Dadis Camara, declared that he had become president of the republic and head of the National Council for Democracy and Development (sic) (BBC News, Wednesday, December 24, 2008, online). He declared an overnight curfew. Within hours, however, crowds came out into the streets cheering and it was clear that the coup had a great deal of support, although condemned both by the regional organization, Ecowas, and the African Union.

Prior preparation is usually much more significant. Its absence can be disastrous. No one in 1961 in the United States seems to have seen the Bay of Pigs fiasco for what it was: a failed attempt to seize political power in Cuba. Considered in that light, it becomes clear that almost every conceivable mistake was made. If its instigators wanted to seize political power, they were especially foolish to announce to the Cubans that the expedition was on its way and they ought to arise against the dictatorship of Fidel Castro. He, as it happened, was still very popular. So the announcement merely served to destroy the advantage of surprise without bringing any other advantages. Other errors included choosing a landing area where the water was too deep, on the wrong side of an inlet so that the troops were unable to escape and regroup as Castro himself had been able to do in 1956 (Johnson 1965).

At the first sight, there does not perhaps seem to be much in common between these events and the great social revolutions, which are usually agreed to have been of major significance. But in practice the same analytical distinctions can be applied in those cases too. The difference is that they are formed, not of single events, but of a chain or sequence of events in which political power is transferred from one group to another. Naturally, such sequences display a considerable degree of continuity, and this often leads historians of the individual sequences to assume a degree of overall inevitability in the way events turned out.

It is precisely here that the comparative study of revolution comes into its own, for it enables us to compare such sequences, which did promote major socioeconomic changes, from many other sequences of changes in political power that did not. Such sequences, typically, fail to result in the classic polarization of opinion and the build up of increasingly radical coalitions favoring change. Instead, they display the characteristic pattern of alternating coups, frustrating the build up of a consistent coalition and leading to a political stalemate. Both accident and design played a part. With the hindsight of history, the modern historian can see Napoleon rising to power, knowing that the artillery officer of 1795, and the First Consul of 1799 will give way to the Emperor of 1804. But at the time it did not appear like that to the people who were actually watching events take place. In fact, the tendency to try to make rational patterns out of discrete events in this way, once they have happened, is a reaction to the psychological phenomenon known as "cognitive dissonance"—the uncomfortable feeling caused by trying to hold two clashing ideas simultaneously leading to an attempt over time to rationalize this by asserting one at the expense of the other. In extreme cases, true believers would continue to hold on to their beliefs regardless of any amount of new information, as in those who deny the reality of climate change.

The second point is that there were also some very sharp reversals even in these revolutions. One of the interesting things about them is that although even the mightiest social revolutions can be broken down into a series of coup-like events—short moments in which political power actually changed from one group to another—there is at the same time evidence of the difference between preplanning and luck. With the hindsight of history, the modern observer can see Napoleon rising to power, knowing that the artillery officer of 1795 and the First Consul of 1799 will give way to the Emperor of 1804. But at the time it did not appear like that to the people actually watching these events take place.

The attempt to overthrow Robespierre was virtually unplanned. His opponents acted on the spur of the moment to seize him for fear of their own lives. Had Robespierre not been disabled by a shot in the jaw, which rendered him incapable of speech, he might have retained political power and even strengthened his own position. The fall of the Directory in 1799, on the other hand, was very well planned, and without the direction of Lucien Bonaparte, president of the Council of the Five Hundred, the proclamation of his brother as First Consul might well not have happened. No blood was shed and the new order of things received general acclamation. Lucien was later rewarded by his brother for his efforts by being banished for marrying an American and went to live in the United States. A direct descendant sat in Theodore Roosevelt's Cabinet.

Certainly, when the Rump was dissolved in England in 1653 it was a well-prepared military operation, Cromwell having placed plenty of soldiers all round the House of Commons. But in 1659, when the military attempted to do the same thing again and tried to enforce their will upon Parliament, then it just did not work. Public support just was not there, as at least one Army leader realized. When General John Lambert in London declared against the Parliament, General George Monck in Scotland held his counsel until he had forced the dissolution of the Parliament. It was only when a new Parliament had been chosen and he was assured of support that he pronounced in favor of the monarchy. He was rewarded with the highest honors, including a Dukedom and a huge grant of land in North America, which eventually became North and South Carolina.

In other words, the same principles (or lack of them) can be applied to almost any situation. Once **sequences** have been broken down into their component **revolutionary events,** it is possible to see their common basis in the gathering of political support a its translation into military terms into a successful revolutionary event. For such an event to be successful it must have leadership, recruit support, have access to material facilities (e.g., weapons, transport), and have well-defined goals capable of being translated into action. Of these, leadership and recruitment will be discussed in detail in Chapter Four, and the question of material facilities, and the part foreign governments play in the provision of them, will form an important theme of later chapters.

Consolidation

Once political power has been seized, its holders face the problem of its consolidation. This is, ironically, the part of the revolutionary process most lacking in a theoretical framework, and yet it is the key to the relationship between the fact of political revolution and the aspiration to social change.

Once again it will be helpful to begin with the consolidation of the coup. When a coup has taken place there are then two major objectives for the coup promoters. First, there is what Goodspeed calls the pursuit stage, the eradication of serious opposition. This makes use of three principal devices—the establishment of martial law; the setting up of revolutionary tribunals to try the enemies of the State, and/or the establishment of a secret police organization, or the use of an existing police organization, to hunt down any potential political enemies.

Secondly, there comes mobilizing general support with or without the acquisition of legitimacy. The acquisition of legitimacy is very desirable but it is not always easy, and many governments have found that the best method is simply to constitute themselves as a provisional government and go on running the country. For as long as they are provisional there is always the hope that they may go away eventually.

Devices that are constantly used in all kinds of military coups for mobilizing general support include some or all the following. First, price and wage fixing. There is no question of fixing prices without wages or wages without prices—the army fix both, usually in their own favor. Secondly, there is the stabilization of the revolutionary forces themselves. If these were left unchanged, there would be—first of all—a problem with the existing regular military forces who are usually too strong to be wholly disarmed and too conservative to be taken over, and if it is a military coup, in any case, they will not allow themselves to be taken over, so the forces that have been mobilized for the purpose of taking over power must be stabilized; that is, either demobilized or incorporated into regular units. And the transfer of law and order to disciplined bodies, properly established police or militia forces is of great importance because as long as there is a purely ad hoc martial law, too many people will be terrified for the economic system to function properly.

Two further stages of legitimation follow. First comes internal legitimation by plebiscite or election or the calling of some kind of convention. Then (not necessarily last and certainly not the least important) comes external recognition—recognition by foreign powers.

Now from this it can be deduced that in the revolutionary situation proper—the consolidation of a "great revolution"—one can expect to find stages of evolution corresponding to these stages; certainly the first and second stage, possibly all three (but cf. Craig 1996). Talmon (1961, see also Israel Academy of Sciences and Humanities 1984) speaks of three stage of the evolution of the French Revolution; one is the stage of "popular enthusiasm," two is the stage of "Jacobin improvization," and the third is the period of "Babouviste crystallization." These phrases need a little more explanation for those not familiar with the history of the French Revolution.

"Popular enthusiasm" means spontaneous mass rising at the beginning—the storming of the Bastille. Then it is necessary to create some kind of more stable form of government and this is done by the setting up of the Committee of Public Safety, the Reign of Terror and so forth, which Talmon calls "Jacobin improvization." "Babouviste crystallization" reflects the crystalliz-ing of a revolutionary set of ideas into a social program in the aftermath of the Revolution. The Babouvistes, followers of the radical leader Gracchus Baboeuf, were the extreme left faction. Though suppressed by the Jacobins and ultimately by the Directory their ideas represent the fullest extent of the revolutionary claims of the period.

The development of popular participation in the French Revolution, as in the Russian Revolution, and in a number of the other great revolutions has been slow. The immediate aftermath of the revolution has been a period of provisional government marked by martial law, revolutionary tribunals and the establishment of a secret police, but not a phase of terror—yet. The immediate position is the setting up of a provisional government which is supposed to be more representative than its predecessor. The turning toward terror, however, is precipitated by two things—first, a consciousness of the internal forces acting against the revolution are stronger than were at first thought, and that this is contrary to the ideological predictions of the promoters of the revolution. And secondly, in all the "great" Terrors—the French Revolutionary terror, the Red/White Terrors in Russia there is also a combination of internal opposition with external attack or foreign threat. In the French Revolutionary case it can be dated to the assassination of Marat; in the case of the Russian Revolution to the attempted assassination of Lenin. Up to that time, such Terrors as there had been in Russia were principally White rather than Red (Calvert 1986, 33–4; see also O'Kane 1991). Brinton (1952) regards terror as resulting from a combination of traditional violence; civilian militarism, that is, the desire of the civilians to subordinate themselves to a truly efficient government with military overtones; the inefficiency of the extremist government itself; an acute economic crisis complicated by class struggle; and religious hysteria.

So the first stage after the change of government is a limited degree of consolidation, the eradication of serious opposition, followed, in this particular case, by terror. And terror is followed, in turn, by Thermidor, of a period/relaxation; decline of persecution, the collapse of moral sanctions, the restoration of government on the old form and the end of plebiscitary democracy. Psychologically this would be the understandable consequence of the effects of being "forced to be free."

Some of these phenomena are extremely interesting, for example, the socially beneficial consequences of price and wage fixing which was one of the elements in the French Revolution. There were also adverse ones from the creation of a new currency by the issue of assignats (effectively paper money), the difficulties of inflation, and so forth, being met by governmental action really for the first time in modern history. These are then followed by a number of much more widespread social changes in the French Revolutionary situation—the same thing happens again in Russia.

Most striking is the destruction and recreation of the national community and of the family of which it is a derivative. The execution of the monarch, destruction of the aristocracy and elimination of the church as a force in politics combine to destroy the "national family," the hierarchical structure of government. The sweeping away of religious and legal sanctions on morals in both cases accompanies the process, atomizing the family and giving the State a direct relationship to the individual. Here too there could be contradictions; in the early days of the Soviet Union the formal rise in the status of women was accompanied by permissive legislation on marriage, divorce, and abortion but not by a lasting gain in full political equality.

In fact, by 1934 the Stalin regime was enacting a new puritanism which in many respects echoed the similar reaction of the Napoleonic period in France. Such a reaction is of course not confined to revolutionary situations. In England, for example, the Victorian period embodied a clear middle-class reaction against the libertarian aristocratic values of the Regency period, and Pitrim Sorokin, among sociologists, has sought to relate all the major political events of war and revolution to an underlying oscillation in history between the "ideational" and the "sensate" society (Sorokin 1937). But the significance of it must be seen in a deliberate attempt to return to the old ways, by stabilizing the structure of the family to restabilize that of the political community as a whole, and, inevitably, to reintroduce the concept of hierarchy, in the Russian case most dramatically shown by the reintroduction of uniform for state employees.

The sharper the reaction, however, the greater the likelihood of despotism. Brinton (1952) believes that Russian despotism owes more to Asia than to reaction, but Napoleon cannot be explained away in this fashion. The fact is that in this case as in others, it is clear that the prerevolutionary state has most in common with the postrevolutionary state. The ultimate postrevolutionary state is remarkably like the prerevolutionary state except that there is a considerable amount of social engineering in between. Secondly, that the great revolutions are rare, precisely because the exact combination of internal civil war, with foreign intervention without a precise military conclusion resulting is exceedingly rare.

Normally one or other of other possible scenarios may be expected to occur instead: that the military intervention is successful; that it is completely repulsed, or that the internal civil war is resolved, one way or the other. And in modern times, the thing that is noticeable is that most violent changes of power are taking less and less time, and as they get shorter and shorter, then the chances of external intervention get smaller and smaller. It may even be that the great powers have become wise to the fact that there is one aspect of the revolutionary situation they could control, and that is they can always stay out of it. Looking at what politicians are capable of on subjects they are alleged to know something about, like economics, one can understand why they cannot be expected to know much about revolutions.

Conclusion

What the value of the Terror might be is much less clear. It is far from clear that it helped French society one whit, to slaughter its aristocrats. It does not seem that the massacres in Russia or in Indonesia have done anyone any good. What is really curious is that they should happen at all . . . this extraordinary facility that human beings have for killing huge numbers of their own species. It has been suggested that this is a fact that directly relates to the nature of political power. Elias Canetti, in *Crowds and Power* (1973) says that the ultimate experience of political power is to stand looking at a field of dead people. The situation is vividly described by Gabriel García Márquez in *One Hundred Years of Solitude* (1978). Whether the power of the situation derives from some kind of perversion or misapplication of the hunting instinct or not Canetti does not consider.

But he does point out that there is a very interesting symbolism associated with prostration before the ruler, for example: the elevation of the ruler in relation to those around him, but most of all, most desirably, where and in many primitive cultures the fact of rulership is associated with complete prostration, with people lying down. And that this kind of utter subjection of one's enemy, feeds the appetite to power, very drastically. Once the ruler actually sees the bodies lying around the place, it is a short step indeed to megalomania. The anthropological evidence that power is very directly related to the idea of large-scale massacres is too alarmingly like the Russian Revolution and the French Revolution for us to ignore it altogether. It is even more true of the Iranian Revolution of 1979. The fear of revolution is the fear of the crowd (see also McClelland 1989).

Revolutions may, therefore, consist of single revolutionary events or of sequences of such events. By examining each in turn, the observer can identify the process of change in each case. Key moments in the preparation, action phase, and consolidation of revolutions involve international action. Such action includes possible support by foreign powers for the promoters, diplomatic or even military intervention during the action phase, recognition or nonrecognition of the new government and support for, or hostility to, the program of change ensuing. The international environment shapes events in other ways too. In prime place stands the globalization of communications. The reporting of events can in itself shape future events and governments find it much harder to control the foreign media than their own.

CHAPTER TWO

Use of Force in the International System

The traditional view of international relations was that it was concerned primarily with the formal relations between the legal entities known as states. The state itself, as the legally constituted expression of the political community, had both the authority, and, if it could command it, the power to ensure its will was obeyed within its own borders. What determined the relations between states, however, was a matter of some controversy. Legally, each state was characterized by three attributes: sovereignty, territorial integrity, and legal equality. In practice, governments intervened constantly in the affairs of their neighbors, the map of Europe was redrawn after each major war in accord with the wishes of the victors, and weaker states might lose huge tracts of territory to stronger ones (Luxembourg) or even disappear altogether (Poland).

Before the emergence of the modern European state system it had been assumed that behind every actual system of state law lay divine law or "natural law." This view was most comprehensively rejected by Thomas Hobbes, whose pessimistic view of man in the state of nature was shared by many observers of the international state system, who saw the relations between states as being essentially ungoverned and ungovernable. The older view survived, to be restated in more modern terms by Immanuel Kant, who held that there were in fact universal moral imperatives governing human behavior even in the absence of governmental sanction. His tract *Perpetual Peace* was the first important work on international relations written by a philosopher rather than by a diplomat or an international lawyer. His view was not, however, acceptable to the practitioners of international relations, on the grounds that they could not make bargains with people when they had no assurance that they would be kept.

Consequently, what has come to be the dominant view of international relations in the modern world is what may be termed the Grotian view, after Hugo Grotius, perhaps the best known of a number of writers on international law in the seventeenth century. Grotius established the view that international society was neither anarchy nor an idealized political community, but a structure of self-interested agreements. Under this view, the breach of any agreement threatened the credibility of the structure of the whole; it was therefore in the common interest of the contending parties to maintain the whole to ensure the effectiveness of any bargain, even if that bargain was not seen as being immediately and directly in one's own interests at that particular moment.

The international community is, therefore, in the words of Hedley Bull, an "anarchical society"—a society or community which is at one and the same time different from national communities in the weakness of its formal rules and the difficulty of enforcing them. It may be worth noting, however, that in the past some national communities survived for long periods unaltered in such a condition, and indeed that the development of strong national governments certain of being able to enforce their wishes in the vast majority of cases is a relatively recent historical phenomenon. Furthermore, since the beginning of the twentieth century an important qualitative change has come over the system, contemporaneously with the extension of the European system to the entire world. For the first time in human history an elaborate network of organizations has been developed to avoid, rather than to resolve international differences. Of these, the most important, as well as the best known, is the United Nations Organization.

The United Nations is not a world government. It has no forces at its disposal to enforce its decisions, and such forces as have been raised for special purposes in localized areas (Cyprus, the Gaza Strip) depend for their continued existence on the resolutions of the member states and, even more importantly, on the willingness of the richer powers to pay for their maintenance. The United Nations, unlike a national government, has no taxing power of its own. Worst of all, although its very existence is supposed to represent the rejection of force in the settlement of disputes between nations, the Charter does in fact specifically legitimate the use of force in "self-defense" (Article 51) as well as in pursuance of a decision made collectively, and so legitimizes a state in frustrating the purposes for which the organization was set up. It is only fair to say that this provision of the Charter was part of the necessary process of political bargaining by which the organization was set up, and the authority it confers is supposed only to last until a meeting of the Security Council can be held. However, in practice it has been extended. It is undoubtedly much better to have the organization with this weakness than not to have it at all, but it would be better not to have it.

The Charter, therefore, in some respects consolidates and in others modifies the structure of international relations as it had grown up in the

3 centuries since 1648. What it did not do was to supersede it entirely. States continued to be legally sovereign, as witness the provisions that the United Nations could not intervene in their internal affairs. Any violation of their territorial integrity continued to be regarded as a legitimate pretext for the use of force even if that violation was merely technical. The smaller states, which increasingly came to dominate the proceedings of the General Assembly after 1960, tried to have their legal equality taken seriously but were not successful. In fact they became more unequal, and the more unequal they became, the more hostility came to be polarized between the wealthy and developed "North" and the poor and underdeveloped "South," adding new and dangerous grounds for conflict to those that already had developed between the East and West camps of the Cold War period in which the United Nations had taken shape.

The fundamental thing about the use of force in the international system of today, therefore, is that it is almost universally regarded as legitimate. It is legitimate, moreover, not just for the world community as a whole but for each and every one of the national actors concerned. There is, in consequence, a considerable range of ways in which states and other actors use force within the international order in pursuit of their individual objectives, notably demonstrations of force, military aid, military intervention, and war.

Demonstrations of Force

The first requirement for the use of force in international relations is that states maintain armed forces; in fact, maintaining armed forces is what states do and war is what justifies their existence. Almost all modern states maintain armed forces of some sort, the few exceptions being Andorra, Costa Rica, Dominica, Grenada, Haiti, the Holy See, Kiribati, Liechtenstein, Marshall Islands, Mauritius, Micronesia, Nauru, Palau, St. Lucia, St. Vincent and the Grenadines, Samoa, Solomon Islands, and Tuvalu. Only four of these have land frontiers with another state. Iceland, Monaco and Panama have only nominal military forces.

Symbolism must not be discounted, however, (as in the case of the Holy See's Swiss Guard, which is not a military force), since it is precisely in the symbolic evidence of the ability to defend themselves against foreign attack that most states see their best protection. In the past, the symbolic demonstration was enough, in that military threats could only be made effective through mobilization, and that in itself gave sufficient time to mobilize in return. Conversely, the deployment of forces by a larger power, or the actual implementation of a mobilization plan, might be sufficient in itself to bring about a desired change of policy in a neighboring state. Thus, in 1907, President Theodore Roosevelt sent the American fleet on a world cruise to avert the escalation of conflict with Japan. But in 1914 Austria mobilized with the ostensible purpose of bringing about a change of policy in Serbia, though actually with the intention of invading it and ending the threat it presented to the multinational Habsburg State by actual subjugation of the Serbs.

There are numerous examples of cases where the mobilization or deployment of forces by great powers have in themselves been sufficient to affect the course of civil conflict. In 1903, United States warships were deployed to make clear to Colombia that the United States was prepared to defend the independence of secessionist Panama. In 1910 United States warships were again deployed to promote a change of government in Nicaragua, an event well remembered in that country when in 1983 the United States government under President Reagan carried out large-scale maneuvers in Honduras at a time when it was already supporting attacks by counterrevolutionary forces based in Honduras against the Sandinista government of Nicaragua.

Technically, neither mobilization of forces nor the conduct of military maneuvers infringes international law, unless the state concerned is party to a treaty or agreement specifically forbidding such actions in the area where they are being conducted. Such treaties demilitarizing specific zones for specific purposes have a long history, and were of particular importance in the regulation of international waterways such as the Dardanelles, the Black Sea, and the Baltic Sea, and in establishing the international consensus on the neutrality of Switzerland, Belgium, Finland, and Austria (1955). The acute state of permanent readiness of the modern superpowers, however, made the question of indirect threats of this kind a much more difficult one to assess, and the problem was compounded by the extensive evidence of clandestine involvement by both the superpowers in domestic conflict in a number of countries.

Hence, today "demonstrations of force" can be achieved in the most indirect fashion by cryptic references to this state of permanent readiness incorporated in politicians' speeches. Since the foundation of the state of Israel, its prime ministers have made regular use of such references to the preparedness of its armed forces, though in 1973 the awareness of them was not sufficient to avert an Egyptian attack. It is also a game that two can play, as President Ahmadinejad of Iran has sought to do, by test-launching rockets which are capable of hitting a wide range of targets in the Middle East and southern Europe.

It is scarcely surprising, therefore, that an extensive mythology grew up on both sides about the actual involvement of the rival superpower in a wide range of political events where such involvement has not subsequently been proved. Examples of this are the United States' charges of Soviet involvement in events in the Dominican Republic in 1965, and Soviet charges of United States involvement in events in Afghanistan in 1979, both of which, if true, were trivial.

Sea and Air Power in Domestic Conflict

In Chile in 1891, congressional forces, supported by the Navy, successfully defeated the Army which had taken the presidential side. However, in modern times, navies have only occasionally played a key role in internal warfare. Lessons can however be learned from various cases, in conventional warfare, where the ability to project force significantly altered the outcome of conflict. The United States was able to use its base on Diego Garcia in the Indian Ocean to increase substantially the amount of force it was able to bring to bear on Iraq in both the Gulf War of 1991 (Operation Desert Storm) and the Iraq War of 2003 (Operation Iraqi Freedom)

British naval power was important in countering communist insurgency in Malaya (peninsular Malaysia). Naval patrols were highly effective in limiting the possibility of resupply to the insurgents by sea and no successful case is known. Less significant was the use of shallow-draught river patrol craft to bombard suspected bases in coastal regions, thus driving them further inland (Short 1974, 371–2). The inability to do this effectively in the very different conditions of Mozambique was one of the reasons for the length of the guerrilla campaign there against the Portuguese. Nor were US naval forces particularly effective in securing control of the Mekong Delta, not through any defect in their swift boats and hovercraft, but because when they withdrew the guerrillas quietly reoccupied any territory they had lost.

Naval forces may, however, play an important role in establishing a second front, and diverting pressure from the principal objective. During the Russian campaign to detach South Ossetia from Georgia in 2008 the Russian fleet in the Black Sea was used in this way against the Georgian navy.

Sea power does not always have to be used to secure a useful political point and so change the balance of power. China is building up a formidable naval presence to enforce its hegemony in the South China Sea in face of rival claims to economic zones. However, at the same time, this enables it to increase pressure on Taiwan, which it regards as an integral part of its national territory.

Most modern governments have at least some air capability, placing insurgent movements at an immediate disadvantage. Given the power of the weapons used, however, the use of air power in domestic conflict is fraught with difficulties, as despite all the claims that are made that force is being employed only in a discriminating manner, large numbers of civilian casualties continue to show that this is not good enough.

The first military use of air power, in this case a balloon, in warfare seems to have been at the battle of Fleurus in France in 1794. The inability to generate easily sufficient quantities of hydrogen seems to have put an end to their further use for the time being. However, with better technical support, balloons were successfully used for observation purposes by the Union side during the American Civil War, starting in 1861, though the difficulties of construction and maintenance remained considerable and by 1863 the experiment had been abandoned. Balloons were used by the British Royal Engineers for observation purposes in both Bechuanaland (now Botswana) and the Sudan in the 1870s and 1880s, and a permanent section formed in 1890 (Royal Engineers Museum, www.remuseum.org.uk/corpshistory/rem_corps_part8.htm#equip accessed October 8, 2009). Observation balloons were much in use by both sides in the Great War, and German forces in occupied Belgium used Zeppelins (a form of rigid dirigible) to drop bombs on Britain; they killed 557 people in 159 attacks, ending only in August 1918, 2 months before the Armistice.

The first known use of aircraft in civil war was in Mexico in 1914, when Constitutionalist aircraft dropped bombs on Federal ships off Topolobampo. They had, however, already been used the previous year in the Second Balkan War and were soon to be employed extensively in the Great War. Following the War, aircraft were employed by Britain to suppress what they saw as insurgency in the Mandate territory of Iraq. But the 1920 rebellion convinced several observers that aircraft could not replace ground troops as the main imperial police force in Iraq. Haldane acknowledged that aeroplanes had proved of great value during the revolt for reconnaissance, close support, pursuit, rapid communication, and demonstration; but he denied that aircraft alone could force the submission of tribes who were committed to rebellion. [Civil Commissioner] Arnold Wilson believed that the main cause of the revolt was the perceived military weakness of the imperial forces after the reduction of the garrison: "to kick a man when he is down is the most popular pastime in the East, sanctioned by centuries of precept and practice." He also suggested however, that the "use of aeroplanes against recalcitrants" had created deep currents of resentment which had surfaced in rebellion (Omissi 1990).

The use of aerial bombing in the Spanish Civil War was to rouse Europeans to the transformation of military strategy they represented, creating widespread pessimism and great fear, while international arms dealers successfully frustrated the attempts of the Republicans to obtain munitions at reasonable cost (Howson 1998). From the beginning of the Second World War, therefore, it was expected that strategic bombing would be used by both sides against military and defense targets. However, after the destruction of Coventry by "carpet" bombing early in the war, Britain retaliated and by the end of the war, with increased bomb weights, the Allies unintentionally killed tens of thousands of civilians in the course of reducing Hamburg and Dresden to rubble. With the atomic bomb, it was of course impossible to discriminate between the military and civilians.

However, air power proved much less effective in counterinsurgency. US bombing of Vietnam proved futile in the attempt to cut off the Ho Chi Minh Trail by which the insurgents in South Vietnam were sustained and resupplied from the North. The extension in 1970 of the bombing campaign to Cambodia proved disastrous, since it brought hitherto neutral Cambodia into the war, and by 1975 the pro-American government had been driven out.

By 2001, the use of helicopters to maximize the effectiveness of ground troops, in civil as in international war, had become a standard practice. They were the key to the rapid advance of US troops in the initial invasion of Iraq. In the very different terrain of Afghanistan, however, they proved much less effective. A worrying development has been the improvement of guided missiles including the very small aerial vehicles known as drones, which are employed, among other things, to assassinate political opponents (usually along with their families, which does not win friends). Guided missiles in Iraq proved much less reliable than expected, and very much more expensive, while the extension of the use of drones to Pakistan has seriously alienated opinion in that strategically important country.

Military Aid

Military aid to allies and client states is exceedingly ancient, and was incorporated naturally in the structure of the modern world system through its extensive practice in Europe before 1815 and in the construction of the European world empires. Thus, military aid to the princely states formed an important part of the strategy of the construction of the British Indian Empire, and a deal between France and Norodom (1860–1904) of Cambodia saved that country from partition but facilitated French penetration of Indo-China.

Aid, whether in the form of arms or their cash equivalent, is a perfectly legitimate transaction in international law where it involves support for an established government recognized by the international community. In such circumstances it can be, and is, carried on perfectly openly, and in no way constitutes an interference by the donor state in the internal affairs of the country concerned. However, it may have consequences for the recipient state that an impartial observer might regard as extremely unfortunate, if not disastrous. United States military aid to the last Shah of Iran, Reza Pahlevi (1941–79) strengthened his increasingly dictatorial rule against his political opponents and fostered an uncontrolled desire for ever greater military expenditure. It played a major role in consolidating the opposition coalition that brought about the fall of the Shah in the Iranian Revolution of 1979 (Halliday 1979, Arjomand 1988, Farhi 1988, see also Foran and Goodwin 1993).

Thus, it was counterproductive in that the Revolution itself resulted in a partial "reversal of alliances" on the part of the new regime. Not only did it reject the influence of US capitalism (Skocpol 1982), but became increasingly committed to changing the international order that made that influence possible (Christopher 1985, Ramazani 1986, Chan and Williams 1994). The effects, unfortunately, have been far more far-reaching. To understand them fully, one must be aware that the population of Iraq, like Iran, is mainly Shi'a, and that some of the most important Shi'a holy places are in Iraq, not in Iran. When, therefore, the secular regime of Saddam Hussein, with US military aid, launched an all-out war against Iran, it immediately became a test which the new order could not lose. But when after 8 years of bitter conflict Saddam Hussein was forced to agree to peace terms, he not only sought to represent it as a victory, but went on to try to recover some of his losses by invading oil-rich Kuwait, on a spurious claim he had in fact previously formally abandoned.

The Iraqis were successfully ejected from Kuwait, but Saddam Hussein remained in power, and remained a check on Iran. However, this unstable situation was totally disrupted by the decision of George W. Bush to invade and occupy Iraq, so that on both secular and religious grounds the "Great Satan," the United States, became the principal antagonist of the Iranian regime. It is hardly surprising, therefore, that Iran has become an important arms supplier both to Hamas in the Occupied Territories and to Hezbollah in Lebanon.

Soviet military aid to the Cuban revolutionary government created a similar reversal of alliances, but involved it ultimately in a long-term open-ended commitment that proved exceedingly expensive and had to be abandoned even before the collapse of the Soviet Union itself. The deployment of Cuban forces in 1975 in Angola and Ethiopia, though perhaps beneficial to the Soviet Union in strategic terms, and certainly valuable in the sense of testing weapons in real combat conditions, has contributed to the militarization of the Cuban government and the distortion of the Cuban economy which a prolonged military commitment involves. Soviet military aid to the governments of Eastern Europe, and the structure of alliance based on it, resulted in the fear of revolution that led to Soviet intervention in Czechoslovakia in 1968 and the enunciation of the Brezhnev Doctrine, by which the Soviet Union was committed to the maintenance of socialist governments and maintaining the fiction of the irreversibility of Soviet-inspired revolutionary change.

Military Intervention

Military intervention can, therefore, be of two kinds; either by "invitation" in support of an incumbent regime, which is generally acceptable under international law, or to give support in the most definite and uncompromising fashion possible to an opposition movement, which, though sanctioned in certain instances (e.g., Palestine, Namibia) by resolutions of the United Nations, cannot yet be said to be generally acceptable under international law.

The relationship between military aid and intervention, on the one hand, and between military intervention and other sorts of intervention, on the other, is a complex one. This topic is therefore dealt with in more detail in Chapter Five.

Military intervention in revolutionary incidents or events has historically often been the trigger for a general war, and such wars have been particularly characteristic of the periods of the so-called great social revolutions (Pettee 1938). Thus, the English Civil War was followed by wars between England and foreign-backed forces in Ireland, as well as with Scotland, the Dutch Republic, and Spain. The French Revolutionary Wars (1793–1803) resulted from the intervention of the other European powers (the Netherlands, Britain, Austria, Prussia, and Spain) in support of the monarchists. The Allied intervention in Russia in 1919–20 in support of the White forces contributed powerfully to the radicalization of the Revolution, and stimulated, rather than allayed, the desire of its leaders to win friends by propagating revolution in Europe and the Far East. And US intervention to oust the Soviet-backed secular regime from Afghanistan led after their withdrawal to the conquest of the country by the Taliban and the accompanying Islamist counterrevolution.

War

In fact, each of these movements owed its origins, at least in part, to the defeat in war of the prerevolutionary government. For war is a distinguishing characteristic, if not **the** distinguishing characteristic, of the international system, and the system is structured by past generations' successive attempts to limit war without, however, relinquishing the right to resort to it in their own self-defense!

War as a contest carried on by force of arms necessarily implies the death of one's opponents. This presents two sorts of problems. Moral problems are raised by the idea of killing individuals who have in themselves done nothing to "deserve" it. Wars, therefore, are justified by their participants in terms of self-defense, self-protection, or the subhuman (i.e., inhuman) nature of their opponents. Tony Blair used this justification for intervention in Iraq, in the form of the need to get rid of a particularly ruthless and obnoxious dictator, though as he should have known, this is not a justification recognized in modern international law. Practical problems arise from the obvious dangers of uncontrolled war. War has, therefore, to be legitimized by some authority acting on behalf of divine providence or the political community, or both.

The idea of war is therefore inextricably linked with the concept of the state (Tilly 1985, see also Skocpol 1985, Cammack 1989, Hall and Ikenberry 1989, Held 1989). This is, however, not, as is often thought, because war is (or has been) an activity solely carried on by states. Rather, the state is the term that we give to the political community when it is organized for war. To conduct war, therefore, is to claim the role of a state, the sole entity that can legitimize an activity that in almost all societies of any complexity would be regarded as illegitimate if practiced by an individual or group on its own account. Armed attempts to overthrow state governments may, therefore, be regarded as a form of "internal war" (Eckstein 1964). The popular term "civil war" has the connotation of being at one and the same time a major upheaval and one which has the political objective of seizing control of the state as constituted, and would, therefore, like internal war, include unsuccessful movements if sufficiently large, but exclude many events in which only small force levels were involved, but which can, as we shall see, lead to profoundly revolutionary consequences. Meanwhile, as far as the international system is concerned, states "retain the monopoly of territory and the near-monopoly of large-scale legitimate force" (Frankel 1979, 55).

War presupposes the existence of weapons. However, until very modern times, weapons were not a specialized form of product designed purely for use in war, and only after the invention of gunpowder did they begin, and even then very slowly, to become so. This change accompanied the development of regular permanent military forces on a large scale. With the development came, for the first time, the need for large-scale plants designed for the exclusive purpose of producing munitions; and it was this, ironically, that was to lead strategists once more to break down the distinction between military and civilian in their urgency to stop-up the sources of military power by strategic bombing. The development of atomic weapons has altered this position in only one respect: that the states on both sides have grown to such an extent that sane military planning assumes the operation of deterrence rather than of retaliation despite the moral problem that for deterrence to be effective, the other side has first to be convinced that its opponent will, if necessary, engage in retaliation that inevitably implies an appalling breach of widely accepted principles of morality.

In one sense, therefore, nothing has changed. It is true, as has been remarked, that human beings now have the capacity to exterminate all human life with atomic weapons, but it has always been true that there have been enough hands to strangle the entire human race. This has not deterred conflict, and it has not stopped wars. Only twice in the entire history of ancient Rome down to Augustus was the city at peace and the temple gates of the god Janus closed. In modern times, Quincy Wright, in his major study, lists and analyzes 278 wars that occurred in the period 1480–1941, wars of sufficient severity to result in substantial casualties (Wright 1965, 650; cf. Richardson 1960). The claim that nuclear weapons prevented conflict in Europe between 1945 and 1979 looks rather hollow in the light of Europe's evident incapacity to intervene effectively in Croatia and Bosnia and Herzegovina. Patterns of armed conflict since 1989 do not support the notion that we are moving into a new era of peace; merely that the incidence of conflict has shifted (Wallensteen and Sollenberg 1995).

In other senses, however, nuclear capability does have important effects which are of special relevance to this discussion. First, it creates the need, not just for weapons as such, but for complex weapons systems to ensure its maintenance, targeting, and delivery. This in turn presupposes a close and constant relationship between government, the strategic armed forces, and the manufacturers, the degree of whose specialization is such that they are now wholly dependent on the one exclusive market for their product. Secondly, such systems are extremely expensive by any standards. In theory, a minimal nuclear capacity can be acquired relatively cheaply which will enable a state to impress its lesser neighbors; in practice it costs a great deal of money and makes that state an automatic target for one or other of the nuclear states. Meanwhile, the ability to maintain "conventional forces" is correspondingly reduced for any given level of expenditure that may be contemplated. Thirdly, such highly specialized forces, and even more such ferociously powerful weapons, are of little or no use in the traditional alternative role of armed forces, namely counterinsurgency. A government cannot put down a rebellion with thermonuclear weapons. Even the use of heavy conventional weapons such as tanks, artillery shells, and bombs may prove counterproductive. Bombing his own capital, if anything, accelerated the fall of Anastasio Somoza Debayle in Nicaragua in 1979. Lastly, as the Falklands Crisis of 1982 demonstrated, nuclear weapons do not deter conventional aggression (Calvert 1982); so that President Reagan's naval maneuvers off Nicaragua in 1983, impressive as the hardware deployed was to the unsophisticated, had little real credibility as a response to the alleged threat of subversion or guerrilla attack (Calvert 2008).

It can be argued, therefore, that the possession of nuclear weapons actually limits a power's ability to respond to threats of insurgency. Support for this view may be found in the history of US relations with Cuba and Vietnam (the Second Indo-China War, 1965–75) and in the way in which Britain, which had successfully contained guerrilla threats in Malaya, Kenya, and Cyprus, was forced to contract its forces in the late 1950s and soon afterwards failed dismally to respond to insurgency in Aden (subsequently the People's Republic of South Yemen and now part of Yemen—Bell 1976).

Lastly, the possession of nuclear weapons does not, it seems, end the long human tradition of glorifying combat with other human beings and regarding it as the highest expression of human courage and endeavor in the face of overwhelming odds. Undoubtedly, the glorification of war has on many occasions been adapted to the services of revolutionary movements which, by terming their members "soldiers" and their forces "armies," seek to legitimize—apparently at least in the eyes of their own supporters—their political ends. Were it not for the glorification of force in war, indeed, the belief in revolutionary activity as a means for settling other political disputes or realizing other political aspirations would lose much of its rationale.

The mystique of war contributes to revolution in other ways too. First, it places undue emphasis on the value of obedience and the military way of doing things as part of one's general service of the state. It would be pointless to deny that in many ways military training is of great value in other occupations. But there are many in which it is not, and often the authoritarian attitudes characteristic of traditional military training prove a major obstacle to the survival of military governments themselves. Politics involves the management of a subtle structure of reward and punishment, persuasion and bargaining as well as command. Thus, the imposition of military ideas can and does contribute to the desire for revolutionary change.

It is a popular belief, secondly, among some conservatives, that universal military training will create a massively disciplined population capable of meeting the challenge of rapid economic growth and expansion. The evidence suggests the exact reverse; in fact such training undercuts the desire to do more than just get by; it emphasizes the value of personal survival rather than the desire to take risks, which is essential to economic growth, by stimulating hitherto untried ideas. It creates a large number of individuals with a degree of resentment against a system that has taken up a crucial period of their young lives with activity that to them is at best inconsequential and at worst thoroughly unpleasant. Worst of all, some of these individuals will have gained, free of charge, something that they might otherwise have had to go far to find: sophisticated instruction in the use of modern weapons and an awareness of their tactical possibilities.

Armies, therefore, are a traditional training ground, not only for the practitioners of the military coup, but for those who take to the hills and become guerrillas, and for those who lead others to the barricades in urban insurrection. The abolition of compulsory military service has gone along with, and may well be a precondition for, the demilitarization of Latin American politics. Against this, it has been argued that in France conscripts resisted the pretensions of their officers to dictate terms to de Gaulle.

Standing Armies and the Problem of Militarism

The belief that military values are the highest expression of human activity is a very ancient one, and it is not surprising therefore to find that it is very deep-rooted. Particularly interesting from the point of view of the student of revolution is the complex relationship between militarism among the military themselves and militarism among civilians.

Militarism is, in the words of Alfred Vagts, "a domination of the military man over the civilian, an undue preponderance of military demands, an emphasis on military considerations, spirit, ideals and scales of value, in the life of states" (Vagts 1959, 14).

Discipline, a strong sense of group mission and esprit de corps are indeed defining characteristics of well-trained military forces. Such a sense of pride could be expected to feed on success and to evaporate in face of failure. In fact, the reverse appears to be the case. The undue development of militarism among the armed forces characteristically occurs as a result of military setback or defeat. By the common psychological mechanisms of displacement and projection, responsibility for such defeats as, for example, the Egyptian defeat in the Arab-Israeli War of 1948–9, is transferred to the civilian government. It becomes, in fact, an argument for greater dedication to military values, not less.

Ultimately, this can, as it did in Egypt in 1952, become the motivation for direct military intervention in politics. It is important to note, therefore, that when Finer writes of military intervention in terms of the "opportunity" and "disposition" the military have to intervene; that in the strict sense the military (assuming they exist at all) *always* have the *opportunity* to intervene, what they may lack is the *inclination*. The very fact of their existence means that they are always intervening, if only at Finer's lowest level of intervention, namely as a lobby. What is different about the armed forces as a lobby is the compelling nature of their arguments (that without increased defense expenditure the country would be laid open to its enemies) and the opportunity that they have, as a branch of government and perhaps the major spending branch at that, to push their case from within. As Finer correctly recognizes, what is remarkable about the armed forces is not that they intervene, but that there are any countries in the world that are not subject to military governments (Finer 1962, 4). "The military possess vastly superior organisation," he argues. "And they possess *arms*."

The weakness of the military position is, however, concealed by the word "superior." Superior in what respect? Certainly superior to any other agency within the state in the ability to project force. But for how long and with what assurance? An army is an integral part of the state, and it depends for its continued viability and effectiveness on the support it receives for the role it assumes from the civilian population on which it depends. Only where this dependence is minimized, either by acquiesence, or by external support and/or funding, or by extreme weakness in terms of social cohesion of politically expressive structures such as political parties, churches, and secret societies, can the military forces be free to pursue their own ambitions. In practice, the desire for military government is as much a civilian phenomenon as a military one, and generals who seize power do so in alliance with and at the urging of prominent civilians representing powerful interests within the state.

We turn, therefore, to civilian militarism, defined by Vagts as: "the unquestioning embrace of military values, ethos, principles, attitudes; as ranking military institutions and considerations above all others in the state" (Vagts 1959, 453) by civilians, even at the cost of their own lives and well-being. It is found, as he himself suggests, in its most pure and least contested form in the later stages of an international war, when the frenzy of patriotic fervor has reached the height at which no sacrifice seems unreasonable in pursuit of the ideal of victory, and it goes far to explain the, at best, weak differences observed by Wright and Haas between democracies and autocracies in their propensity to go to war (Wright 1965, 828–41; Haas 1965).

Civilian militarism may involve acceptance of the military claim to preeminence. But it seems as if it may also develop independently, forcing the military, often in circumstances unsuitable for successfully waging war, to live up to the expectations suddenly thrust upon them. So we find civilian militarism not only in Germany but also in Britain in the First World War, and not only in Japan but also in the United States, in the Second. In both cases, the exigencies of war forced the substantial expansion of the horizons of government power, making natural after the war what had been regarded as dangerous hitherto. It is easy to think of such an expansion in purely administrative terms, and that is precisely how in general it has tended to be regarded. Much more important is the way in which a sustained high level of crisis consolidates support for an incumbent government, enabling it to sustain a continued war effort far beyond what might objectively be planned for in time of peace. But administrative considerations cannot altogether be overlooked. A key reason for the acceptance of military government is the desire to short-cut the complex and unpredictable bargaining procedures of a fragmented society, in which bureaucratic structures are only partly developed and administrative jobs are seen as the personal property of the individual officeholder. In such societies, and they are the majority of the world's societies, the military forces offer the one arbiter of politics to which powerful interests can appeal in order to liberate themselves from the bonds they feel are limiting their potential.

Military intervention, once secured, creates new problems. At the lowest level, reliance on unconstitutional use of force permits it to be used freely against individuals according to the whim of immediate military commanders.

At the middle level, recent experience shows that military concepts of national security, particularly when linked to interservice rivalry in the control of the political process, can lead to the unrestrained use of arrest, torture, and execution against the supposed enemies of the regime.

But at this level and at the top level there is, once the armed forces are enthroned, no further arbiter to which appeal may be made, with the sole, intangible and all-too ineffective exception of international public opinion. In the age of superpower competition the operation of such international sanctions as exist against such regimes depended on the stand of the bloc leaders, the superpowers.

With the end of the Cold War, this seems to be have given way once again to a classic nineteenth-century pattern of "spheres of influence." In August 2008, Russian forces used the pretext of defending their own citizens to send forces into South Ossetia and Abkhazia. Both regions lay within the boundary of Georgia, but Georgian relations with Russia had deteriorated after the election in 2004 of Mikhail Saakashvili, who had promised to integrate the regions more effectively. Georgia launched an aerial bombardment and ground attack on South Ossetia on August 7, 2008. Georgian forces controlled the South Ossetian capital, Tskhinvali, for part of the following day. Russia then poured thousands of troops into South Ossetia, and launched bombing raids both over the province and on targets in the rest of Georgia. The conflict resulted in a significant number of casualties and enabled Russia effectively to incorporate the disputed territories, seriously compromising Georgian independence.

The Coup

The coup is something so alien to British politics that there is no English word for it, and it is often wrongly confused with a related concept, that of coup d'état. But "coup d'état" means, in the strict sense, a seizure of a disproportionate share of the state power in a sudden stroke of force **by the existing government**. The coup is essentially a tactical military operation with a strategic political motive. Hence, it is not something that anyone can do. It derives from the very special nature of the military as an institution.

In the first place, the military are an arm of government; indeed in earlier times in all states, and again in the new states, they are overwhelmingly the most important branch of government. They combine exceptional resources born of the need or desire to defend the state with the symbolic importance they therefore can claim as custodians of national independence, unity, and purpose. Because their business is national security, they have the right to keep all that they do secret, and this gives them a unique ability to conspire against the authorities, be they civil or military.

Secondly, military forces have a very distinctive form of organization, centered on a special group, the officer corps, who are trained and recruited separately in order to ensure the automatic and unquestioning obedience of those they command. Educated together in special establishments from their early adolescence, the officers have a strong sense of esprit de corps and are overwhelmingly influenced by the concept of their membership of the armed forces as an organization. Indeed, such is the esprit de corps of each service, that inter-service rivalry, where the army, for geostrategic reasons, has to admit the existence of other services to the political process, is one of the few factors acting to restrain military intervention or prolonged military control of politics. For the military officer, military service is much more important than any other formative influence; so much so, in fact, that some Third World Marxists have actually wondered if the armed forces do not constitute a separate class, with interests and motivation of its own.

Thirdly, therefore, in a politicized army, participation in military politics becomes for the individual officer not merely an option but a necessity, such that his entire personal career, on the one hand, and the future of the social order, on the other, both come to be regarded by him as subordinated to the needs of the military institution. This in turn becomes an institution that is very highly bureaucratized (cf. Feit 1973), in which the highly structured nature of the military society makes the conduct of the military coup increasingly formalized. It therefore ceases to be a military action for military motives, and becomes instead, by degrees, a highly stylized demonstration of military power designed at one and the same time to remove an unpopular government from power with the minimum of fuss and military casualties, and at the same time to make it clear to the civilians that they must not and will not be allowed to intervene on their own account. It is this that accounts for the soldiers at street corners, guards on public buildings and rounding-up of student and trade-union leaders that characteristically accompany a military coup.

Military coups may be fronted by military officers alone or by a junta composed both of military officers and prominent civilian politicians. But they are never led by civilians alone. No one can hope safely to suborn the military unless they are a member of the military (and not always then). Yet it cannot be assumed even by the armed forces that they can successfully take over political power without someone realizing what they are doing and trying to stop them. And it is an observation repeatedly confirmed by experience that it almost invariably seems to be known by a government beforehand that a military coup is under preparation. The main difference between countries in which military coups are successful, and countries in which they are not, seems to be that, in the former, there are so many military coups being planned at any given moment that a government cannot possibly plan to anticipate all of them.

A classic example occurred in 1974 in Bolivia itself, when promoters of two coups—a right wing one and a left wing one—tried to seize power simultaneously. The result was that, no sooner had the government been overthrown, than the successor government was in turn overthrown . The whole sequence took only about 24 hours, but the whole point of it would be missed if one did not realize that there were two actions going on at the same time. One consequence was that the outcome was particularly bloody. Usually military coups result in few casualties and in Latin America in the twentieth century three quarters of successful coups have been bloodless (though the other quarter have not).

Finally, even at the level of the coup the problems of preparation do not concern the military aspect alone. When the military set about preparing a coup they have to carry out certain kinds of political activities as well. They have to engage in negotiations (*trabajos*) ("works") with key power-holders and make bargains (*compromisos*) (Finer 1962).

The problem with such agreements reached by clandestine negotiation is that, being completely illegal, they are not always adhered to. This, in due course, gives fertile grounds for the next military rebellion, which is one reason why when countries start having military coups, they tend to go on doing so until and unless strong external pressure is exerted upon them to stop. When no-one can trust anyone else, and all bargaining is conditional, very rapidly the foundations of political stability are altogether eroded. Stability in the political system is based on the assurance if you do X then Y will result. (E.g., if you pay your taxes, you will receive social security when you are out of work.) Once this link is broken, it takes a long time to restore. And even a military government depends on its ability to communicate with regional military commanders and important provincial power-holders.

In the coup-like seizure of power by the Bolsheviks in Russia in 1917, Trotsky made extensive use of the ability to cut the incumbent Kerensky government off from peripheral military installations by simply cutting off the telephone and other services. And after the coup, the promised Constitutional Convention was put out of action altogether because a technician turned off the lights and went home and they were all left sitting in the dark! Hence, Trotsky (1966) argued later that the real center of power, the real key to the control of the modern state was its communications. But the pieces of this doctrine were first picked up not by Trotsky and his followers, or indeed by communists in general, but by Mussolini. The famous Mussolini "March on Rome" depended on the development of this technique which was not only the control of communications, but the saturation of communications, by a blanket of misleading messages to the effect that the Fascists were marching on Rome and were going to take over. This so scared the incumbent government that they collapsed without much resistance, and the King called upon Mussolini to form a government when he arrived peacefully in Rome by train.

It was Curzio Malaparte, an Italian newspaperman who had in fact seen this Mussolini technique in action at first hand and later embraced Fascism, who wrote in 1927 a book on coups (Malaparte 1932), in which he too stated that the key issue was the control of communications. To avoid the problem of actually fighting the government, one simply blew up the communications network and the government would collapse. Malaparte was partly right in that communications are obviously important, but he was also seriously wrong. It is possible to put the communications network out of action to a considerable extent but most governments do in fact have a considerable back-up facility, and nowhere more than among the armed forces. Secondly, the monopoly of communications that might have been possible in 1917 is no longer practicable, certainly in any developed country. Ironically, a system originally devised for military use, the internet, seems finally to have put an end to the possibility. Moreover, communications work both ways, so it is not just a question of putting communications out of action for the incumbent government, but maintaining them for the revolutionaries. In 1918, Lenin, for example, was able to use the telephone as Kerensky had not, to rally the troops to the defense of his government.

Again, the symbolic importance of targets was not as fully recognized by Malaparte as it was by Trotsky. It was not sufficient for the October Revolution simply to cut the Kerensky government off; it was necessary for the Winter Palace to be captured in order to demonstrate to the people of Petrograd that power had in fact been seized. In Mexico in 1915, Venustiano Carranza was able effectively to control something like nine-tenths of the national territory, in so far as anyone could control the national territory of Mexico at that particular time, but he could not maintain a viable government in Mexico City itself. Hence, until he had actually succeeded in capturing the national capital, he was not able to convince outside observers and a large section of the population that he was, in fact, effectively in control. This is even more true of the smaller countries than it is of large ones like Mexico.

And lastly, on the purely military aspects, there is the question of the arena. Luttwak suggests that the perimeter of the arena should be defined by roadblocks or other means, so that the military activities going on inside cannot be hampered by inconvenient problems like the arrival of reinforcements from the neighboring town. He conceives his entire strategy in terms of the governmental defense of this perimeter, which the coup forces have to penetrate rapidly and without warning.

Now this does not, in fact, happen. Where, in the past, the military have got into the habit of making military coups, there is more often than not a barrack very close to the center of the capital city with a good route direct to the center of government, for example, Campo de Mayo in Buenos Aires. The armed forces, therefore, are already so near to the center of power that they do not have to worry about things like roadblocks and there is no question of forces actually coming in from outside. In the case of the cuartelazo, the "blow from the barracks," the barracks that the blow comes from is right behind the presidential palace.

The principal political problems of the coup revolve around the thesis of destabilization versus restabilization. Here there are two basic and opposing theses; the first one, which will here be termed the "Malaparte thesis," that there is a technical separation of government from their command structure and that the seizure of power mainly involves the neutralization of communications, and so the neutralization of the government. The emphasis is therefore on "soft" communications targets and their neutralization. The second is Luttwak's thesis which emphasizes the "hard" strategic targets which are of both physical and symbolic importance, with communications treated as a secondary prerequisite to the acquisition of the arena, in which the main battle for the control of the "hard" targets will be fought out.

Neither of these two writers seem to think a great deal of the human targets of the coup, but in fact it is they who are the key to the whole exercise. The rapid removal of the president of the Republic by way of the military airfield to the nearest point of the globe where he is likely to be welcome is, in fact, the most common form of all military coups and there are numerous examples. A celebrated one that went wrong, was the case of Alberto Lleras Camargo, president of Colombia, who was seized by a small force of military rebels, flung into the back of a jeep, and driven off rapidly toward the airport to be put on a plane. As they drove past the front of the presidential palace they were stopped for speeding by a traffic policeman who looked in the back, found the president of the Republic there, called up reinforcements and freed him. So the coup failed.

The human targets, therefore, are the key to the political success of the coup, which is basically about removing the officials of the existing government. The key word is "removal." Political assassinations are not distinct in their effects from coups but coups do not normally mean the assassination of leaders of governments. Nor are coup promoters normally very bloodthirsty. In practice, deaths during coups are usually accidental or, one might say "incidental" to the main purpose. It is very seldom government leaders who get killed in coup-prone countries, and exceptions like the deaths of King Feisal of Iraq (1958), Salvador Allende in Chile (1973) or William

Tolbert in Liberia (1980), are in fact conspicuous precisely because they are exceptions.

After the coup, the next question is "how is political power acquired?" First, the source of power comes from the removal of the existing source of power. Then political allegiances necessarily have to re-form around the new rulers. If the former government is in flight, then it cannot command allegiance in the way that an effective functioning government can. Coups frequently fail if incumbent governments take fast evasive action and then simply call upon their established political support to rally to them. Even the most unstable government in Latin America survives often until the sixth, seventh or eighth attempt to remove it.

Luttwak (1968) produces three preconditions for a successful coup. First, "the social and economic conditions of the target country must be such as to confine political participation to a small fraction of the population." This is realistic, because a coup most usually does not occur in countries with broad political participation. Where coups have occurred in such countries, they have generally occurred (as in 1940 in France) in cases of grave national emergency, when, in other words, participation was momentarily suspended. Though Uruguay, where political participation had been broad for many years, sustained a violent deformation in its government in 1973, this deformation (termed, appropriately in some ways, a "soft coup") was not a military coup in the sense in which, for example, the fall of Allende in Chile was a military coup, but the establishment of indirect military control of a figurehead civilian government. The operation of the broad participation itself varies the terms in which the seizure of political power is possible. It has to take place in a different kind of way and with a much greater degree of mass participation.

The second condition is that "the target state must be substantially independent and the influence of foreign powers in its internal political life must be relatively limited." If intervention is possible, the coup may be halted or reversed. Thus, in 1963, the government of Gabon was overthrown by a military coup. President Mba, however, was able to get word through to the French; the French rushed in an expeditionary force and set Mba back on the presidential chair.

The third condition is that "the target state must have a political centre. If there are several centres these must be identifiable and they must be politically, rather than ethnically, structured." One could infer from this that military coups in Nigeria are likely to go wrong. And the evidence of what has happened when there first was a military coup in Nigeria in 1966 shows that this was probably substantially correct. All kinds of things went wrong; the coup failed to impose a new regime, although the Head of State, General Ironsi, was killed, and the dislocation of the state was such that it was one of the major contingent factors in the secession of Biafra and the ensuing Nigerian Civil War of 1966–7.

Fourthly, "if the state is controlled by a nonpolitically organized unit, the coup can only be carried out with its consent or neutrality." In other words, if it is a military government, the military have to support the coup or be neutral, and the same can be presumed by extension for a secret police organization. The existence of a powerful repressive secret police in a country would suggest that coups can only be carried out there with their tacit consent or even connivance. This raises interesting questions about the events of 1991 in Russia.

Quite apart from the many technical questions impeding replacement of governments, it is doubtful whether there is in fact a very wide range of governments that would automatically be obeyed by the state machine. Luttwak claims: "The apparatus of the state is therefore to some extent a machine which will normally behave in a perfectly predictable and automatic manner. A coup operates by taking advantage of this machine-like behavior during the coup because it uses parts of the state apparatus to seize the controlling levers and afterwards because the value of the levers depends on the fact that the state is a machine." Common sense, however, suggests that it cannot be assumed that, for example, in a normally strongly right-wing country a very strongly left-wing government would necessarily be obeyed, or vice versa, and in practice this does not appear to happen.

It would clearly be extremely awkward if no one realized that a coup had in fact happened, and went on as before. Coup promoters therefore necessarily make use of the media to issue a statement of goals. Usually they accompany this by proclaiming a period of curfew which results in complete immobility; forcing upon people a reappraisal of their predicament in circumstances in which they are exposed only to official statements, generally interspersed by patriotic music.

To sum up, therefore, there are three aspects of restabilization. It is, first, necessary to stop the revolutionary forces in their takeover of power, or else the coup promoters would be in trouble. It is, secondly, necessary to get the state bureaucracy functioning again and to get the state operating like a state. And lastly, it will be necessary to get the public back to work, a problem which is not confined, of course, to the events of the military coup.

However, the most important thing about the military coup lies in its relevance to revolution. Where military coups are easy, the armed forces seldom fail to make use of them to preempt any significant social change since it might threaten their own privileged position in a system which enables them to exploit the state. The slightest hint of revolution, and they are alert to intervene. The problem is that by preempting moderate social change in this way, they may be hastening the time in which they are faced with something much more challenging. As Goodwin (2008) argues, too may people may come to believe that there is no other way out.

Urban Insurrection

Urban insurrection is clearly distinguished from the other two forms of warfare. First, unlike guerrilla warfare, it occurs principally in cities, and secondly, unlike a military coup, it involves armed mass uprisings, and this is its basic distinguishing feature. The existence of urban insurrectionary movements of more or less spontaneous character is associated particularly with the so-called great revolutions, and in particular, with the French and Russian Revolutions. Features which are related to the question of armed mass uprising are as follows:

1. First, the existence of a condition of dual power; that is to say, the creation by mass action of competitive political organs, or the enlargement of existing organs, into a political structure (competitive with the existing regime). Examples are the Paris Sections, the Russian Soviets, and trade union movements generally, in conditions in which they have been associated with revolutionary mass action.
2. Secondly, the phenomenon of the general strike, first employed in Italy in 1907. There have been numerous examples of countries in which general strikes have occurred since, and one theorist, Sorel, held that the general strike itself was the truly proletarian way to overthrow a government and to bring about political change (Sorel 1950). However, general strikes in this particular context tend to be associated with mass action, or to be a form of mass action which is particularly associated with the involvement of the proletariat and therefore of particular interest if one is studying revolutions from a Marxist ideological base.
3. Lastly, convention leadership, that is to say, leadership of the movement by a large body in which alternative policies are publicly canvassed, be it a party organization, a central committee organization, or a body such as the National Assembly or the National Convention in France.

There are precursors of modern urban insurrection in the numerous urban movements of early modern times, for example, the Fronde in France but if one wants to study the history of urban insurrection one must draw a sharp line and accept that the definitive example for all later purposes has been the French Revolution of 1789. The Revolution itself was a product of the shifting coalition of political forces which was continually acting in opposition to mass unrest, and mass unrest periodically erupted into political action and impinged upon any attempt to try and create a stable political system. So that, in fact, the most democratic of the French revolutionary Constitutions, the revolutionary Constitution of 1791, was never put into practice, because it could not survive in opposition to the actual physical power of the Sections which led eventually to the setting up of the Committee of Public Safety.

There are six cases of mass action determining events between 1789 and 1792. Two are right at the beginning, in 1789: the storming of the Bastille on 14 July, and on 5 October, the march on Versailles when the royal family was brought back to Paris by the crowd. Then in 1792, there is an important series of four incidents. First came the unsuccessful attack on the Tuileries on 20 June which was repulsed, the King covering himself with great distinction. On 11 July, mass action broke up the Paris Council and destroyed the municipal government of Paris, thus laying open the way for the lack of central control which led to the storming of the Tuileries on 10 August. That, in turn, virtually meant the end of the monarchy; and lastly, between 2 and 7 September, followed the so-called September Massacres in which a great many people perished who were not aristocrats, still less royalty. The massacres had little or nothing to do with political outcomes. They were the occasion of the paying-off of old scores. But the September Massacres led directly to the creation by the National Assembly of the Committee of Public Safety.

Once the Committee of Public Safety had come into existence it is significant that the future course of the revolution no longer involved mass action on a successful level. The next major uprising against the French revolutionary government, the Bread Riots of April 1, 1795 (12 Germinal), were suppressed. So were the riots of 20 May (1 Prarial). Finally on the famous Day of the Sections, October 5, 1795 (13 Vendémiaire), the crowd was dispersed with the celebrated "whiff of grapeshot" by a young artillery lieutenant newly known as Napoleon.

People had, however, already learnt from the French Revolution the lesson of the effectiveness, as they thought, of mass action. It was believed that mass insurrection on a sufficient scale was, in fact, the distinguishing feature of those revolutions that were successful. In 1830, Charles X was overthrown by a mass rising of Parisians who seized the Hotel de Ville and raised the barricades on 29 July. Thiers, the parliamentary leader who had led the protest against Charles X's dictatorial acts, was completely out-flanked: the parliamentary protest was not the immediate cause for the fall of Charles X. Similarly, between 22 and 24 February 1848, a spontaneous revolt sufficed to topple Louis Philippe. And the lesson was, therefore, reinforced for most Frenchmen and a great many European observers that revolutionary action meant mass urban action.

Two other incidents offered different lessons. First, between 23 and 26 June—the "June Days" of 1848—a further rising occurred against the Provisional Government. But the National Assembly gave dictatorial powers to General Cavaignac who suppressed the revolt with considerable brutality. The "June Days" therefore ended in massacre.

Secondly, the leader of the parliamentary revolt in 1830, Thiers, was the man who became head of the Provisional Government of France on the fall of the Second Empire in 1870. And it was he who was the first modern statesman to understand the roots of the problem for previous governments confronted with revolutionary mass action and how to counteract it. When Thiers was confronted with the appearance of the Commune on March 18, 1871, he already had troops in Paris, where they repeated the example of previous detachments, except for the fresh troops led by Napoleon and Cavaignac, and began to fraternize with the spontaneous revolt which they encountered. The fraternization was in itself sufficient to stop Thiers from successfully suppressing the Commune on 18 March. Thiers, however, responded to this in the way that has become standard practice; that is to say, he withdrew his forces from the city to training camps outside Paris, weeded them out and reconstituted them. When they next went in there was no time for fraternization to occur and the Commune was suppressed. It is only fair to point out that the Commune was, throughout, very much on the defensive. It could only have come into existence as a result of the military occupation of France by the Prussians, and was only possible as a form of government because of the power vacuum following the defeat of France and the long siege of Paris during the winter of 1870–1. The Prussians would not have allowed it to spread, but were happy to have the French incur the responsibility of suppressing it. So it was as a result of this experience that Engels wrote his famous remark in the introduction to The Class Struggles in France, 1848–50 "let us have no illusions about it, a real victory of insurrection over the military in street fighting, a victory as between two armies, is one of the rarest exceptions" (Marx and Engels, 1962, I, 130).

Now the reason for this historical introduction is quite plain when one considers what had to be, logically speaking, the attitude of socialists in general to most of the important revolutionary movements in the latter half of the nineteenth century and the early part of the twentieth. It might have been logical to discard the idea of urban insurrection altogether, but there were powerful ideological reasons why this should not occur, and people who toyed with the idea of resorting to the coup on the one hand, or mass peasant uprisings on the other, were denounced. For it would be extremely difficult for any uprising against an established government to claim mass support unless the mass support was visibly forthcoming. Once the example of mass support had been shown by the French Revolution, then its absence would, for the first time, have been noticeable.

The dilemmas are well indicated by the Comintern manual on urban insurrection published in English under the title of A. Neuberg, *Armed Insurrection* (Neuberg 1970). "A. Neuberg" is a pseudonym for the Agitprop section of the Comintern under the direction of Palmiro Togliatti, and the manual was prepared in 1928, and published in German, bearing the imprint of the City of Zurich and the imaginary publisher Otto Meyer. In fact, the only things that were accurate about its original description is that it was about armed insurrection, and it was actually published in 1928. This seemed to be a particularly favorable moment for condensing the experience of the early 1920s into handbook form and making it available to the comrades for their instruction and it went out with an official seal of approval from the Comintern, with, however, certain criticisms of its actual content.

It begins with two theoretical chapters written by Piatnitsky. Piatnitsky was then the organizing secretary of the Comintern but was liquidated by Stalin during the 1930s. The theoretical chapters trace, in context, the Bolshevik directions for revolution. He was primarily concerned to argue, against Karl Kautsky, the German Social Democrat leader, that only through violence could the bourgeois state be overthrown. Having picked up the quotation of Engels mentioned above, he then continued it according to what is supposed to be Engels' original text, which Eduard Bernstein had cut out, arguing that street fighting would continue to be important, though because of the disadvantageous situation as against the regular military—by this time very much better armed than they had been back in 1848—this would have to be compensated for by other factors.

Secondly, Engels seems to argue that it was unlikely that urban insurrection would play a major role at the beginning of a great revolution rather than later on—in other words, a revolution would have to be initiated by some other means and then mass uprising would perform an important part in it. Such a formulation safeguarded the claim to a "leading role" of the communist party.

And thirdly, he claims that open attack was likely to be preferred to the passive barricade tactics. With the perfection of the machine gun, such a strategy was likely to be suicidal, and the interesting thing is that having taken note of the quotation, the manual itself then proceeds to argue that all will be well if, and only if, the time is ripe and the insurrectionists depend on the support of the "advanced class" (Neuberg 1970, 42). Assessing the situation therefore becomes a major problem for a Bolshevik wishing to carry out an armed insurrection who needs, first of all, to find out when the time is right. So the next four chapters of the manual are chapters of case studies, dealing in turn with the Reval uprising (the reader will not find Reval on a modern map; it is now called Talinn), the Hamburg uprising, the Canton insurrection and the three Shanghai insurrections. The reason for the detail and interest in the Chinese examples is because Ho Chi Minh (or, as he was then called, Nyguen Thanh) was one of the authors of the manual.

There follow three chapters on political preparation for the insurrection and two chapters by Tukhachevsky on the military tactics to be followed. The political problem basically revolves around the military question. A legitimate criticism made by the Comintern of its own manual was that it concerned itself too much with the military and not enough with the political.

An entire long chapter, to begin with, is devoted to the subversion of the military. The army, it says, is the key element in the organization of the state. Upon its stability and its general condition depend the stability of the state as a whole. It points out that the military was not adequately subverted at Reval where, indeed, the insurrectionists made a number of other mistakes including not being ready in time. Worse, communists had wasted the opportunities they had had for subverting the military in Germany, where the military under the Weimar Constitution was unusually open to penetration. Normally, military forces are protected to a considerable extent against casual encounters with civilians, and in any case are retrained in barracks so that subversion is very difficult to achieve. The manual argues that the reason why this has not been adequately done is that their people are waiting for revolution to happen spontaneously in the aftermath of a great war and they fail to realize, they say, that revolutionary situations also arise in times of "peace" (quotation marks in original Neuberg 1970, 153). And the military, they suggest, can be easily subverted by two means: first, the use of situations which are, in fact, specifically military in content; in other words, where the military have been defeated, and that rankles. And secondly, by supporting what they call the partial demands of the military, which will stimulate the class struggle in the army. This is done by asking for better pay, better living conditions, etc. At the same time, the manual warns the comrades who are engaged in this action; first, that it is extremely dangerous but, for that reason must in fact be stepped up, not down; secondly, that the bourgeoisie will do anything, simply anything to avoid revolution, including getting the soldiers drunk in order to keep them in line so that subversion will be very difficult. Interestingly enough, it devotes precisely two paragraphs to the party infiltration of the police, despite the fact that it claims that there was considerable sympathy in police circles for the party in Germany in 1923, when the police were highly politicized and there was a social democratic government in office.

Subversion of the military is only one part of the preparatory organization recommended by the manual, the other part is the organization of the proletarian force, the Red Guard. Here, the first problem is getting hold of recruits. Neuberg stresses that, as Lenin advises, the Red Guard can only be formed when the seizure of power is "on the immediate agenda" (Neuberg 1970, 172). The bourgeoisie will not allow the creation of a Red Guard while the situation has not yet become one of civil war and they will endeavor to prevent it by every means possible. Then, even if a skeleton Red Guard is set up with cadres, it will still take months to make it into a really effective fighting force. Yet, it may at the same time (and this is the intrinsic paradox of the book's approach to armed insurrection) have to take the brunt of the fighting until the bourgeois army is disarmed or begins to waver.

The second problem is that of armaments. Clearly, the bourgeoisie (for which read "the established government") is not going to permit people to arm themselves unless they think they are on their side. Yet it is Lenin's view that the insurrectionists must immediately arm, and must start building up stores of arms as early as possible.

> The contingents . . . [Lenin says] must arm themselves as best they can (rifles, revolvers, bombs, knives, knuckledusters, sticks, rags soaked in kerosene for starting fires, ropes or rope ladders, shovels for building barricades, pyroxylin cartridges, barbed wire, nails against cavalry, etc., etc.) Under no circumstances should they wait for help from other sources, from above, from the outside; they must procure everything themselves. (Neuberg 1970, 177)

Where from, Lenin, and the manual, do not say, but in modern times the competition between suppliers has become more intense than ever before.

The next problem is, how are the rebels trained to use them? And this really is the nub of the question, not satisfactorily resolved by the manual. If you want to train people for urban insurrection, it believes, they should disguise themselves as members of an ex-servicemen's organization or drill in secret. Very little adequate guidance is given as to how this might be done. Instead, then, they go on to the military problems. These two chapters are written by Marshal Tukhachevsky who was, at that time, second in command of the Red Army. As is well known, Tukhachevsky disappeared in the course of the spectacular show trial of 1937, but was posthumously rehabilitated by Khrushchev (for what that is worth). It is particularly interesting to find that Tukhachevsky diverges completely from the idea that armed insurrection will only be used in the later stages of a revolution. He claims that from the beginning that the struggle will take place in the cities and that it is during this period that the insurgents have to create the Red Army to consolidate the revolution and to extend it territorially (Neuberg 1970, 185).

Then he goes on to discuss its distinctive problems. There are four principal ones: first, in urban fighting there is no front line. This can cut both ways because a regular soldier may not be any more happy in the city than the army of the proletariat. Secondly, the army of the proletariat will not be ready; the "regular army of the proletariat" is created, and must be created in the course of the struggle for power. Thirdly, on the other hand, insurrection modifies, and indeed subverts the army of the ruling class (the established government).

Lastly, he argues that because they are making use of untrained amateur soldiers the communists have both their advantages and disadvantages; they have to achieve superiority at the start, avoid the defensive, and provide a series of continuous successes. If they do this, the untrained nature of their fighting force will give them extra fighting power, in other words, they will not realize the fantastic odds that they are overcoming. Specific suggestions then follow; there are a large number and the manual is very detailed.

It is clear that Tukhachevsky had thought out the problem of urban insurrection extremely clearly, and the only problem was how it would actually be put into practice. First, armed workers (he points out) could very easily take over all the secondary targets like banks, workplaces, railway stations, and installations that do not actually need armed fighting men to take them over, because they are not normally guarded. Secondly, then, he points out that the forces of the government can be disorientated by picking off the leaders, and he goes into considerable discussion to try and prove that this is not a terrorist action and therefore reprehensible, but is in fact quite Leninist; that one should concentrate on picking off the leaders and killing them as quickly as possible.

Thirdly, at the start, surprise is necessary. This can be achieved by detailed reconnaissance of the circumstances and by preparing an adequate fighting force for the tasks in hand. At Reval, for example, there was detailed reconnaissance but its execution failed. At the Officer Cadet Academy they succeeded in disarming those on the ground floor, but apparently the force which was meant to disarm the first floor did not turn up in time, and the cadets there were able to hold out. The trouble was that, having had this slight setback, the revolutionaries failed to change their plans. Instead of swarming through the building with the forces they then had at their disposal, they fell back disheartened, withdrew, and lost an important stronghold.

Neuberg points out that timing is extremely important and should always be set in advance. To rely on signals such as cannon shot or rockets or suchlike to launch a revolt, as the Bolsheviks did with the *Aurora* in 1917, is a great mistake because people are unlikely either to see them, to hear them, or to pay any attention to them. Apparently, in the Bulgarian insurrection in 1923 this actually happened. Someone was supposed to fire a cannon as a signal for the rising. The gun went off but people in one part of the city heard it while people in the other part did not and the result was disaster (Neuberg 1970, 211).

This section of the manual concludes with the discussion of defensive actions, on the realistic grounds that the proletariat may not, even given these instructions, succeed in carrying out successfully an urban insurrection, but it can all be used as training for the future. Clearly, even Marshals of the Soviet Union treat their forces with the same kind of disregard for life that generals do in other countries. Tukhachevsky told them cheerfully how to build barricades, how successfully to throw bombs at tanks, dig holes in the ground, and stick it out for the sake of the cause to the final hour. The manual concludes with some words from Ho Chi Minh on how to prepare a peasant uprising, the argument for this being that it is a very useful thing to have going on in the background, while the Red Guard is occupied seizing the cities.

This manual was published, as noted above, in 1928. Between 1928 and 1989 there were several urban insurrections but practically none of them were successful. This suggests that there is something wrong with the idea of urban insurrection altogether. By an odd coincidence, the interesting examples are in states with communist governments, which reinforces the view that it was not by pure accident that Tukhachevsky and the old Bolsheviks who were behind the writing of this manual were among the first people liquidated in 1936–8. The most interesting examples since Stalin's death are the East German uprising of 1953, the Hungarian uprising of 1956, the risings in Poland in 1944, 1953 and 1970 (the last of which, of course, was successful in the overthrow of Wladyslaw Gomulka), and the fall of Ceausescu in Romania in 1989. All these are examples in which there was large-scale mass uprising, where the manual workers played an important part, and played very much the Tukhachevsky way—taking over the secondary targets and indeed, even making use of blasting charges, pits for tanks, gasoline bombs and all the other things that Lenin long ago suggested workers might use if they wanted to take political power. About the only thing they did not seem to use were pyroxylin cartridges.

Civil War and the Failure of Revolution

There have also been a number of abortive communist revolts in other countries, the most interesting of which is the series that occurred in Indonesia: the rising of 1928 (the same year as the Tukhachevsky manual was published); the Madiun uprising of 1948; and the abortive uprising (Gestapu) of 1965, which, if genuine (and there are reasons to believe that it might not be) was a complete disaster. The interesting thing is that, if it was genuine, looked at in the light of the Comintern manual, it fulfilled to a nicety the kind of conditions which the manual laid down.

Obviously there is a fundamental theoretical problem for a Marxist, as to whether he is going to persist with this very dangerous technique which has proved so disastrously unsuccessful in so many situations; whether he adopts a putschist strategy, or whether he goes for guerrilla warfare. Putschism in a sense was the choice of Lenin himself. In October 1917 he took political power by an organized coup in which the urban insurrection element was, practically speaking, minimized. He tells the Central Committee, after the plans are made, of using the existing military forces, many of whom are regular army units, that had already been subverted. One alternative is to go to the other extreme and adopt the guerrilla way, whether it be the Maoist, Castro, Guevara or whatever version, according to taste.

A second alternative, and the one currently in vogue, is to abandon the notion of armed uprising altogether and to rely on the popular vote. The election of Hugo Chávez in Venezuela in 1998 has given him a mandate for change which any postrevolutionary government would envy. It is the ultimate irony that throughout Eastern Europe and the former Soviet Union communists have, since the early 1990s, been returning to power with a popular mandate achieved in free elections in open competition with Western-style political parties.

CHAPTER THREE

Wars of National Liberation

Nationalism and Empire

Wars of national liberation are as old as recorded human history. The Battle of Bannockburn, the union of the three forest cantons of Switzerland (1291), the French Wars in Italy after 1494 and the rise of the Dutch Republic after 1581 each contributed to our modern notions of liberty and laid the foundation of thought for later attempts by communities to establish their own form of self-government. It is with the French Revolution in particular, however, that historians tend to associate the rise of that phenomenon known as nationalism, which has so much affected the history of the last 200 years.

Nationalism is the belief that a nation, that is to say a community of persons united by a common religion, language and/or culture, should be expressed in political terms by the creation by its members of a state, a political entity independent of other political entities. It is because the statesmen and politicians of revolutionary France laid much emphasis in their public speeches on the concept of the French nation, as a ground for their legitimate exercise of political power, that this period is seen particularly to have influenced the identification of nationhood with statehood. Ironically, in French a very clear distinction is made to this day between the two concepts. English, on the other hand, confuses the two, and English-speakers talk of "nationalization" because they lack any comparable verb derived from the word "state." The French Revolution, too, is an important historical turning point for another reason. Before that time in Europe, dynastic states created a sense of nation among their inhabitants. After that time, people who regarded themselves as nations, for example, the Poles, the Germans, and the Italians, sought to create new states for themselves (Minogue 1969, Seton-Watson 1977).

After 1945 a large number of new states came into existence as the nineteenth-century colonial empires fell apart and former colonies became independent. Of those of Great Britain, France, the Netherlands, Belgium, Spain, and Portugal only tiny fragments, mostly islands, remain. The dissolution of the Portuguese colonial empire in the mid-1970s seemed to mark the end of the main phase of decolonization. The United Nations Committee on Decolonization, the so-called Committee of 24, continued to occupy itself with the problem of a few remaining disputed territories, but its interest reflected the pressure of a few interested parties rather than any very important strategic anomaly. Such pressures not surprisingly met with the near-automatic approval of the bulk of the members of the General Assembly, themselves ex-colonies.

Such disputes were in the age of the Cold War fertile ground for the two superpowers, as they maneuvered for political advantage and alliance in what was then generally known as the Third World and is now increasingly termed (outside the United States) simply "the South." Here history is interestingly at variance with public image. The United States was once "the first new nation," and her war of national liberation, termed in the United States itself "the American Revolution," both preceded the French Revolution and contributed to it, and has much in common with it. With its rise to world standing in the twentieth century already established, however, the United States came in much of the Third World to be seen as a conservative power, maintaining a system of alliances with reactionary rulers in what many left-wing writers regarded as a "neoimperialist" relationship. As early as the 1930s the United States began to divest itself of the formal structures of nineteenth-century empire, by promising independence to its dependencies it has maintained ties of financial investment and control which enable the United States to obtain the support she wants and to draw all the financial benefits she attributes to the possession of colonies without a formal link. As Marxist writers put it, the age of colonialism had given way to the age of imperialism (or neoimperialism).

The former Soviet Union, on the other hand, was the successor state to the Russian Empire, acquired by military conquest and subjugation. It was created in 1922 as the political expression of the reconquest of those parts of Central Asia and Central Europe that tried to secede after 1917, and was added to by the military conquest of the Baltic States during the Second World War, and the annexation of large parts of Poland and Romania. In 1989, of all the nineteenth-century empires, only that of Russia remained intact and by 1991 it had disintegrated. The problem was that until then the Soviet Union professed to be a Marxist state, ideologically committed to the support of movements for national liberation, and ready at all times to denounce the United States as an "imperialist" power, regardless of the latter's strong support for the dissolution of the European colonial empires.

This view was often uncritically accepted in the Third World, where there was no history of recent Russian penetration and where some national liberation movements had, since 1945, been able to receive Soviet ideological, if not military, support. Since the United States has been officially precluded in many cases from following suit, owing to its alliance with the metropolitan powers concerned, the Soviet Union was able to use this as support for its view of the United States as an "imperialist" power. It was also uncritically accepted in the former Soviet Union itself, so that the first stirrings of nationalism in the Baltic States and Moldavia/Moldova were met by the Soviet leadership with a puzzled combination of hesitation and incomprehension.

The contest between the superpowers for influence among rival Third World states, and the problem of whether or not to support their aspirations, was not new. Very similar considerations underlay the concept of the "balance of power" in Europe in the nineteenth century, and the pressure to create the European colonial empires in the first place. Despite the collapse of the European empires, the position today is, however, complicated by the fact that, although in some places nationalism is a strong and potent force in the Third World, in other places, notably in Africa where the present state boundaries are the artificial creations of European statesmen and map-makers and so cut across religious, linguistic, and ethnic boundaries, the existence of the state has again preceded the emergence of the concept of nation. To create such a concept has therefore been the work not only of charismatic nationalists such as Nkrumah in Ghana or Kenyatta in Kenya, but also of military administrators such as the successive leaders of Nigeria or of Somalia. All nationalism, to be successful, draws heavily on local symbolism, a sense of differentness. Hence, its successful achievement creates a sense of individuality among such leaders and renders them much less willing than they might otherwise have been to enter any wider political grouping.

Such fragmentation has contributed to the division both of the African continent and of the Arab world. The latter is particularly remarkable, since the unifying effect of Islam has historically been strong. Yet even with its heightened sense since the mid-1970s revival, the only issue that effectively still unites the Islamic states remains their hostility to Israel. With the effective ending of the period of the creation of new states, all such regional groupings have in any case been settling down into a more routine era of diplomacy, in which relationships were less likely to be disrupted by the emergence of any new counter in the power balance. The only remaining possibility for a sudden change of pattern, therefore, was a major revolution in one or other of the component states. Such a revolution occurred in Germany at the end of 1989, but not so far in a major Third World state, given the peaceful nature of the transition to majority rule in South Africa.

Fighting for Independence

The age of wars of national liberation, however, will continue to influence such future developments, and it will therefore be useful to have a look at the special features of such wars.

Wars of national liberation are a type of revolution in that they involve the seizure of power by the use of force. They differ from a purely internal event in that the goal sought is secession, the creation from a province of the former "empire," of a new state as an independent actor in the international system. There are in fact several other ways in which states can become independent. States can become independent by attenuation, that is to say, the weakening of ties with the metropolitan state to the point at which the metropolitan authorities recognize that independence is already an accomplished fact: such states are, for example, Canada, Australia, and New Zealand. They can become independent by political negotiation and peaceful agreement such as Norway, Iceland, and the majority of British and French colonial territories since 1945, among them Ghana, Nigeria, Cameroon, Upper Volta, and Côte d'Ivoire. In terms of recent history, this is now by far the commonest method by which independence has been achieved. They can, exceptionally, declare independence when separated from their mother country by the exigencies of war or the occupation of the metropolitan countries themselves. This was a major cause of the early movements toward independence in the Latin American states and was the determining factor in the independence of Syria and Lebanon in 1941 (formally recognized in 1946). Only in a relatively small number of cases, 36 of the cases that occurred between 1901 and 1960 (Calvert 1970b, 139), has independence gained by the use of force or convincing threat of force by separatist movements, and these cases include those in which the force was provided by a state of international war. Similarly, in the latest wave of secessions, neither Slovenia nor Slovakia presented a convincing threat of force, and despite continuing tensions in Georgia and Armenia, the use of force played only a limited role in the disintegration of the Soviet Union.

Separatist movements have one great advantage over other revolutionists. Their goal of separatism is compatible with the survival of the incumbent government of the metropolitan country, which therefore need not press the fight to a conclusion and can if it wishes enter into negotiations for the termination of the active phase of conflict on terms acceptable to both sides. Such has been the pattern in the majority of cases since 1945, though in the case of Aden (South Yemen) and some of the ex-Portuguese territories no such settlement was in fact achieved before the metropolitan state decided to cut its losses by withdrawal. Despite some obvious hesitation, this was also the course followed by the new Russian government of Boris Yeltsin in respect of territories outside the Russian Federation, though attempts to secede from the Federation itself, notably in the case of Chechenya, were strongly resisted.

As the earlier cases remind us, separatist movements may, in addition, have the great advantage of operating in a territory that is not contiguous to the metropolitan state, and which the metropolitan government therefore finds it much harder to reinforce. Where, as in the case of Spain and Britain, the acquisition of sea power was an important factor in the creation of an empire, loss of sea power was an important factor in its dissolution. The British Empire was unusually dispersed. Most other imperial powers have sought to expand in a limited area of the world, either on land, like Russia or Austro-Hungary, or across inland sea as in the case of France or Italy, for each of which states such expansion represented the logical next stage of an expansion already completed on land. The loss of sea power was an important factor above all in the case of the Netherlands and Indonesia, where Britain had in fact helped reconquer Java at the conclusion of the Second World War, at one stage making use of the only troops available, namely the defeated Japanese (Drummond 1979).

Where such separatist movements occur close to the territory of another major power or superpower, the chances are great that they will receive clandestine support from that power, as in the case of China's support for the communists in Indo-China, between 1949 and 1954.

The disadvantages of separatist movements stem mainly from their weakness in face of the strength of the metropolitan country. A country controlling a large empire is in a position rather like a central bank facing a run on the banking system. Faced with pressure from one direction at a time, it is in a position to bring to bear such force that local pressure cannot hope to compete with it. Faced with pressure from all sides at once, it may have no option but to give way. Thus, as J. Bowyer Bell (1976) points out, Britain was in a relatively favorable position after 1945 in that the challenges to its central power came one after the other. Though the force at its disposal was not always sufficient to overcome armed insurgency, therefore, in almost all cases it was able to ensure a settlement more favorable to its interests than would otherwise have been the case. Bell identifies the cases of Ireland, Israel, and India as the three experiences that taught British governments to develop flexible responses to the problem of disengagement, showing them the advisability of creating representative institutions with which negotiations for independence could be successfully concluded and of avoiding the situation in which the home government was directly confronting a direct challenge to its own authority, such as was the case in Palestine.

A consequential weakness of a successful separatist movement may well be the fact that it stimulates in turn provincial or regional demands for separatism, such as led to the secession of Bangladesh from Pakistan and the unsuccessful moves for the secession of Biafra from Nigeria or the Cabinda enclave from Angola or Nagorno-Karabakh from Armenia. The history of Latin America in the nineteenth century offers a particularly striking series of examples of such a progression; from, for example, the secession of New Granada from Spain, to its dissolution into the three separate states of Colombia, Ecuador, and Venezuela, and finally to the secession of Panama from Colombia, which was at the same time constantly troubled by similar secessionist movements in other provinces. In this respect the case of North-East Ulster/Northern Ireland is not exceptional. What is unusual about it is that its claim to separateness takes the form of close identification with the metropolitan state, Great Britain.

National Liberation and the International System

To understand the relationship between national liberation and the wars (and civil wars) to which it gives rise it will first be necessary to consider further the historical development of the international system after the French Revolution.

Between 1815 and 1914 the world order was dominated by the great European Powers. Those in the center of the Eurasian land mass expanded on land; those on its fringes by sea. They did so at the expense of non-European empires such as Turkey, Iran/Persia, and China, as well as by the conquest and subjugation of "unoccupied" territory.

The term "empire" itself has an interesting history. Originally, before 1805, there was only one European empire, the (Holy Roman) Empire, which had historically enshrined the universal concept of a world empire. By claiming the title of Emperor, Napoleon was therefore asserting a universal primacy; ironically it was this act which made the concept of empire a divisible one. Hitherto, the rulers of Turkey and Iran had been accorded their own special titles (Sultan, Shah), as were the multitudinous rulers of the Indian states. Now to the rulers of China and Japan were added the formal titles of the rulers of France, Germany, and Great Britain (in her person as Empress of India), and the new word "imperialism" was coined to designate the desirability of creating and maintaining empires. Only later was the use of the word reversed by Hobson (1902) and Lenin (1916) to give it an undesirable connotation (see Hobson 1968, Lenin 1967).

At the beginning of this long period new states came into existence that were accepted as such and did not become part of the great European empires. But the majority of them were concentrated in the Americas, where the isolation of distance and sea communication allowed a largely independent order to be established, without, however, challenging the existing possessions of European powers other than Spain and Portugal. Serbia (effectively independent since 1805) and Greece (independent since 1822) maintained their independence in the disputed area between Turkey and Europe known as the Balkans, where they were to be joined in due course by Romania, Bulgaria and, just before the First World War, Albania. In the Far East, only China, because of its size, Japan, an island Empire, and Thailand, able to play off Britain against France, retained independence, while the European states encroached on both China and Thailand as they had previously done on Turkey and were to continue to do so in South West Asia during the First World War. In central Asia, Iran and Afghanistan survived the struggle between Britain and Russia. In Africa only Ethiopia survived the first wave of European penetration, though at a serious loss of its traditional territories.

Between 1914 and 1945 the world order continued to be dominated by European powers. Britain, France, and Germany were separated from Russia (now the Soviet Union) by the "Balkanisation" of Eastern Europe, where the Austrian and Turkish Empires had disappeared almost, leaving only modern Austria and the enclave of Turkey-in-Europe. The rising power of the United States had come to dominate the western hemisphere, but its involvement in the First World War and its brief period of formal empire building (Hawaii, Samoa, Puerto Rico, the Philippines, the Canal Zone, the Virgin Islands) had ended and its withdrawal from world involvement had been accompanied by strong support for the dissolution of rival empires, just as protectionism at home had been accompanied by the policy of the "Open Door" in China. Meanwhile, with the creation of the League of Nations, the first serious attempt had been made to constitute a new world order based on the formal equality of sovereign states, in which the former colonies of the European powers (Canada, Australia, New Zealand, South Africa, India) would take their place by peaceful evolution.

The states in the Middle East (Iraq, Syria) and Africa (Namibia) that did not proceed directly to independence after the First World War were given a wholly new status. Despite the all-too evident desire of the governments of Britain and France to add them to their formal Empires, and their tendency afterwards to treat them as if they had in fact been so added, they were instead constituted as League of Nations Mandated Territories. In other words, they were to be administered by the victorious powers in such a way as to further their transition to independence at an early period. In the meanwhile, in the former Turkish territories of the Middle East in particular, Britain and France were able to retain control of a strategically sensitive area on the route to the Far East, but also to exploit the very considerable resources of oil that lay below the desert sands.

The considerable irony of treating these territories as ones which required a period of development prior to independence was not lost on either their rulers or their more educated citizens. Countries such as Iraq and Syria had been seats of advanced civilization while Europe was in its infancy. Not only did they resent the assumption that they were not able to govern themselves, but in religious circles, particularly those surrounding the Grand Mufti of Jerusalem, Haj Muhammad Amin al-Husseini, in the British Mandated Territory of Palestine, there was a special resentment that the rule of Muslims had now passed into the hands of infidels. Religious leadership was, however, fragmented, following the secular revolution of Mustafa Kemal Atatürk in Turkey and the abolition of the Caliphate, on the one hand, and the rise of fundamentalist Islamic leadership under Ibn Saud of Saudi Arabia (Abdul Aziz bin Abdur Rahman al-Saud) on the other. Nationalist feeling also grew strong in the strategically key country of Egypt, which had already enjoyed relative independence in the early nineteenth century, and where a powerful historical symbolism was also available for nationalist exploitation.

Despite the formal agreements embodied in the mandate system, the rivalry for influence between Britain and France was barely checked, and the antagonisms generated by the First World War alliance and its aftermath made it difficult for the two powers to act in common. The world order of the inter-war period, therefore, was much less stable than that of 1914, and efforts to reestablish the principle of balance of power in face of the rise of Hitler led only to the Second World War. Though both Britain and France appeared among the four victorious powers in 1945, France had been occupied and Britain humiliated in the Far East. By 1946–7 it became apparent that a new bipolar world order was emerging in which neither of the two new major powers, the United States and the Soviet Union, had any interest in conserving the old colonial empires.

In striking contrast with its predecessors, therefore, the new world order has been marked by the disintegration, not the development, of formal empires. At the same time, it is clear that each of the two superpowers have sought in this situation to add to their own spheres of influence, or, at the least, to deny new states to the sphere of their rival. They have, however, sought to do this in rather different ways.

The United States, faced with what it saw as a challenge from the Soviet Union, responded by making use of the traditional instruments of diplomacy.

Basic to the structure was a system of formal military alliances. The traditional claim of primacy within the western hemisphere, known as the Monroe Doctrine, was multilateralized by the creation of two organizations: a military alliance (the Rio Pact) and a regional organization within the United Nations committed to applying on a regional basis the United Nation's mission of collective security, namely, the Organization of American States (OAS). In Western Europe the formal alliance, the North Atlantic Treaty Organisation (NATO), had a consultative counterpart in the so-called Western European Union, but this failed to generate support, and was eventually to be superseded by the European initiative to create an Economic Community (1957) on a much narrower geographical basis. Outside these two areas, the strategy of formal alliance was relatively unsuccessful; though by a direct alliance the United States took over directly the traditional links of Britain with Australia and New Zealand (Australia, New Zealand, United States Security Treaty [ANZUS]), alliance structures for south-east Asia foundered on local neutralism (South East Asia Treaty Organization [SEATO]) and initiatives for the Middle East created more trouble than they were worth, in view of the growing resentment at United States' support for Israel (Middle Eastern/Central Defense Organization [MEDO/CENTO]).

Outside this structure, the United States concluded a large number of bilateral military agreements. These formed one of two bases for the extensive use of aid programs in the long term, in a sense merely a natural extension of the wartime systems of military aid that had led up to and included Lend Lease. The other, the provision of economic aid for civilian development, was new. It began with the Marshall Plan, a successful initiative to restore the war-damaged industrial base of western Europe, from which, under Soviet prodding, the Eastern European countries that had at first been willing to participate, dissociated themselves, as did the USSR itself. It was later to extend, in Latin America, Africa, and south Asia, into a gigantic attempt to promote new industrial development and so to win friends among the new states.

The structures of aid and alliance were extended at the same time as the United States as the world's largest concentration of finance capital had emerged by default as the banker and creditor of the noncommunist world. By the later 1950s this was to give rise to increasing complaints among the new states that their position had not really changed. When Ghana, for example, became independent in 1957 its leader, Kwame Nkrumah, who was initially influenced by United States black consciousness and Christian symbolism, adopted the saying "Seek ye first the political kingdom." By the time of his deposition in 1966 he was already author of a sequel to Lenin, *Neocolonialism, the Last Stage of Imperialism* (1965). Its theme, echoed by others, was that political independence was not enough, for visible control by colonialism had simply been superseded by an invisible control of finance capital and dependence on market prices set by the developed powers. The ultimate banker of this system and largest consumer of raw materials, the United States, thus became a "neocolonialist" power. Only much later, under George W. Bush, were Americans again ready to openly embrace the notion that they were, and should rightfully be, an imperial power.

Dependency and Neocolonialism

In the late 1960s and 1970s the so-called dependency theorists were to carry this theme a stage further, arguing that by maintaining the existing economic order the United States and its developed client states were in fact actively promoting the underdevelopment of the Third World, which they argued was a necessary condition of their own development (Frank 1969, 1978; Cardoso and Faletto 1979). Aid and investment, therefore, far from promoting the long-term growth of the underdeveloped world, was actively seeking to continue its state of deprivation. The two streams came together in mid-decade in demands for a "New International Economic Order" from, in particular, the then presidents of Mexico and Venezuela on behalf of their colleagues of the Third World (Arnell and Nygren 1980).

There were, of course, always public figures in the United States prepared to argue that the formal structure of aid was a denial of traditional American practice; that the structure of private investment was as benign in its effects abroad as at home. What was not always realized outside the United States was that the government of that country, by the nature of its political system, lacked any effective check on investment abroad. "Neocolonialism," therefore, if it existed, was not a system in the sense of being consciously guided and directed. Hence, if it worked in favor of the United States, that was fortuitous, though certainly not unwelcome to the US government. The rising economic power of Japan, South Korea, Taiwan, and Hong Kong certainly seemed to show that the dependency thesis that the development of existing powers was incompatible with the development of latecomers was quite incorrect.

The Soviet Union, as might have been expected from a country that had been invaded and had suffered badly from the ravages of the Second World War, initially took a very different attitude to the outside world, which it saw as a fundamentally hostile territory. Only in Europe did it constitute a formal military alliance grouping, the Warsaw Pact, to match that of NATO. Far from receiving aid other than military, its members were required in many cases to pay reparations to the USSR itself, and their economic recovery was correspondingly delayed. This serious shortage of economic resources and its lack of productive capacity prevented it from developing an aid program comparable to that of the United States, though in the 1950s it was to make a number of spectacular moves to enlist key support, notably by the agreement to finance the Aswan High Dam in Egypt in 1956 when western experts had doubted its value or desirability (cf. Feinberg 1983).

Having no stake in the existing diplomatic order, the Soviet Union returned to its traditional revolutionary posture in encouraging revolts in the colonial empires, for which purpose a new organization, the Cominform, was constituted to replace the Comintern, which had been dissolved as a gesture of wartime solidarity with Russia's allies. It began with the advantage that in certain areas such revolts had already begun before the war's end, notably that in Indo-China against the French (the "August Revolution," or First Indo-China War) and that in Indonesia against the Dutch. In the former case, Ho Chi Minh, a committed communist, was able, even with Chinese support, only to hold the northern part of Vietnam at the first peace settlement in 1954. The neutralist regimes of Sihanouk in Cambodia and of the Laotian princes, however, that emerged at the same time represented a useful strategic gain for the communists in the region and displayed much the same blend of nationalism, neutralism, and self-conscious rapprochement with the USSR as did the regime of Sukarno in Indonesia or the self-consciously even-handed government of Pandit Nehru in India. By the late 1950s, therefore, the Soviet leaders had come not only to be received with respect in a much wider range of countries than had been the case with Stalin, but also in turn to recognize the validity of a "non-aligned position," though this last they continued to regard as only a half-way stage to a committed socialist position recognizing the Soviet Union as the leading anticolonial force.

Between 1959 and 1961 the Soviet camp received the unexpected addition of support from Cuba. Because of its strategic value to the Soviet Union in the confrontation with the United States, this addition was welcomed, even though it proved very costly in continuing economic support. In due course it was admitted to formal alliance with the Soviet Union and became a member of Comecon. After this, and with increasing speed in the 1970s, a number of other newly independent states: South Yemen, Somalia, Angola, Mozambique, Guinea-Bissau, and Cabo Verde, proclaimed themselves Marxist states and aligned themselves with the USSR without in the first instance the spur of an actual Soviet military presence or the close support of its assistance across a land frontier. Thus, the Soviet Union came to acquire an extended group of client states which looked to it for aid, which might, as in the case of Angola, involve open military assistance or, worse, as in the case of Somalia, be incompatible with support for a neighboring Marxist regime, namely Ethiopia. In this way the Soviet Union began for the first time to incur the disadvantages that had previously been associated with the world-wide commitments of the United States, which, by a coincidence, was at the same time seeking, under the Nixon/Kissinger leadership, to withdraw from some of its more exposed positions. The immediate consequence of this last was the eventual victory in 1975 of communist forces in Cambodia and Laos as well as South Vietnam.

It must not necessarily be assumed that all national liberation movements in the post-1945 period necessarily involved one or other of the superpowers, even though it was generally believed at the time that this was the case. Events have since shown that the movements of the 1940s, then often attributed to "communist infiltration," had in fact a strong nationalist content, and that attempts to transpose the methods used in one area, Vietnam for example, into others often proved unsuccessful. In the more recent period, the Third Indo-China War between Vietnam and China, the Ethiopia-Somalia contest for the Ogaden, and the Argentine attack on the Falkland Islands have all confirmed the primacy of nationalism over ideological affinities. The international system of the day has set some bounds for the pursuit of nationalism. The phenomenon itself remains varied and unpredictable.

The Pursuit of National Identity

The pursuit of political independence has been historically a prime objective of nationalists since the Dutch Revolution. The concept of nation, it seems, has the same ability to legitimize in its supporters the willingness to resort to armed struggle as has religion, and, as in the case of the USSR itself in the Second World War bears witness, more power than that of the state. But how does such a struggle actually begin?

The first prerequisite is one of the three criteria for nationhood; linguistic, religious, or cultural identity. The term "ethnic" is often used, but is in practice hard to define meaningfully except in terms that admit a large proportion of the other criteria. Besides, there are cases such as that of the United States or Brazil in which it is clearly not at all appropriate.

What Anthony Smith calls the "bearers" (Smith 1976, 21) of nationalism are therefore crucially important to its appearance, since it is necessary not only that these criteria exist in a given area, but that they come to be seen as important. Such individuals are characteristically of the intellectual elite, well-educated and with experience of life abroad that has thrown into relief for them their own sense of cultural separateness. Cultural identity, it seems, can only be realized in opposition to something else. At the same time, a sense of cultural identity does not preclude extensive borrowing from the dominant culture of the area, particularly where such aspects are not seen at the time being as of crucial significance, or are invested with other desirable properties, for example "modernity." In fact, a crucial factor in the emergence of leaders of independence movements seems, on the contrary, to have been their access to higher education in the metropolitan country; something shared by leaders otherwise as disparate as Nehru, Nkrumah, Sukarno, and Dr Hastings Banda.

The leader of an independence movement, in short, must combine not only cultural identity but also proficiency in the dominant culture which enables him to deploy it against its proponents and gives him confidence to do so. In the post-1945 period his or her claim to authority among his followers was characteristically defined by the colonial authorities, who sent him, as the British did Kenyatta or Makarios, into detention or exile as an attempt to reduce the leader's impact on the nascent nationalist movement and to remove what was essentially regarded as a focus of disaffection.

In an earlier period such leaders might have been less fortunate. They themselves might have been executed, like Jose Martí within weeks of his return to Cuba in 1895. Their followers might have been suppressed by military force and then executed, as by the Russian General Paskievitch who in 1831 could say "L'ordre règne à Varsovie" ("Order reigns in Warsaw") because his guns had ensured that it did. Attempts to disengage national communist movements from Soviet domination in eastern Europe in Hungary in 1956 and in Czechoslovakia in 1968 were in similar fashion ruthlessly suppressed by Soviet military power. The Hungarian leader, Imre Nagy, was imprisoned and shot, as earlier were nationalist resistance leaders in the Baltic States and the Ukraine. On the other hand, the shooting of the leaders of the Easter Rising in Dublin in 1916 had exactly the effect of consolidating what had previously only been a weak national movement into a strong armed force, entirely alienated from the sources of government authority; and democratic governments, such as that of Lloyd George in post-1918 Britain, found public opinion unwilling to support long-term repressive measures of such a drastic nature. Such an option, therefore, did not lie open to the post-1945 governments of Britain, France, the Netherlands, and Belgium.

A militant resistance movement, if it is to present an effective challenge, needs a source of arms. In the case of the post-1945 governments these came from the colonial powers themselves. They had been supplied, as in Burma, Malaysia, and Indonesia, to use against the Japanese. The same was true in the first instances of the levies hastily raised to support the republic of Vietnam in 1945. Only later did it become possible for some of the enormous quantity of arms also supplied by the western powers to China to be redeployed secretly to aid the resistance struggle in south-east Asia. Western sources seem always to have underestimated the indigenous contribution to the success of such movements, and to have overestimated the amount of physical aid received from China and/or the Soviet Union. They were to do the same in the 1960s in evaluating the guerrilla movements in Latin America, a mistake shown even more recently in the Reagan administration's persistent belief that the Farabundo Martí National Liberation Front (FMLN) in El Salvador was receiving large arms shipments from Cuba via Nicaragua, despite clear evidence from arms captures that insurgent arms were overwhelmingly of NATO origin and supplied by the United States.

Lastly, once arms were available, an effective strategy had to be found for their use. Again, the indigenous importance of Truong Chinh (1963) in Vietnam, and even more notably the noncommunist Nasution (1965) in Indonesia, is very clear. Nationalist movements have not in general operated to a grand strategic plan. Instead, they have relearned the lessons of war by trial and error, aided by two principal sources: recollections of their former past, as with Moshe Dayan in Israel, and the military manuals of the metropolitan forces themselves, as with the first Irish Republican Army.

Where they differed from internal revolutionary movements, is that they did not necessarily have to achieve military victory. As the number of calls on the resources of the metropolitan states increased, it was sufficient to ensure that they were not themselves defeated. The case of Portugal presents only the most spectacular of the instances of the period in which growing war weariness caused a dramatic political reversal (*Sunday Times* Insight Team 1975) leading to an agreed settlement; other examples being the agreement on the independence of Indo-China in 1954 and the Evian Agreement leading to the independence of Algeria in 1962. It is this combination of military and political strategies that was most strikingly elaborated in the course of the period.

At the beginning of the period, there was strong public support for the United States for the war against the guerrillas in the Philippines and in Britain a series of colonial wars and in particular the "Hola prison camp" scandal failed to become an issue in the 1959 General Election in Britain. In France, however, the fall of Dien Bien Phu brought about a drastic public reappraisal of the situation that had led its defender, General de Castris to allow his forces to become "bottled up" without hope of escape, and enabled the Mendès-France government to cut French losses by withdrawal. The United States during the Vietnam War fell into the same trap of attempting to use traditional military strategy in a guerrilla war.

The Johnson administration was thrown into disarray and the president driven to resignation by the Tet offensive of February 1968. It is an irony that in military strategic terms the Tet offensive was in fact a severe defeat for the Vietcong and the North Vietnamese, while in political terms it was a decisive turning-point in their favor. For the simultaneous seizure of strong-points in many cities in South Vietnam led to a fierce counterattack that cost the lives of many well-trained communist cadres without any hope of achieving the instant seizure of power. But, paradoxically, the fact that such a hopeless gesture could be attempted at all was taken in the United States as a sign of American weakness and precipitated a major political crisis.

The Nixon administration, relying on much greater firepower than had been available to the French in 1954, tried to cut the Vietcong supply route (the "Ho Chi Minh Trail") by strategic bombing, and extended the war to Cambodia in a vain attempt to achieve total denial. Despite protests the administration was, however, able to retain adequate support based on its professions of peace-seeking at the negotiating table in February 1972. It claimed to be seeking the Vietnamization of the war, but in the long run this only helped to destroy all confidence in the ability of the South Vietnamese themselves to defend their own country. In the end the Nixon administration was left with no choice but to accept a humiliating withdrawal and the transfer of the Indo-Chinese territories to communist control, which it then sought to blame on the US Congress. How far this result was intended is very hard to assess. Fraternal support for the Vietcong had existed in the United States since the late 1960s, but remained always very marginal as an element in the United States peace movement. It is also probable that the North Vietnamese overestimated the strength of the peace movement as a whole, at least if they believed their own propaganda.

It is instructive to contrast the way in which for 11 years the Salazar government and its successor in Portugal managed, with only a tiny fraction of the resources available to the government of the United States, to sustain an antiguerrilla campaign, not only in Angola, but also in Mozambique and Guinea-Bissau. Control of the media and censorship of reports from the fighting zone minimized the effect of the fighting on public opinion, which in any case had no public expression in political form. The sole prominent political opponent of the regime within Portugal, Humberto Delgado, was secretly murdered on the Spanish frontier by the PIDE, the Portuguese

Secret Police. World opinion, too, had only a minimal effect, as Portugal's NATO allies were unwilling to deny it the supplies of arms and ammunition needed to continue the campaign, for fear of a general communist takeover in southern Africa. It was, therefore, only among the armed forces of Portugal, where the true picture was known, that war weariness could be translated into political form, the result being the Revolution of 1975. Again, however, there seems no reason to suppose that this was for the insurgents a deliberately planned outcome, however welcome.

Once the colonial power (or equivalent) has withdrawn, as this last case shows, the consequences of wars of national liberation are by no means over. They have the effect of creating a distinctive style of political leadership in the new state which is the product of war, operates in a military mode and is particularly intolerant of internal opposition, which it regards, not as a valuable political discovery enabling a good government to maximize its political support, but as a colonialist encumbrance holding back national development. Where the struggle has been particularly fierce, opposition has been entirely eliminated; elsewhere it has been curtailed over time (Calvert 1976).

In the majority of cases the independent states have quickly adopted a presidential style of leadership, with the focus of power and public attention on a charismatic leader. Where there has been more than one such leader, as in Zimbabwe, the one who is in office at independence moves to eliminate his rival. Robert Mugabe did this by sending the Fifth Brigade into the tribal lands of the supporters of Joshua Nkomo. There is a strong incentive for such leaders to become radicalized, since by doing so they avert any imputation that they were acceptable to the outgoing colonial government.

Such a style of leadership draws both on traditional sources in adopting, like Jomo Kenyatta, the emblems of traditional chieftainship, and on modern ones in attending the military parades and recalling the days of glory of the armed forces and their struggle. As the history of the Francophone African states in the early 1960s shows, all independent states are at first extremely vulnerable to military coups. Even the tiny army of ex-Dutch Suriname, only 300 strong, was able to seize control of the political system from the elected prime minister, Henck Arron. But states that have already been militarized run in addition the extra risk of being involved in a major internal civil war, as disappointment grows at the actual outcome of independence and its inevitable failure to deliver all that the supporters of independence individually hoped from it. With much better communications, the new states have been far more successful in achieving speedy centralization than their predecessors in Latin America, who spent much of the nineteenth century locked in a conflict between centralists and federalists. However, there is every reason to suppose that the same pressures still exist, and account for the movements for regional autonomy or separatism that have been characteristic of India, Burma/Myanmar, and the Philippines, to name but three very different examples.

A newly independent state with a substantial military capability already in being, moreover, enters the international system not just as a client state but as an actor in its own right, capable of acting as a local or even regional power. It must therefore have regard not only to the global balance and its effect in its region, but on the internal dynamics of the situation in which it finds itself, and it is in any case going to be approached very soon to return the favors its neighbors may have done on it by giving tacit or active support to its struggle for independence. Thus, Nigeria, despite being itself torn by civil war and tribal conflicts leading to a demand for secession, could not but help becoming a focus for its African neighbors, and as an oil-rich state assuming a leadership role within the Organization of African Unity (OAU—now the African Union). Zimbabwe, on the other hand, came to independence already locked into confrontation with South Africa, and, suffering from the depletion of civil war, was frustrated in its attempts to achieve the successful revolution of the whole of southern Africa that its leader may have dreamt of before independence. Like Mozambique, strong pressures later operated to drive it back into alliance with the West. In Mozambique, only inept handling of the situation by the Reagan administration in the United States cut the process short and delayed progress until the fall of the apartheid regime in South Africa.

In the New World Order, wars of national liberation continue, though attention has shifted to new zones of conflict. As a result, the major powers will continue to have regard to the problems they present for international stability. Indeed the prevailing economic model of free trade has actually facilitated them by making it even more difficult to control the global trade in arms and ammunition. It does not follow, however, that in all cases success will be rewarded with recognition.

Ironically, successful nationalism coupled with military experience creates a strong demand for a command economy. Economies, however, do not necessarily respond well to command, and no government can put into the ground the mineral or energy resources that nature has failed to provide. The desire for economic independence, then, tends toward the creation of economies that replicate the features of existing ones, but in weaker form: the same emphasis on heavy industry, import substitution, and control of what foreign investment may be permitted, but a weaker state to enforce such policies. It is this combination of weaknesses in face of the developed economies that emerged in the 1970s as the main burden of complaint of the proponents of the New International Economic Order.

However, the collapse of the Soviet Union, the new role of the United States as a "lonely superpower" and the continuing political divisions that the post-Cold War situation embodies made it very unlikely that such a dramatic change could be achieved in the near future—if at all. One consequence of this is likely to be the buildup of resentment in provincial areas of the South against the hegemony of national government. Though as in the case of the Zapatista revolt in Mexico this may be capable of being contained within the existing political order, it is almost inevitable that in some instances it will not. The Kurds of Iraq, for example, are unlikely to wish to risk the loss of the virtual autonomy they have fortuitously gained as a result of the Iraq War but there are many other Kurds in Iran and Turkey who would wish to join them. The future of Kashmir remains a perennial problem for both India and Pakistan. Where the very definition of nation is contested, agreement on a political settlement is exceedingly unlikely.

Guerrilla Warfare

Guerrilla warfare is at least as old as fifth-century China, but it was difficult to distinguish from ordinary warfare until very recent times. The introduction of heavy artillery from about 1780 onwards changed the nature of "conventional" war; it has not changed the nature of partisan or guerrilla warfare.

The major change has been the disappearance of the siege, though it has since reappeared at Sarajevo and elsewhere in Bosnia. With the disappearance of the siege, regular forces revert to mobile combat and the guerrilla has an opportunity to attack them. Guerrilla warfare is often wrongly thought of as being alien to the European tradition. But it is in Europe that the term originated, in the Spanish War of Independence which broke out on May 2, 1808. The rising followed Napoleon's successful invasion of Spain and Portugal, the capture of the Spanish Monarchy by the French and the imposition of Napoleon's brother as ruler of Spain; and it was a war of independence in the same sense as the Serbian War of Independence or the Egyptian war against the Turks or any other early-nineteenth-century nationalist war.

The Spanish War of Independence, however, notably depended on two kinds of fighting. The Spanish component, which had largely been preempted by the success of the French invasion and the capture of the regular seat of power in Spain, consisted of the organization of irregular forces. These were, in turn, sustained by Spain's allies in the field, the regular forces under Arthur Wellesley, later First Duke of Wellington, who started out from Portugal and eventually drove forward into Spain, supported by the "little war" or "guerrilla" of the native Spanish irregulars, until able to engage the French troops in a series of decisive battles.

The guerrillas gave rise to a Spanish mystique. They were the Spanish component; they were the element that actually represented the Spanish contribution to the War of Independence. As Raymond Carr says in his history of Spain, the war "gave liberalism its programme and its technique of revolution. It defines Spanish patriotism and endows it with an enduring myth. It saddled liberalism with the problems of generals in politics and the mystique of the guerrilla" (Carr 1966, 105). Their success was, therefore, directly related to a political party within Spain, that is, the *liberales* or Liberals, as they became more familiarly known later. Their appeal was nationalistic in flavor in that it called upon the resources of the support latent in the Spanish countryside for a fighting force that would drive the French out.

One very important point about the Spanish uprising was that it did secure a very early though largely symbolic victory, which is often important in a long drawn-out contest. The first Spanish victory occurred in July 1808, at Baylén, and it was a product not just of Spanish prowess but of French incompetence. Napoleon thought that the conquest of Spain was a secondary matter that could be entrusted to inferior troops, and he sent one of his most loyal but least able marshals to command them. However, with good troops they won repeatedly. The pressure that this put on the Allied effort was extremely divisive. Time and time again Wellington believed that he was being betrayed by the Spanish and his irregulars, whereas time and time again the Spaniards believed that the English were merely pillaging the country and doing very little toward its liberation. In other words, there was, from the beginning, a dichotomy between the irregular forces of the Spanish and the regular forces of the allies and the French were able for a time to exploit this.

Yet the liberation of Spain required both: the guerrilla was essential to the defeat of the French. "It was this continuous resistance, feeble as it often was, which broke Napoleon's doctrine of maximum concentration in the attempt to solve contradictory demands of operation and occupation in the hostile countryside" (Carr 1966, 108). Spain would have been powerless without Wellington's field forces; Wellington could not have operated with such a small army without the diversionary effects of Spanish resistance.

It was the Spaniards who proved Wellington's own maxim, "the more ground the French hold the weaker they will be at any point." With allowances, this could almost have been written by Mao Tse Tung. The guerrilla element in the Spanish War of Independence converted the enemy's strength into weakness. It wore down the French and it destroyed what should have been their greatest strategic advantage, their concentration. By concentrating forces, the French finally found they had increased their dependence on their supply lines rather than decreased them. As they increased their dependence on their lines of supply so the lines of supply themselves became more critical and were correspondingly more vulnerable to Spanish operations.

The Spanish guerrilla war was in fact one of the largest recorded in terms of the size of the forces. The Spaniards deployed up to, perhaps, 50,000 men altogether, organized in bands of up to 8,000—a very substantial force indeed, and hardly what we would now today regard as a guerrilla force. But even then it proved very difficult to use them other than tactically. They were a raw force and because of the very poor communications, the use of guerrillas in coordinated military activities proved almost impossible. They operated primarily as independent units. Even then the French were able to hold them at a certain level because the French enjoyed means of communication superior to any other nation in Europe at that time. They had interior lines of communication and they made use of the semaphore. From semaphore towers on every hill they could signal with moveable apparatus from one hill to another, which of course was very much quicker than the guerrillas could signal to one another by runner or on horseback. So that superior communications were the secret of the long French resistance rather than the concentration of military forces that went with it. US forces used both the heliograph and the telegraph in their successful campaigns to end resistance to their expansion toward the West.

But the guerrillas also had one very important additional effect. Their function was to reoccupy areas evacuated by the French and to impose a "patriot terror," bullying the population into resistance. Each time the French moved out of an area the guerrillas would move in, fill the vacuum and punish any French collaborators, thus ensuring less collaboration next time the French came by. In other words, the possibility of being vulnerable to a terrorist movement once the French had gone away was something that severely restricted collaboration with the invading forces.

Three reasons explain the attention given to this single case. First, the instance is unfamiliar. Secondly, it explains the origins of the word. Thirdly, it has a very definite, direct relationship with three of the major modern areas of insurgency. All are former Spanish territories and the communication links between them and Spain are quite manifest. In fact, they are so manifest that caution is required, because it may not be that the idea of guerrilla warfare was actually transmitted from Spain to its colonies. It may merely have been that the social conditions in the colonies were similar and that most of them copied the same kind of methods.

First, there are the Latin American countries which generally became independent in the nineteenth century. Here, in fact, the legacy of guerrilla warfare goes on throughout the nineteenth century. It is responsible to a considerable extent for the ultimate defeat in 1825 of the Spaniards in Peru itself, where Spaniards enjoyed a considerable degree of support; but their support was gradually eroded by irregular forces operating over a very wide area. Later it brings the liberals to power in many countries, as in Guatemala in 1870. And in resistance to foreign attack, it is very successful in wearing down the French occupation in Mexico in 1864–7. These are three examples of the use of guerrilla warfare tactics, which confirm the value of the method in Latin America itself in the nineteenth century. Another legacy of the Spanish War of Independence in general politics, a product of war with very small forces, was that of the *caudillo*, the military leader of the nineteenth century. It is one of the major disadvantages of guerrilla warfare that it tends to place military leaders or militarized leaders in politics.

Cuba was the one state in Latin America that did not get independence with the rest. In fact it was known as *La Isla Siempre Leal* ("The Ever Loyal Island"). But in 1868, at the time of the collapse of the Spanish monarchy and the imposition of the republic in Spain itself, the rather conservative Cubans got impatient. They decided it was now time for them to fight for their independence and they were helped in this by sympathizers in the United States. From 1868–78 there followed the Ten Years War—a war of independence which in fact did not succeed. Cuba did not have a surviving indigenous population. It did have a large, mainly Afro-American population descended from imported slaves. Since slavery was still legal in Cuba at this period this was a powerful reason for other countries to support the War of Independence in Cuba for purely idealistic reasons; but it was not yet sufficient to bring success.

In 1895 the War of Independence was resumed as the result of a small expeditionary movement led by the famous patriot Jose Martí. Martí, whose poetry is still read today, was not only an inspiration to the movement of Cuban independence, but he was also its first real leader (Martí 1968). His career is remarkably similar to the career of all kinds of other guerrillas and can serve as a typical example.

First of all, he was jailed at 17 years of age for laughing at some Spanish soldiers. One could compare Andrew Jackson, later president of the United States, who at the age of 14 was ordered to black the boots of a British officer during the American War of Independence. When he refused to do so, the officer hit him across the face with his sword, leaving him scarred for life. He later turned out to be the American hero of the Battle of New Orleans (1815). Martí was luckier, he was merely put in jail. After he got out he fled, left Cuba and built a Cuban revolutionary party among exiles in the United States, which he financed by going on speaking tours. In February 1895 he landed in Cuba with his pocket edition of Cicero and a couple of revolvers. Sadly, he soon fell into the hands of the Spanish authorities and was put to death; but his separatist movement survived. In his last letter to the people of Cuba he expressed his main fears; first that, the danger of Cuba lay in that, when it attained independence, it would fall under the dominance of a military leader, a military *caudillo*, like the other Latin American countries; and secondly, that in any case, it was too near the United States not to be subjected to its power, like David to Goliath (sic).

Martí's inspiration stirred again in two experienced military leaders who had both fought in the Ten Years War. Gómez and Maceo recruited from the rural areas groups of black and poor white forces, the classes which had traditionally taken to the hills when there was no economic future for them. And they received through filibustering, arms sent in small ships from the United States, which the Spanish fleet could not intercept.

The Spanish forces faced, among other things, bad roads—since they had foolishly not built any—jungle war, rain, and disease. They sent there instead (as always on these occasions) a General, General Weyler, to pacify the Cubans by military means. Weyler set about pacifying them vigorously, with all the guns he had available. To prevent them receiving supplies he herded the civilian population into *campos de reconcentracion*, or concentration camps. It should be noted that, when originally invented, "concentration camp" meant a place where the civilian population was concentrated: only since 1944 have the words "concentration camp" inevitably come to be interpreted as a euphemism for "extermination camp." They are two very different things, and it was Weyler who seems to have used concentration camps for the very first time, not, as may be found in some textbooks, the British in South Africa.

Weyler was subject to abuse from all sides, not only from Spain, but from the United States. He is quoted as saying, rather bitterly "How do they want me to wage war? With Bishops' pastorals and presents of sweets and money?" (Carr 1966, 385). With Martí killed in battle, the whole picture could have been black indeed for the Cubans if it had not been for two fortunate events. First, Canovas, the prime minister of Spain, was assassinated by an Italian anarchist in 1897. When his government fell apart, the liberals were converted to the principle of autonomy but were unable to form a working coalition to continue the war. Finally, the United States picked a quarrel with them over the explosion which sank the USS *Maine* in Havana harbor in 1898. The Spanish-American War broke out, and the Spanish were resoundingly defeated. Cuba was freed, but only as an American protectorate. The *Maine* was towed out to sea and scuttled. This experience was later to shape the course of the Cuban Revolution after 1959.

The third area affected by the Spanish experience is that of the Philippines in south-east Asia which, between 1898 and 1902, waged a guerrilla war against the Americans. The reason was that the Americans had bestowed their forces in readiness for the Spanish-American War in such a way that they had forces in all major Spanish strongholds and an obvious one was in Manila Bay in the Philippines. This was the only south-east Asian colony of Spain and it was also an important naval base. If the Americans pulled their ships out of the Pacific to send them to the Atlantic to fight against Cuba instead, then they would risk having to fight a two-ocean war. What they did was to direct Admiral Dewey, who happened to be in the region, to attack Manila Bay and capture it, surprising the Spanish so that resistance collapsed very quickly.

The capture of Manila Bay therefore left the US government in nominal control of the Philippines, but the Philippines, of course, now wanted to become independent too. They in turn therefore had to be pacified. It took 4 years to end guerrilla resistance but it was done. And so the Philippines remained an American possession down to 1946 when they became independent. In the years between 1945 and 1948, however, a further guerrilla movement arose which, though to a considerable extent preempted by the American decision to give the Philippines independence in 1946, necessitated the commitment of American forces, available as a result of the end of the war in the Pacific.

Thus, the Philippines in the postwar period forms one of the four major areas of insurgency in south-east Asia; the other three being the Indonesian War of Independence, 1945–8 (Nasution 1965), the August Revolution in Vietnam, 1945–54 (Giap 1965) and the Malayan Emergency, 1948–60. There are distinct resemblances between all these movements, and so great was the similarity in fact, that at the time they were generally put down to communist machinations. Certainly there were communist moves to encourage revolt and there were substantial communist elements in all these movements. But there was also, though not greatly appreciated at the time, a great reservoir of feeling for independence. The western powers had been humiliated in the Pacific; they had been soundly defeated by the Japanese and humiliated in Singapore. The loss of prestige which this meant was in itself sufficient to result in independence for Burma and hasten that of other Asian colonies.

The development of guerrilla warfare seems to have come easily for the British, probably because they did not maintain a large standing army as such. Where they did maintain a large standing army, in India, there was the greatest possible resistance to any irregular warfare. In the Second World War Wingate and his Chindits operated quite naturally on the further side of the Indian Empire, purely on native wit and their experience of the First World War, but they were always greatly distrusted by the establishment in India itself. Yet in doing so they drew on this native tradition, and the role of one man in particular, T.E. Lawrence (1926). It has been suggested that it is with Lawrence, as far as the Western tradition is concerned, that guerrilla warfare actually developed from being just a convenient technique into a doctrine about how to wage war by every possible means.

Lawrence's theory about guerrilla warfare is interesting because he emphasizes two points. First, that the main purpose of guerrilla forces, unlike conventional forces, is not to engage the enemy. They must be capable of protecting themselves against the enemy and they must harass the enemy, but they must not engage the enemy. There is no thought here, therefore, of using guerrillas as partisan forces in the sense in which, for example, Clausewitz would have permitted their use; nor in the sense which Mao uses forces, so that they will actually be developed into a conventional army. Rather, Lawrence is thinking of a political process that will make it politically inexpedient for the Turks to remain in possession of the Arabian states. Secondly, to attack the enemy is to destroy their supplies and lines of communication; to destroy their machinery is to destroy their importance and to destroy them. Lawrence's small forces, drifting around "like a gas," were particularly at home in the Arabian territory as they could easily disappear into the civilian population. If guerrillas are to do this they must have a civilian population to disappear into. In South Vietnam, when everyone of fighting age was called up for military service, the only people actually left, who could sink into the background, were women and children—hence the very widespread use of children on the insurgent side in South Vietnam. Boys who are not yet old enough to be called up are still able to shoot people, but they have to be trained first. Also, in Arabia in Lawrence's time, space was a tremendous advantage; there were no aircraft as yet, and his forces could hide in the desert where no one could pursue them, since they did not have the transport.

Although Lawrence was very much a sideshow in the First World War and guerrilla tactics were used nowhere else in the War other than Tanganyika (now Tanzania), they did turn out to be very important even so. For one thing, the tragic, heroic nature of Lawrence's career made him a very attractive character. He knew the right people, and he wrote well, so that the next generation in Britain grew up feeling that Lawrence had been badly treated, and so he had. And secondly, the Second World War was not a static war like the First World War. In mobile war, states collapsed very quickly, leaving a great deal of their social structure intact. It was possible to keep guerrilla forces in being on the edge of the main theatres of conflict to perform an important role in holding down regular troops. And the Chindits, who at first proved unpopular with the British regular military establishment, afterwards turned out to be very much more valuable than people realized, and in fact they helped protect the flank of India itself.

Guerrilla tactics had an added disadvantage, which was not fully realized until after 1945. It made, not only politically active, but also militarily active, a great many local inhabitants who, after the war, had been conveniently issued with British guns, trained in military techniques, who, in addition, had had 4 years' free experience in fighting the Japanese. They were then able to enforce their own political opinions, which they proceeded to do, rifle in hand. The result was the Malayan Emergency. The wartime Malayan People's Anti-Japanese Army (MPAJA) was simply transformed into the Malayan Races Liberation Army (MRLA), and aimed at the British instead of the Japanese. Its veterans took out the same guns as they had used before, disappeared into the jungle, and set to work. Again the technique was very similar to Lawrence's, to blow up the roads and railway lines. To keep the railway lines clear, cars were run up and down the lines 15 minutes in front of every train. At first the guerrillas blew up the armored cars; later they let the armored car go by and there was a good chance that when it had gone through the train would be there, so they could attack the train itself. In 1950 the High Commissioner, Sir Henry Gurney, was ambushed successfully, though quite unintentionally, since it appears from the captured documents and the information that later became available that they thought they were ambushing the military commander (Short 1974).

Sir Henry Gurney's death in fact saved a great number of British lives. It forced them to turn their weakness into strength by adopting a systematic antiguerrilla campaign strategy—the Briggs Plan. Guerrillas must resist the temptation to strike too soon or in the wrong place and, as again in the case of Guevara's expedition in Bolivia, alert the government to the urgency and the necessity of doing something about them. Circumstances often dictate that such guerrilla movements are ultimately defeated. Far more have been defeated than have been successful.

The same period saw the emergence, with Mao Tse-tung, of a new kind of guerrilla warfare as a political technique. Mao profited from indigenous Chinese experience and his extensive knowledge of Chinese history and of the Chinese past. Secondly, the heroes whom he followed (and he did follow heroes) were specifically Chinese heroes who had fought against foreigners. Thirdly, Mao's technique of guerrilla warfare was tested, as it were, and given its baptism of fire, in combat with the Japanese. The Sino-Japanese War of 1937–45 is the real beginning of the Second World War. For Europeans it began in 1939, for the Americans and the USSR in 1941, but for the Chinese it began in 1937, if not in 1931, when the Japanese originally invaded Manchuria. And the alliance of nationalist partisan forces through the countryside was not only the natural, but the obvious thing to do. They were fighting an international war against the Japanese: it was a war of national liberation.

The theory behind it, developed in Mao's tract *Guerrilla Warfare*, which appeared in 1937 (Schram 1963), is based on a three-stage model. It begins, first, with organization, consolidation, preservation of base areas, and creation of a network of sympathizers by the training of volunteers and the agitation and propaganda in the surrounding countryside. The second stage envisages the progressive military expansion of the base areas, making use of sabotage, liquidation of "collaborationists" and "reactionary elements," and the seizure of medical supplies and equipment from forces, from outlying police posts and weak columns. The expansion of the base areas, then, is affected by sabotage, liquidation of "collaborationists" and "reactionary elements" and the seizure of arms, ammunition, and supplies. And this is in fact very close to Lawrence's view, also worked out in actual combat. The theoretical expansion of the peripheral liberated area, however, was quite unLawrentian, as Lawrence did not believe in the liberation of areas at all, as being quite contrary to his notion of effective guerrilla warfare. The question is, was Mao right or was Lawrence right? For Mao, the expansion of the liberated areas takes place by a useful technique of expanding the militia faster than the regular army. It is the militia that sabotages the immediate surrounding countryside, liquidating collaborationists as it goes. Because there is a regular military effort behind it, it expands rapidly through the countryside in what is termed the "oilspot technique."

The climax is the destruction of the enemy by the transformation of guerrilla forces into an orthodox military force capable of defeating the government in pitched battles. This will be supplemented by the protraction of the phase of development into conventional forces and the retraining of the military under cover of negotiations. Enormous hysteria was raised in the West after 1968 that the Americans could not possibly take seriously the desire of the Vietnamese for peace. The Vietnamese, happy and peace-loving people that they were, were no doubt sincere in their desire to negotiate, even if in doing so they negotiated away some of their own positions. But they also proceeded to reorganize the guerrilla forces in South Vietnam into conventional forces so they could hold strategic lines, under cover of the negotiations. When that failed, in 1972, they called in the North Vietnamese army. Mao himself emphasized that the use of negotiations would be for purely military purposes, to wear down the opponent's morale and allow time to regroup and resupply. Quite understandably, modern governments are therefore very suspicious of invitations from insurgent movements to engage in a dialogue. In the recent conflict in Sri Lanka, once 6 years of negotiations with the Tigers had broken down, the government strongly resisted any calls for a ceasefire until they had achieved their military objectives and Prabhakaran and his chief aides were known to be dead.

Mao's work is based on three basic preconceptions. First, the doctrine of strength and weakness: to turn one's weaknesses into strength and the enemy's strength into his weaknesses. This is done by a number of means, but primarily by surprise. The expression is "Uproar in the East, strike in the West"—a technique older than Mao, and probably older even than organized government in China. The second preconception (the most dubious one) is that guerrillas will have full information and that the government will have no information; that the guerrillas will succeed in denying all information about themselves to the government while, through their own network of sympathizers, laying open the strategic and tactical state of the government to themselves. As an ideal this is excellent, and under conditions of international warfare this is probably very nearly possible. But times have changed since 1937. Aircraft were already in those days reaching a sufficient level of sophistication to be used successfully as spotters, for example, in northern Mexico in 1938. Now the major powers have earth satellites, infra-red detectors, guided missiles, thinking bombs, drones, and napalm. Psychological warfare has been developed, and many governments have not stopped short of using torture. The chance of a guerrilla being able to deny all knowledge of his activities to the government is now in fact very much less than it was in Mao's time. So anyone following his advice will be in trouble, unless they remember that guerrilla warfare is not mainly to defeat the enemy but it is to mobilize the people and to turn them into a revolutionary force. This is the great difference between Mao and anyone else, except perhaps Lawrence, who regarded the Arab role in the fight against the Turks as being an essential part of creating Arab nationalism.

There is little practical detail in Mao. There are, however, the Three Rules and the Eight Remarks. The Three Rules are that "all actions are subject to command," "do not steal from the people," "be neither selfish nor unjust"; they are general precepts. The Eight Remarks are specific ones, which are as follows:

Close the door when you leave the house; Roll up the bedding in which you have slept; Be courteous; Be honest in your transactions; Return what you borrow; Replace what you break; Do not bathe in the presence of women; Do not without authority search those you arrest.

"It is only undisciplined troops who make the people their enemies" [says Mao] "and who like the fish out of its native element, cannot live." Elsewhere he says that the guerrilla moves among the people and is sustained by them like the fish in water.

For more detailed practical information on guerrilla warfare, therefore, many revolutionaries were to turn to Cuba, the Cuba of Fidel Castro and Che Guevara. Che Guevara, an Argentine by birth, had studied medicine before traveling via Bolivia and Guatemala into exile in Mexico, where he met the Cubans planning their return to their homeland. In actual combat he became a military leader himself, directing the crucial "Battle of Santa Clara" which in late 1958 proved the decisive psychological stroke in the campaign against President Batista, and shortly after victory he wrote his account of the campaign (Guevara 1968b) and a short handbook for the guerrilla fighter (Guevara 1967). Both stress the very practical approach he brought to the subject, but the latter also enunciated three principles which were to be of much greater theoretical appeal. They were as follows:

1. Popular forces can win a war against the army.
2. It is not necessary to wait until all conditions for making revolution exist; the insurrection can create them.
3. In underdeveloped America the countryside is the basic area for armed fighting. (Guevara 1967, 2.)

This was a heady message for his admirers. It was not necessary, they believed, to create a party (or even a trained army) and Guevara himself rejected the idea that his followers should come from one social class. All that was needed was a small group of guerrillas. This was the theory of the *foco* (focus), a small group as the vehicle of social revolution, elevated to a doctrine by a French-born professor of the University of Havana, Regis Debray (1965, 1969). It was to exercise a profound influence on insurgents in Latin America and the rest of the Third World well into the 1970s, but as Guevara's own death in Bolivia showed, it was dangerously wrong.

Why then was it so popular? Some of the reasons were of course cultural: it was a call to battle that could hardly be rejected without seeming faint-hearted. But much of it was its seeming practicality. So much of what Guevara wrote was very practical indeed:

A small notebook and pen or pencil for taking notes and for letters to the outside or communication with other guerrilla bands ought always to be a part of the guerrilla fighter's equipment [he wrote]. Pieces of string or rope should be kept available; these have many uses. Also needles, thread, and buttons for clothing. The guerrilla fighter who carries this equipment will have a solid house on his back, rather heavy but furnished to assure a comfortable life during the hardships of the campaign (Guevara 1967, 55).

As Luis Mercier Vega wrote, the book is "rather a strange mixture of traditional precepts, an elementary expose of the principles of military training for NCOs and recruits, nostalgic descriptions of life in the open air among men, and the kind of enthusiasm engendered by ex-servicemen looking back. In particular, there is a sort of exaltation of sweat, steaming feet, and suchlike, which would bring back memories for any 1914–18 veteran or infantryman with experience of something besides asceptic [sic] war" (Mercier Vega 1969, 76).

Conclusion

The seeming practicality disguised the invalidity of the theory. It was true that in Cuba the guerrillas had come before the party, but then not very many people before 1959 had realized that they were fighting for a party. At this stage not even Castro himself could be described as a Marxist-Leninist, despite his later claim to the contrary. More seriously, the Cuban Revolution was not in fact a victory for guerrilla warfare, for its contribution in practical terms was minimal. What eventually defeated Batista was the mass with-drawal of support by the workers in the cities and the inability of the regime to control the organized plantation workers, which had no real parallel even elsewhere in Latin America.

When it came to the test, however, in the Bolivian campaign, it is hard to say whether the trial of guerrilla warfare failed because of deficiencies in the theory or practice, as the evidence of different accounts (Guevara 1968a, González and Sanchez Salazar 1969, Harris 1970) agrees that almost every mistake that could have been made was made. On the strategic level, the decision to pick Bolivia, on a false analogy with the Sierra Maestra, took no account of the rigors of the climate and the mountains. There were peasants in Bolivia, certainly, but they had benefited from the Revolution in 1952 and had no wish to risk their gains. Besides, they were suspicious of white-skinned bearded Cubans (or Argentines), who reminded them too strongly of the Conquistadores who had taken their lands in the first place. Even if the focus had been successful, Bolivia offered too weak a base from which to advance on the rest of Latin America, as they plainly hoped.

On the tactical level, errors were legion. Guevara's Cubans had learnt Quechua, at least, so that they could talk to the Bolivians in their own language, but they picked as site for operations Ñañcuahuazu, where the peasants spoke Guaraní. They attacked a government force before they themselves were ready to defend themselves. They took endless photographs of themselves, which, with much of their other supplies and the vital evidence that linked them to Cuba, fell into the hands of government forces. Even the most trivial mistakes proved fatal; for example, "Tania la guerrillera," apparently both a KGB and an East German agent in her spare time, was killed because she wore a white shirt in the middle of the green jungle and presented a perfect target to her pursuers. And Debray's own visit confirmed the importance of the group to the Bolivian authorities, but not before it had shown up the weaknesses of the group's position: "The Frenchman," Guevara himself wrote, "was somewhat too eloquent when he described how useful he could be to us outside" (Guevara 1968a, 132). Che himself clearly tried to keep up morale as long as possible, ignoring the uncomfortable realities. Thus, he wrote on 30 April that a dog, "Lolo died a victim of Urbano's temper: he threw a rifle at its head." In his analysis of the month of May he wrote that "the dogs have shown themselves to be incompetent and have withdrawn to civilization" (ibid., 151, 164).

The failure of the rural guerrilla dream was to lead to a brief attempt to transpose its principles to the urban setting—to create, in short, a new form of insurgency called "urban guerrilla" warfare (Oppenheimer 1970). As the sudden death of its chief figure, Carlos Marighela showed, its theory, sketchy as it was (Marighela 1971), was even less securely founded. Urban terrorism could be a considerable nuisance to a government, but at no time did it threaten its survival, and it did create a powerful reaction in favor of repression. It is not, however, to be confused with urban insurrection, which has quite a different history and rationale.

CHAPTER FOUR

Leadership and Recruitment

Leadership

In legal theory, international relations is concerned only with the relations between states. Critics argue that it is a holistic process involving also International Organizations (IOs) and Non-Governmental Organizations (NGOs). Revolutionary movements are organizations in this sense until and unless they become governments. In practice, dialogue between organizations has to be conducted by human beings, and states and organizations are personified through their leaders. Revolutionary movements are no exception.

Leadership is a critical variable in the success or failure of revolutionary movements. But Eric Hoffer, in *The True Believer* (Hoffer 1951, 129 ff.) says that revolutions need three types of men (sic): men of words, fanatics, and men of action. Men of words are required to make people aware of the deficiencies in their existing political condition, to alert them to the deficiencies of the existing social order. Fanatics are required to risk the consequences of actually attacking the existing social order and bringing it down. To reshape it they need to be single-minded, dedicated men who are prepared to tear away at history with their bare hands. But men of action are also required, to reconstruct. Revolution for Hoffer, as for most modern writers, is not simply a question of tearing down; it is a question of reshaping, rebuilding, building up.

Hoffer is talking, in fact, about the element of leadership. He does not imply that revolutions are made *solely* by men of words, fanatics and men of action. He is talking about the leadership of revolution. It is true that revolution is not practicable without the mobilization of a considerable body of men and women. But the fact is that some kind of direction is required; even collective leadership is leadership. But looking for a single type of leader in a revolutionary situation is a waste of time. As revolutions are complex events, or sequences of events, their leadership frequently *is* plural and changes in the course of time. Revolutions are not, as was at one time believed, merely the product of a single, individual motivation. Moreover, unless individual leaders, whatever their personal psychological drives, call up some kind of response in a body of supporters, they cannot become a revolutionary leader, or indeed a political leader of any kind.

There are special problems in the study of revolutionary leadership, such as those raised by the necessity for concealment or for surreptitious action. This means that sometimes people who appear to be the leaders are not necessarily in fact the true ones: General Mohammed Neguib in Egypt, for example, who was selected as nominal leader of the Free Officers because of his prestige among the armed forces. But this is a practical problem of research. In addition, most of what has been written on this subject in the past has been rather conditioned by the authors' own social backgrounds and interests. With both these points in mind, the social origins of revolutionary leadership will be considered first, and next the psychological ones.

The Social Origins of Leadership

Pettee (1938) suggested that the origins of the revolutionary impulse lay in the realization of "cramp" a peculiar word which now be rendered as "frustration" (as in "frustration/aggression"). "Cramp," for Pettee, is the realization that one is not able to achieve what one would like to achieve, that one is restricted in one's possibilities. What then determines the revolutionary's response, it appears, is his/her class or ethnic or other origins. As Brinton has pointed out, the leaders of great revolutions often come from the second social rank and they step into the political vacuum left by the overthrow of the existing government (Brinton 1952, Calvert 1970b).

Military coups often follow a blockage of promotion. It is true that commanders-in-chief of armies frequently lead military coups but it is equally true that many other leaders of coups are people of a superior rank somewhere below the top; in other words, they feel that they are aspiring to something beyond this. The self-promotion of colonels, as in Egypt and Libya—and indeed in the case of Liberia, Master Sergeants—confirms that there are similar social pressures operating at lower military levels also, but that middle-ranking officers are more prone to develop radical views. It is often suggested that revolutionary leaders emerge simply from personal frustration. The biggest possible argument against this is that a great many people spend most of their working lives being frustrated in terms of promotion. And yet, most people never become revolutionary leaders. One must account, in other words, not just for the leadership element, but also for the revolutionary element. Many approaches to revolutionary leadership are misleading because they have concentrated in the first instance on the fact of revolution, and have tended to neglect the organizational aspects which are as important in revolution as in anything else. One of the earliest studies of leadership found that what was termed the democratic style of leadership was the most effective in actually producing results, because it minimized the tendency to arouse aggression and encouraged people to work together (Lewin, Lippitt, and White 1939).

For example, the career of Napoleon has been held out for many years as an example of the career open to talent (*carrière ouverte aux talents*). It has been taken for granted that the French Revolution offered him an opportunity to rise to the top in a way he would not otherwise have been able to do. But there is little evidence for this because Napoleon was already in the French army by 1789. Furthermore, he had already gone through military college and was an officer, which suggests that he was not blocked from promotion, and given his age at the time (30) he had the seniority one would have expected. What he needed was the opportunity to show his abilities and to shine in war. And the French government was still royalist when it began the war which opened the way to a policy of military conquest which, such was the surprise of all the other states in Europe, was unusually successful. Because it was unusually successful, the opportunities for military promotion were extremely rapid. Napoleon was to add to them by reviving the classical military title of Emperor.

Napoleon, too, had chosen the right specialism. He was an exponent of the new and important art of artillery and artillery was the key to success in war at this time.

On the other hand, as evidence of his uniqueness, it has been pointed out that he was Corsican by origin. Corsica, formerly Italian, had only very shortly before become part of French territory, making him a French citizen. This is true, but Cardinal Mazarin, who was ruler of France in all but name from 1643 to 1660, was also Italian by birth, and he attained his position, a century and more before Napoleon, by a completely different kind of promotional ladder and one which had nothing to do with revolution. So this suggests that having Italian origin was not an obstacle to holding power in prerevolutionary France and therefore the fact of Napoleon's success in postrevolutionary France is not necessarily a recommendation for revolution as a vehicle for promotion.

It was not necessary to be unprincipled (like Talleyrand, whose sole principle was to survive) in order to work for the French Revolution. Men of ideas did in fact find the old regime stifling. They spent a great number of years explaining why, but not just because it was stifling them. What, after all, could a Rousseau reasonably complain about a France which lionized him, feted him, gave him every sign of respect, distinction, talked about his books all the time, raised him to consideration in the salons of the great, and so forth? But the fact is that he had the capacity which many other writers have had, to realize the weaknesses in the situation for other people and the potential social consequences of these weaknesses. "Man is born free but everywhere he is in chains," he wrote, and yet he did manage to find somewhere reasonably tolerable to live himself (McDonald 1965). On the other hand, the writers who expounded these idealistic critiques of French society before the French Revolution were not the people who directed it. The Abbe Sieyes is the only writer of any consequence to have played a major role in the French Revolution and he was soon to seek exile. Condorcet, on the other hand, was actually executed after a long imprisonment in the Temple, in which he managed to realize only the first part of his masterwork what was to be his masterwork—a sketch of human progress from the beginning up to the time of the French Revolution, in eight parts. The men of words only provided the preconditions for the French Revolution.

The works of Robespierre and Danton show us the revolutionaries in action, but they are not works in the conventional sense. Robespierre's interpretation of Rousseauism as a revolutionary ideology is an ad hoc interpretation. He is busy expounding in the circumstances of the moment what he feels people ought to do next, and why they ought to do it. Therefore, he is one of the fanatics rather than one of the men of words, the men who reduce all problems to the simple question of disposing of the government. Sweep away the vestiges of the past, such men argued, government included, and the new order will emerge. All that is lacking, they suggested, is that these restraining conditions should be swept away, and then liberty, equality, fraternity would reign (Scurr 2006). The degree of idealism in this viewpoint is hard to assess because it is so much constrained by the obvious over-simplification of the problems of human nature, the problems of living in societies. Societies have not got any simpler since 1789.

To sum up, what kind of leadership was required first, to bring down the old regime; secondly, to destroy the vestiges of feudalism; thirdly, to create the new French state; fourthly, to establish a new social order? Put that way, the emphasis will be on leaders as exceptional individuals. But these are of course separate, if related, problems, and the history of the French Revolution shows that a different kind of leadership was found for each, even though there is an institutional continuity between these forms of leadership. If revolution is basically as an act of applied aggression (though not simply an act of applied aggression), then it is rather easier to see why it becomes, as such, a relatively neutral vehicle which allows the acting out of various kinds of impulses arising from diverse social causes.

It is even rather questionable whether there is any clear class interest. One has to remember that even Marx had to allow for the fact that the proletariat may not be aware—and indeed in his day was not aware—of their role in the scenario for the future that he was writing, that they would have to be instructed and guided. One of the basic problems that Marxists have never been able to agree on, not even within any one trend or persuasion of Marxism, is the precise role of the communist party in revolution as opposed to the "leading role" of the party after the event. What if, as in Cuba, for example, the party is not created until 2 years after the seizure of power has actually been consummated (there was a Communist Party in pre-1959 Cuba but it supported Batista)? Some Cubans then suggested that the party somehow, retrospectively, guided the Cuban revolution (Goldenberg 1965). This view was later quietly dropped. The party now guides the destinies of the state, without explaining exactly how the party came to exist. In another successful revolution, Nicaragua the Communist Party formed only part of the coalition which achieved the successful overthrow of the Somozas. Despite the prominence of one or two individuals, the postrevolutionary government was never communist. And the Party formed part of the center-right coalition supporting Violeta Barrios de Chamorro in the elections of 1990.

Of course there are obvious reasons why one should wish, in the Russian context, to emphasize the direction of the party. The party in Russia, or rather the small group of conspirators surrounding Lenin, was a minority interest which was seizing control of the revolution, directing it much more rapidly on its course than anyone could have previously anticipated, and telescoping the "bourgeois" and the "proletarian" revolutions forecast by Marx. Moreover, Marx expected some kind of alliance between the proletariat and the most "advanced" section of the bourgeoisie, the revolutionary intelligentsia, which would have otherwise no clear class interest as such. If the intelligentsia is going to guide and then direct the proletariat of which it does not form a part, for Marx it must be because it realizes that this is what the trend of history indicates it will do, and not because it has common class interests as such.

However, under any of the definitions of class that are widely accepted, there remains a conflict between class interests and class origins. Class origins of people who take part in revolutions, the evidence suggests, tend to conform to the general distribution of classes within society—in other words, people who take part in revolutions are much like people who take part in any other kind of politics. They take part in rough proportion to the social origins of people within society, as will be seen later.

Similarly, the displacement of class-by-class is not a displacement of a complete set of individuals by another complete set of individuals of different class origin. It was Lenin, not Marx, who first attempted to redefine revolution as a displacement of one class by another class. Marx himself spent a long time discussing "revolutions" that were not, in fact, displacements of class-by-class, and never pretended to be. But in considering the Leninist interpretation of Marxism, one must remember, therefore, that when he says "displacement of class-by-class" he is talking about control, not composition. In fact, even after the Russian Revolution a substantial number of people remained in government who had been there before and, as Lenin himself pointed out, continued to collect their salaries on the 23rd of each month.

The question of to what extent the control in any given revolution is absolutely transferred from one side to the other remains one of the very interesting enigmas of history. And of course it does raise the question that, if there are bourgeois survivors in postrevolutionary Russia, then is it because in fact no complete displacement took place? Or is it purely due to the fact that the city tends to bourgeoisify [or civilize] the people who live in it?

The Psychological Origins of Leadership

Biographies of revolutionary leaders tend to assume some kind of psychological motivation, but this is often still at a very simplistic level. E.V. Wolfenstein (1967), for example, who makes use of a Freudian scheme, emerges at the end with the conclusion that the qualities of the leaders he studies are ruthlessness, dogmatism and self-determination, flexibility, toughness, and sound administrative ability. The conclusion is not very rewarding, except in the point about sound administrative ability. Looking at revolutionary leadership, the people who stand out are in fact those people who were able to administer. In other words, they were not only able to create a new system but, like Stalin the bureaucrat, to run the system which they had created. This was because they did not adopt the system as it was, but had learnt the trick of changing the rules of the game to suit their own abilities.

The development of modern psychology is very accurately reflected in the development of psychological theories of the origins of revolutionaries. Earlier views are now largely of curiosity value, but mention should be made of Jung, who in his *Psychology of the Unconscious*, first published in 1917 (Jung 1933), introduced the notion of "primordial images" or "archetypes." There is an interesting parallel between his theory of archetypes and the Weberian concept of traditional authority, just as there is between the Freudian view of leadership and Weber's charisma, and between Weber's notion of legal-rational authority and the interchangeability of leaders envisaged by Trotter (1953).

To play such a role may require what William James (1907) termed "tough-mindedness." This involves the ability to lead with confidence, to be unaffected by doubt but able to point the way to others. This was translated, by Adorno and his colleagues (1964), into the concept of "authoritarianism" and the "authoritarian personality," and related by Eysenck (1963) to political preference. How far authoritarian tendencies qualify a person to lead a revolution is of course a central question. At first sight, it seems they must be invaluable. But too much authoritarianism makes a person inflexible, unable to respond to circumstances, and therefore incapable of being followed. So a successful leader would be a person with a fairly high degree, but not an excessive degree, of authoritarianism—fairly normal, then.

Ideally, one would wish to analyze individual revolutionary leaders clinically. In the past, the people who most wanted to know about leadership were military officers, and they designed tests that were designed to identify military qualities. This limited the general value of the information gained, although it will be of some interest to us because revolution is at least in part a military activity. But to seek to examine a revolutionary leader clinically would probably lead to a considerable amount of trouble. Moreover, it would not necessarily be very rewarding, since something called leadership has no meaning in itself. Leaders have to be leaders of *something*. And leadership varies, therefore, with the nature not only of the individual, but of the group of which he formed part, the situation confronting it and the task to be performed. This, the situational approach to leadership, came to the fore in Psychology in the years after 1945 and now represents the consensus view (Turner 1991).

In the meantime, people who write on *politics* still tend to think of leadership in terms of drives, and instincts, rather than groups and situation. The consensus of the literature is as follows: leaders, on average, excel the group average in intelligence, scholarship, dependability, sociability, and/or socio-economic status. The revolutionary leader is not saying: "here am I, the ideal person to lead the political system as is," s/he is saying: "modify the job, and I'll show you which way to go." So the revolution in fact is about modifying the political structure so that it can be led by new people and new elites.

In between the leadership, the "directorate," and the followers, the revolutionary organization or movement, there are bodies, organizations, groups which can be classified generally as "staff." The organization of a revolution, like the organization of anything else, depends on its implementation. It is not enough just to stand up on a soapbox and announce that the revolution is at hand. It is necessary also to create some form of organization that operationalizes the political views that the revolutionary wants to express.

In the Leninist view, the reason why revolution succeeds is because the organization is created. The precise goals can be redefined, can be reorganized at any time, depending on circumstances. What matters is how they are actually put into effect. And this certainly is no less important than the question of which direction the leaders are leading in the first place.

The Mass and the Crowd

As with political leadership generally, we might expect leadership in revolutionary situations to begin with small-group behavior, with how certain people come to gather small groups around them, to generate forces for the changing of society within these groups, and to organize mass action. The question of the interaction between the leadership and the mass has already implicitly been dealt in consideration of the crowd and the Freudian view of the relationship of the leader to his followers. But this is to go beyond the limits which experimental psychology will permit, into a field in which one cannot produce hypotheses capable of being tested by the process of actual experiment.

From the historical view, there is a great deal that has been written about the actions of revolutionaries in individual revolutionary situations. The problem is relating it to different situations and different historical accounts, and particularly to that most dramatic manifestation of revolutions: the crowd. Not all revolutions have been shaped by the mass mobilization of crowds. However, in one of the most recent examples, the Iranian Revolution of 1979, crowds played an essential role, both in the fall of the Shah and in the rise of Khomeini, and the fear of the crowd is still a major factor in leading many people to oppose sensible change, on the rather specious grounds that it may get out of hand.

The traditional view of conservative historians was that when crowds became threatening, some kind of demonic possession had taken place. Peaceful peasants or jolly apprentices had suddenly been seized by some kind of malign spirit of envy which drove them to revolt against their masters, overthrow the fabric of the state, destroy the structure of society and redistribute wealth. One finds a much higher degree of sophistication only when one gets down to the study of the crowd in specific historical circumstances. Everett Dean Martin (Martin 1920) was quite explicit that what was distinctive about the behavior of the crowd was the condition of mind of the individuals, resulting from a mutual consent to do the forbidden thing. The crowd decided what was permissible and what was not, so no one did, and each could feel that they had got the support of the crowd.

This is the reverse of the political theme that can be found even in nineteenth-century studies, the crowd as mass action equated with "the common people"; the crowd as an expression of popular will. The French Revolutions of 1789, of 1830 and 1848; and indeed all the revolutions of that surprising year 1848 were characterized by crowd action. The one common assumption that all historians seemed to take for granted was that these crowds were somehow made up of "the common people," whoever they may be. It was therefore very interesting to find in George Rudé's *The Crowd in History* (1964) that his view of the crowd in the French Revolution and in England in Luddism and Chartism, and anywhere else where he had studied it, is that on the whole, the crowd is a group of sober citizens, including craftsmen, journeymen, and apprentices. In fact, it is representative of the more solid classes; it is skewed toward representation of the more well-to-do, as a political party is. It is not a carbon copy of the total population.

Furthermore the crowd not only was not invariably a mob of social outsiders who had suddenly risen in revolt against the structure of decent orderly society (which was always implicit in all previous studies of crowd action, particularly those written by academics), but showed quite different characteristics from one incident to another. The crowd differs. In, say, the situation of the Reveillon Riots, where people were rioting about the price of bread, there was a predominance of wage-earners because this was what affected them most closely. In the march on Versailles it was the market women who led the crowd and in the attack on the Tuileries, the action which actually brought down the structure of the French monarchy, the people who dominated the crowd were the workshop masters and the apprentices. For this was an industrial action, resulting from the galloping inflation created by the issue of paper currency (assignats) and the general incompetence of the French government at managing its economy. So that although in each case crowd action takes place, the crowds in each case are different.

Thirdly, one of the extremely interesting things about the French Revolutionary crowds is that, quite apart from their class composition, they were unusual in other respects. First, the members were unusually old by the standards of the time; the average age of the crowds at the siege of the Bastille was 34, as near as can be ascertained, on the basis of those who joined up in the Paris Sections, where close records were taken. Obviously, these are not wholly reliable; there must have been a lot of people who got into the records who were probably not there on the day and indeed may not have even been in Paris on the day. But Paris in 1789 was still a relatively small city. People must have known fairly well who was there and who was not, and must have had to produce witnesses, so this is as good a study of the composition of the revolutionary crowd as is ever likely to emerge. And 34 certainly was old in 1789. The crowd at the Bastille was not made up of the teenage thugs of the late eighteenth century. Its age composition disproportionately included the maturer and more responsible members of society.

How do we know? Well, people had to sign the book when they enrolled in the Paris Sections, and it is clear that a very substantial number of them could write. In fact, measured by their ability to sign their names, rather than make a mark in the book, literacy runs in some of these records as high as 80 percent. However, mass education was by no means one of the features of prerevolutionary society in France. So the *sansculottes*, in other words, who from then on turned out at all the major junctures of the Revolution until 1797, were not, by modern standards, the working class. They were indeed very much the bourgeoisie, seemingly confirming the Marxist view that the French Revolution was a bourgeois revolution, and a forerunner of the modern followers of populist leaders such as Peron's descamisados, or Vargas' *o povo* in Brazil.

Now the problem with extrapolating from this study of the crowd is that the circumstances of the French Revolution are undoubtedly unusual. The fact that much is known about what happened when crowds were gathered together in the French Revolution does not mean that all is known about recruitment in revolutionary conditions. How all these people gathered together, how much their action was an impulse, or how much the product of long-term circumstances, is not certain. Moreover, on many later occasions attempts to reenact the French Revolution in other circumstances did not come off. For example, on at least one occasion, in 1830, the French government survived because a timely shower of rain dispersed the rioters, and it was to do so again in Algiers in 1961. The crowd is unreliable from the revolutionary point of view, and the fact that it is effective in certain circumstances should not be taken as indicating that it is by any means the sole vehicle through which revolutions come to express themselves. Crowds really are a key part of the action only in the unusual condition termed urban insurrection, and even since 1961 the capacity of most police forces to control and to disperse crowds has been increased out of all proportion.

The Gordon Riots of 1780, which did not bring down the British government, originated in organization, peaceful at least by eighteenth-century standards. The crowd was formed from the mass rallies of a body called the Protestant Association, which the fanatic Lord George Gordon, a younger son of the Scottish ducal family, was organizing in resistance to the rumors which were then current that Catholics might perhaps be allowed to vote or perhaps have some representation in the state. He opposed this and, since he was a good orator, whipped up enormous numbers of people into a frenzy of hostility. This mass hysteria culminated in one of his huge rallies which descended on the Houses of Parliament and, among other things, pulled the Archbishop of York out of his coach. (Only the fact that he was grabbed by well-wishers and passed from hand to hand over the top of the crowd saved him from being mauled, but one or two other peers were badly hurt.) In the end, the crowd, frustrated, turned on Newgate Prison, broke it open, released a lot of prisoners, and burned down a distillery. Eventually the whole thing broke up when they started drinking the spirits that poured out of the burning distillery, and people fell about, blind drunk in the street, and were easily dispersed by government troops (Hibbert 1958, Babbington 1991).

A sharp distinction can be drawn between the crowd as such that is, all the people who happened to be present in front of the Houses of Parliament on that day in 1780 and the *effective crowd*, the people who happened to be engaged in political action. The whole point about a crowd is that it is a very substantial body; it is very difficult for crowds of any size to achieve anything very complicated. Given the size of the crowds, given their haphazard nature, given on the whole their political responsibility, which must lead them in general to want to maintain the existing system with only small amendments, and given the fact that too many hands simply cannot move the levers of the state in anything but the crudest sense of the word, it is clear that, when it comes to collective action, anomic groupings of any kind lose out to formal organizations. Therefore, most later revolutions have been organized and led, or captured and taken over and directed, by formal organizations. The structure of recruitment into formal organizations is a very different matter from the informal mechanism of crowd formation.

As noted above, historical instances show that by far the most common element that participates in political revolutions is the professional armed forces—the most disciplined, best-organized, and most well-trained sector of the population. They seem to be followed by civilian institutional groups, that is, groups of civilians, frequently working with the military, sometimes working independently, who have a common interest by virtue of their occupation or work. Least important and least significant are the civilian associational groups, whether the political parties or organizations like Lord George Gordon's Protestant Association. The pressure group is the weakest element and the weakest source of revolutionaries.

Taking Sides

This then leads to the question of the sociological factors determining recruitment. Dahrendorf talks of latent interest groups in society, and regards these as being fodder for mass action where the shared exigencies of the group appear salient (Dahrendorf 1961). The problem with this is, determining, first, what shared exigencies are, and secondly, at what point they become salient. Once more, in examining revolutionary action it is clearly very difficult to determine whether it is revolutionary or not until a revolution has actually happened.

First among shared exigencies is the deprivation of economic resources, as cited by Marxists. If revolutions are created by mass action in the Marxist sense, they are created by the fact that the proletariat is being increasingly deprived of the means by which it lives; the proletariat which is itself defined as being that section of the population which has no economic resource except its children (*proles*) and its work. Increasing deprivation, therefore, leads to the desire for revolt, the circumstances in which revolt is possible, but there is still no effective revolt until the point at which it is given direction and "made aware" of its state of deprivation.

Durkheim, deriving many of his ideas from another aspect of Marxist thinking, in particular Marx's theory of alienation, appears to regard the impulse for revolutions as arising from deprivation of identity (anomie). People in modern societies, unable to regard themselves as individuals by the nature of their society, therefore, turn to mass action as a means of redressing this deprivation (Durkheim 1965). This view has been developed further by the elite theorists. In both Mosca and Pareto the shared exigencies arise from deprivation of access to power (Meisel 1965). The individual who cannot attain political power will turn to mass action as a vehicle for his or her demands.

For the individual, in each of these three cases, the common factor is deprivation of educational advantage. It is the one thing on which everyone appears to be agreed. The most serious deprivation is illiteracy, or, secondarily, functional illiteracy (i.e., one has enough education to be able to write one's name or read a newspaper headline, but is effectively unable to make use of the cultural mechanisms of one's society). The next most serious is an inadequate basis for assessment of one's own circumstances. It is education that allows the individual to handle the mechanisms of social control by making up his own mind about things and forming his own views. If the mechanisms for social control were wholly effective, a functionalist would argue, clearly, revolution in any broad sense of the word must be impossible, because people are unable to form a view that is contrary to the generally held views of their society, and it is impossible therefore for them to wish to revolt against it.

The question is, what is the role of education in revolutionary conditions? Clearly, it is no accident that Rousseau, the principal theorist of the French Revolution, was the author not only of *The Social Contract* but also of *Émile*.

The philosophical basis for the development of revolutionary ambitions lies in an awareness of the inadequacy of society to provide the mechanisms by which people can obtain access to economic resources, identity, or power, as the case may be. In each case, the vehicle remains education.

How far then is it necessary for revolution to take place for this educational process to have reached? Smelser regards the revolution proper, the chain of circumstances that formed the French Revolution or the Russian Revolution, as being primarily concerned with the reorientation of the fundamental norms of society. It is not sufficient for anything less than these to be changed. Indeed, revolutions are about even more than that, about changing the fundamental values of society, about altering its entire intellectual basis (Smelser 1962). There have been revolutions that have developed initially from rather more limited objectives, but have gone on to lead people to question the assumptions on which their society was based. This can be seen, for example, in the period from 1830 to 1848 in France. In 1830, the July Revolution, there was a simple change of monarchy and a belief that political changes in themselves are going to be sufficient. In 1848, although the political changes are dramatic enough, the abolition of the monarchy and the introduction of a Republic was accompanied by the setting up of national workshops under the assumption that the state has now taken on the responsibility for providing work for the unemployed. This is a new sphere of activity for the state and the basis of all subsequent ideas of the role of the state in social welfare.

The change of values, as such, however, does not necessarily lead people to political action. In certain circumstances, and perhaps in most, it leads participants directly to mass action but not necessarily to regime change. A common form of the desire to change the values and norms of society is, for example, the religious revivalist movement, which is not necessarily revolutionary and may indeed be counterrevolutionary. For action to become revolutionary in the political sense of the word it must first involve the further step of the identification of exigencies with the policies of the government of the day. It is not sufficient to feel that the values of society have to be changed, it is necessary for people to have determined that it is the government itself that is maintaining those values through the establishment of norms that implicitly demand the maintenance of values to which they no longer adhere.

The extent of the impact of this decision depends on the extent to which it is felt possible to change the government. The true importance of Marx lay less in his belief that revolution is a vehicle of social change (because many people always have believed that), but in the belief that it was certain to result in historically inevitable and hence favorable social change. And it is this belief that proved at one and the same time to be Marxism's greatest strength and its greatest weakness. The historical examples of the degree and direction of social change which are possible in revolution, now that more historical examples are available than were known to Marx at the beginning of 1848, are distinctly discouraging. So too is the limited extent to which postrevolutionary governments have been able to tackle the problem of relative deprivation.

Deprivation (Gurr 1970) is related to expectation. The Davies J-Curve is a simple attempt to model this in purely economic terms (Davies 1962); revolution breaks out, Davies argues, when a massive gap emerges between expectation and reality. But the problem is that in revolutions observers cannot know what people's expectations are because a revolution is not definable as such until it is over. They cannot ask them beforehand: "What did you expect?" In the circumstances in which some people are attracted to a revolutionary movement, what matters is not just how many are so attracted, but how many people are attracted to any other possible solution, and especially, how many people are attracted to the policies being pursued by the state (cf. Gamson 1975). Who is to be recruited into the revolutionary movement may be less important than who is being alienated from the government. In what sense, therefore, do people feel a government is failing to fulfill their needs? And how small a carrot do they need from the government, in fact, to become totally apathetic? Because if the majority of the nation is apathetic then a relatively small governmental elite may choose to battle it out and the result can go either way.

The opposition, it follows, has to create a winning coalition. How easy is this, and in how many ways can it be done? Marx saw this winning coalition as resulting from the fusion of the direction, the sharpness, and the organization, which the intellectuals could lend to the movement of the proletariat, with the mass power of the proletariat itself, the people who produced goods. They were the fundamental element of the coalition, but they could not be effective without direction. There has been comparatively little work done on the possibilities of other coalitions; there is a great attraction in numbers and the proletariat looks on the face of it very promising as a source of support. Yet it was Engels himself who pointed out that in fact the bourgeoisie was the most revolutionary class (Marx and Engels 1962). It was from its ranks that the men who were actually overthrowing governments came, engaged themselves in the process of reshaping society so as, he argued, to liberate the productive forces implicit in the bourgeoisie itself.

Not until Hitler in the twentieth century constructed his own lower-middle-class military coalition did it become fully obvious how this particular aspect had been overlooked. The idea of the massed power of the workers had blinded people to the fact that other alternative coalitions within society can provide sufficient foundation for the seizure of political power. In modern Brazil, as in modern Argentina, there has been a very deliberate attempt to reshape society on the basis of a very different sort of coalition, overriding the interests of the workers in the interests of a nationalist goal (O'Donnell 1988). Such a middle-class alliance with the military in fact owes many of its roots to the same kind of forces which in the past, in other circumstances, created, for example, left-wing movements in Germany in 1919–20 and in the Russian Revolution, but in the Brazilian case it was followed by the peaceful election of a left-wing president (Bourne 2008).

All governments are the product of a successful coalition. The success of the elite assures that of its coalition. It does not have to carry out a revolution because it is already in power. It can be deduced that this is the kind of political alliance that has the most chance of success.

Lastly, then, the individual motivation of the recruits needs to be identified. Why do so many people follow revolutionary leaders? Leaders certainly may be maladjusted, they may be narcissistic, they may be crazy, but surely all their followers cannot be?

First, it may be accepted that all organized society implies a degree of what Putney and Putney (1964) called "normal neurosis." There is no real alternative but to adjust to a society which demands that you compromise at every turn on what you would like to do. If society changes, people adapt.

Beyond that, there are three views as to the relationship of leaders to followers, to the task and to the situation, from which have been derived different models of the way in which the leader may in fact relate to the followers, and the followers to the leader.

Freud argued for cathexis. The follower identifies with the leader as his/her "ego ideal." S/he would like to be the leader and identifies with the leader, as being something that s/he would like to be and could be. The leader therefore becomes a cathectic object (an object of desire).

Secondly, people they can accept leadership because the leader represents for them what they would like to be but cannot be. They cannot run the 100 yards in world record time. They are not liable to win a gold medal at the Olympic Games. They are not likely to become prime minister. They are not likely to land on the Moon. But for them the leader is doing what they would very much like to do; and not just what they would like to do but cannot. Eva Peron's rich furs and jewels represented this sort of vicarious satisfaction.

A third kind of leader, who is also a common type in revolutionary situations, is the leader who acts out what people ought to do but are not really trying to do. The religious leader, such as the Ayatollah Khomeini, is typical of this. People do not really want to be good, moral, or uplifting, but it salves their conscience considerably to have other people going around being good, moral, and uplifting. They do not really want to attain the standards of sainthood, but they are very happy to venerate a saint, whom they can feel they are trying to live up to without actually having to go through the strain of doing it.

A fourth explanation can be found in the mechanism of projection. The follower has psychological problems—to be human s/he must have psychological problems. S/he therefore projects his/her psychological difficulties on to figures who represent authority. Such followers act out their complexes and use the mechanism of projection to externalize. And because they project their difficulties on to figures representing authority, they develop a degree of opposition to those figures, and so follow a leader who will oppose those figures.

The fifth explanation is to be found in the concept of authoritarianism. Authoritarianism is generally seen as being a statement about leadership. But the point about authoritarianism as a concept is that it is more significant, if anything, as a statement of why people *accept* authority. According to Adorno and his colleagues, authoritarianism in the follower leads him unquestioningly to accept what the leader does, leads him to wish to submit to decisive statements about what is to be done, thus enabling him to avoid having to take psychological initiatives to determine his own place in the world. As Michels (1959) argued, the mass want the burden of leadership removed from them, and are collectively grateful.

Now these five views are each statements about how some people do act in real situations. But another aspect that has become very much part of the modern psychological armoury is the fact that people substitute practical action with dramatic action, in circumstances in which one either cannot see or prefers not to see a path of action that is realistic.

People act out roles, and accept leadership because it does something they are used to. Each accepts the most appropriate role within one's ideal of what society is about. All take part in the play because the play helps pass the time; the play can be used as a substitute for the more uncomfortable problems of reality, or because it is generally more fun.

No one of these five explanations perhaps satisfactorily applies in full to any real person. Each of them has some relevant aspects. But one further contribution which seems to be of particular interest in the revolutionary situation is the question of why any of these psychological mechanisms should particularly relate to revolution as opposed to anything else. In other words, why do people suddenly develop the urge to go out and fight, when they are shown the way?

The fact is that revolution is essentially a product of the lack of alternatives. People who can change their government do not waste time venting their feelings on it; they simply change it. If they feel they can change society the frustration that causes aggression disappears.

The Subculture of Violence

In assessing the risk of revolutionary change it is an important question whether there is, or is not, a preexisting culture, or subculture, of violence in society, on which revolutionary movements draw. The fact that sociologists have spent much time discussing the nature of such a culture or subculture stems from its relevance to the practical tasks of administration presented by the existence of homicide and group violence. Both of these do, in some degree, relate to revolutionary activity, and the sociological evidence, which suggests that there are sharp differences between different societies in this regard, is therefore of considerable interest to any student of international relations.

Wolfgang and Ferracuti (1964) made use of the United Nations' statistics on the rate of homicide in different societies. On the figures presented, Mexico ranked top, and Colombia second. Both were countries in which revolutionary activity has historically been important; in Mexico during the period of the Mexican Revolution, and in Colombia during the period of the Violencia in the late 1940s and early 1950s. On the same figures, the United States ranked very high, but, perhaps significantly, not as high relative to Europe as is often thought. The general rate of homicide and violence in the United States bears reasonable comparison with those for European countries, the more spectacular newspaper comparisons usually being made with the figures for US cities, for example, those for New York and Chicago.

The example of the United States, therefore, does not necessarily disprove the relationship between a high level of violence and the incidence of revolution. But in any case this is not necessarily the point. The question is not whether they are directly related, as political scientists have tended to assume, but whether the existence of group violence lends a particular range of possibilities to potential revolutionary movements.

Group violence is used as a general indicator of political *malaise* and has been examined in detail by sociological writers. In the wake of the assassination of President Kennedy there was much detailed study of the relationship between group violence and political action in the United States, and the

National Commission on Violence (Kirkham et al. 1970) showed that "the level of assassination corresponds to the level of political turmoil and violence in general" (p. 294). They based this generalization on a study of a number of other countries, statistically analyzed. Moreover, "in comparison to other nations, the United States experiences a high level of political violence and assassination attempts" (ibid., 294). This suggests that the comparison with revolutionary behavior has to be regarded with some suspicion, since the United States is not generally considered to be a strong revolutionary nation. They also observed the widespread existence of vigilantism in the United States. They observed that historically such spontaneous quasi-legal behavior by citizens was related to "the right of revolution" reiterated, for example, by Engels. But in the American context it appeared to be less related to the right of revolution, in view of its low relationship with what it termed to be revolutionary violence in United States values, and its high relationship to the persistence of individualism generally in American society, a factor which is undoubtedly unusual among world societies and not to be taken as typical.

There are two principal comments that can be made on the report of the National Commission. First of all, there have to be considerable reservations with regard to the gross figures on which it is based. In Mexico, as in other Latin-American countries, physical violence is strongly and positively equated with masculinity and toughness. It is not, therefore, regarded as socially unacceptable (Stevens 1974). But violence in Mexico was characteristically individual before the rise of the large drug syndicates, and its homicide rate fell despite this from 14.11 in 2000 to 10 in 2008. In Colombia, its high level reflected the major feuds between contending parties (Fals Borda 1965), but the homicide rate in Colombia has also fallen from 63 per 100,000 in 2000 to 36 in 2008. So the nature of violence, as between individual and group violence, therefore needs to be clearly distinguished.

However, there has to be some reservation about the actual reporting of figures on such a controversial issue. In Mexico, where violence is not disapproved of socially, there appears to be relatively little impediment to its reporting, and it has to be presumed that the government of Mexico is not unwilling to let these figures be generally known. In practice, however, most countries simply do not report such figures, or, if they do, include them in a general reserve category where their significance is lost. Obviously, in such societies there may be considerable reluctance to report. Social violence is not the only phenomenon which appears to be affected by the reluctance to report—a similar example is the rate of suicide which is reported as high in Russia (32.2 per 100,000) and low in Mexico (4.1 per 100,000—World Health Organization 2008).

It is therefore necessary, it seems, to qualify one's assessment of the incidence of violence within society with some other indicator which is more easily generalized. A significant one, probably, is the use of force by government, given the interactive nature of the revolutionary process. Government use of force is much more widely reported, and much less amenable to suppression than generalized statistics on individual violence drawn over a large area, but it does present its own particular problems and, again, governments may be unwilling to have such data made publicly available.

The significance of the use of force by government is in the first instance the evidence it presents about the role of violence in the dominant culture. The dominant culture is the official culture of the rulers of the society, in relation to which, in Marxist terms, the cultures of other subordinate classes are formed. Such cultures can, therefore, only be fully understood in relation to the dominant culture. In turn, the formation of subcultures stems from the impact of the dominant culture on its rivals as it changes according to the socioeconomic conditions of the time. The fact that the rulers come from groups, and the three most significant forms of group threat may be conveniently subdivided as gang behavior, social banditry, terrorism, and external attack.

Gangs, Bandits, and Pirates

Gangs have long been seen as a possible source of ready-made revolutionaries. However, gang behavior, especially in the young and adolescent, is generally seen as normal in human societies, and even as functional; it lies at the basis of many courtship rituals. And as with other human behavior, integration into the gang involves the management of aggression (Lorenz 1966, Tiger 1969, Morris 1969). Lorenz regards such management as being the control of a "failsafe" mechanism to protect the group against sudden attack, and therefore basic to the existence of the group. Its management normally, he suggests, involves externalization on fixed objects, whether another gang or an individual.

There is of course considerable doubt as to whether aggression is in fact "normal" in the human condition, whatever that may mean. And, indeed, many progressive thinkers are unwilling to accept that it may be. However, it seems fairly generally agreed that such behavior, aggressive behavior, is of particular significance in human societies which have become urbanized. A good deal of literature exists on this aspect, for the understanding of which it is not necessary to have held very strong views one way or the other on the basic function of aggression in human societies.

It seems that there are several possible responses to the existence of aggression in urbanized societies. The most obvious is the acceptance of it as normal. Empirically, it appears that there is an irreducible minimum of violence which cannot be totally eliminated, at least in the present state of our knowledge of human society, and therefore a degree of acceptance, though it may not much help those involved in the violence, will at least keep the rest of us happy.

The second response is the therapy of the individual, and the satisfaction by this of individual needs.

A third response is social concern about the future of an increasingly urbanized society ("mass society") by sociologists who expect "meaningless" violent behavior to increase. Remedial action proposed includes promotion of community action groups and other small organizations to mediate between individuals and society.

In the context of revolutionary change, pessimism about such developments stems from the belief that such societies are characteristically a prey to mass movements led by demagogues of potentially revolutionary sympathies (Chakotin 1940, 38). Here the cry is for defense, rather than for therapy, though once again it takes the form of individual alertness and awareness. Such mass movements have been seen by their hostile critics as being virtually "political gangs" and their relationship to the study of gang behavior is therefore of particular interest.

Sociological study of gangs, however, does not suggest that they form an important reservoir of violence available to be tapped by revolutionaries. On the contrary, gangs represent in the main the development among predominantly working-class youth of a subculture within which they can be at home, and from which they can withstand something of the pressures to which they are otherwise exposed from the dominant culture. They are, moreover, highly localized, being rooted in the local communities of which they form part, and are conditioned to a temporary and cyclical existence by the relentless pressure of the need to conform to the working week. They do not, in short, exist independently of the structure of society as they find it, and economic necessity ensures that they cannot do so. Their aggression, where it exists, significantly, is focused on rival gangs rather than on the structure of authority in the state as a whole (Hall and Jefferson 1977).

Adult gangs are not very different. Their endurance does involve political awareness and organization to a level that ensures that they assert themselves in the political management of the communities of which they form part. Failing that, they are no more durable. Al Capone was apprehended in the end not for murder or robbery, but for tax evasion. Such organizations, however, far from being revolutionary in effect, have a particularly strong influence on maintaining the existing order of society, for it is by its maintenance that they can alone hope to survive and to make money. Most studies of gang behavior carried out for sociological purposes that groups are, in effect, from a political point of view, virtually proto-political communities, which substitute for remote and/or inaccessible authorities (Fromm 1960).

This view is so widely held that it comes as some surprise to discover that there are exceptions. A significant one, however, is provided by Yablonsky, who in his study of the so-called violent gang demonstrates that it is in fact almost totally asocial. Moreover, the violence associated with it is in fact mostly talk, as the members of it are so asocial that they lack both the organization and the ability to cooperate in order to organize successful combat (Yablonsky 1962). The element of organization, therefore, is obviously intrinsic to political, as opposed to purely asocial behavior, and it is precisely this element which in the past has received so little attention.

Banditry is quite a different phenomenon. To start with, banditry is essentially a rural activity, and its relationship to behavior in modern urbanized societies is still uncertain. Hobsbawm (1972) argued that, far from being just criminals, alienated antisocial elements, the bandits of the past, operating in rural communities, were a defined professional group. This thesis seems to be well supported by the evidence and to be entirely acceptable. He went beyond this, however, to talk about what he calls the "social bandit," motivated not just by loot but by desire for social justice. Of these he identifies three types:

1. The *noble robber* or "Robin Hood." His characteristic is that he robs the rich to give to the poor. It is, of course, true that most bandits prefer to rob the rich since they have more money, but undeniably many of them do not choose to give their money to the poor. This is where banditry, as a noble career, appears such an attractive vehicle for the revolutionary, and yet there is little or no evidence that such banditry has in fact ever served a major revolutionary purpose. In the best-known case of northern Mexico, it is not the bandit but the politician who in fact succeeded in promoting those revolutionary changes, political, social, or economic, which ultimately form the political significance of the revolution (Wilkie and Wilkie 1970).
2. The *haiduks*. These are primitive resistance fighters or organized guerrillas, and they have a characteristically political motivation, being primitive only in the sense that they are operating in underdeveloped societies in which banditry is a natural form of self-expression.

3. The terror-bringing *avenger*. He exists in the public consciousness because
    he rights by his own form of instant justice wrongs which society is
    either powerless or unwilling to right.

As ideal types, these three are useful, each of the roles described plainly
being of some significance in extending or limiting the political appeal of a
specified actor, though it must be observed that they do in fact overlap. Hence
a primitive resistance fighter such as Pancho Villa springs into prominence
first when he acts to avenge a wrong, in this case, traditionally, the rape of
his sister, and gains in his later years a reputation for generosity and open-
handedness which is the hallmark of a noble robber. It appears, however, that
the particular form of political action taken will depend on a number of
things, of which the most important is no doubt the individual's own make-up
and capacity.

But banditry as a general social phenomenon is another matter entirely.
The practice of banditry is aided specifically by geographical remoteness
and the absence of roads, particularly those open to governmental forces.
But it is more specifically related to a type of political remoteness, especially
where jurisdictions are complex, badly delimited, or the subject of competition between states. In feudal society a bandit can easily become the founder
of a government, and indeed of a whole state. In modern times, Hobsbawm
notes, the social bandit has disappeared, to be peasant guerrilla leaders such
as those of the movements described in Wolf (1970) in Mexico, Russia,
China, Vietnam, Algeria, and Cuba. In modern times the guerrilla leader has,
therefore, taken over many of the characteristics of the bandit and, it may
be presumed, something of the same mystique and political support. But,
significantly, banditry does not transplant to the cities, where the characteristic feature of political action is terrorism.

Piracy has never really gone away in the Straits of Malacca, where the
combination of a narrow shipping channel and many islets and river mouths
afford pirates numerous hiding places. Many of them are Indonesian, but the
Republic of Indonesia, with more than 40,000 islands, lacks the naval forces
effectively to cope with the pirates. Though both Indonesia and Malaysia have
long opposed any foreign intervention which might succeed in bringing the
problem under control, the Indian Navy has in recent years helped reduce the
incidence of attacks considerably (Chalk 1998). Since the turn of the century,
shipping faces a new problem in the form of the "failed state" of Somalia,
which has become the base for a new generation of pirates in the Arabian
Sea, preying in the main on large cargo vessels for which they can expect a
large ransom.

Pirates are a considerable nuisance and present a very real threat to the sailors who have the actual task of navigating pirate-infested waters. However, the case of Somalia in particular shows that they are not at all interested in changing the existing states of affairs, since it is precisely the weakness or absence of the government that allows them to flourish.

Terrorists as Revolutionary Leaders

Terrorism, a phenomenon common in modern urban societies, is regarded by most dwellers within such societies with abhorrence, though the majority of them are unwilling to risk themselves personally by expressing this abhorrence openly. A small group of people, normally active in it, approve of terrorism as a possible cleansing influence in a society which they see as being hopelessly out of control. And it may well be that others than Hyams (1975) can take a longer perspective in regarding it as a "cathartic fever incident to civilization" (Hyams, 189). Terrorism is capable of description, delimitation, and even classification (Wilkinson 1974). It seems to be less easily capable of control (cf. Wilkinson 1978).

Wilkinson sees the close relationship between government and opposition as lying at the root of his classification of terrorism, for which he has three categories. These are revolutionary terrorism, subrevolutionary terrorism, and repressive terrorism. Of these, the second and third categories relate to the government and opposition, respectively; the first, however, is a more complex phenomenon embracing both. And it is significant that it is extremely difficult to draw a clear boundary line in any given set of circumstances between the use of one, and the use of the other, for the two do seem indeed to be so closely related that they cannot be separated.

Wilkinson deals with a number of different situations in which terrorism is used. Acts against those deemed unworthy, often for religious or semireligious motives, closely relate to Hobsbawm's category of the avenger. Acts against an indigenous autocrat or tyrant, a purely political phenomenon, suggest the resistance fighter and go with the absence of any legal organized opposition, capable of expressing itself within any nonviolent political process. Resistance to so-called totalitarian societies, and the use of terror against the liberal democracies in order to undermine them and subject them to totalitarian rule, are opposite sides of the same coin, but in the post-Cold War period the notion of totalitarianism has lost whatever value it may once have held. Finally, acts intended to secure liberation from foreign rule direct our attention outwards beyond the confines of the state and shade off into subrevolutionary terrorism at the international level.

Of course, we are concerned with not just how terrorism is used in various circumstances but why terrorism should become to be used as a weapon at all. Here it seems particularly important to devote attention to the psychological origins of the individual, for the psychological origins of terrorist action seem to be in general terms those common to agitators, namely the displacement of private motives into public life (Lasswell 1960). Specifically, it lies in what Erikson (1968) describes as the rejection of negative identities ("images of self") and their elimination from other social groups in which they appear. Since this involves the actual killing of individuals, it is necessary for the psychological stability of the individual to redesignate the members of such social groups as subhuman, a process which Erikson calls their designation as a "pseudo-species." But this in turn can only be supported in the individual by an elaborate psychological mechanism designed to prevent the breakdown of his own identity in the face of actions which he has been instinctively taught to believe from an early age to be essentially barbarous.

The question is, however, has he in fact been taught to consider them barbarous, or has the society in which he lives allowed him to perform such acts? The urban terrorist appears to serve no useful social purpose beyond pulling down the fabric of society for others to build in its place. It is hard to think of any major domestic terrorist who has in fact become the successful leader of a political movement. Generally, terrorists, if they become political leaders, seem to have been those who have not themselves personally taken part in political action. The successful general does not risk his own precious life in the cause, he leaves that to others.

Terrorist methods, as noted in Chapter Three, have frequently been employed in the course of movements of national liberation. It is such movements, therefore, that offer the most striking examples of the importance of education in the perpetuation of political stability or instability. Undoubtedly, great national heroes may serve as powerful examples in a unified political culture for the maintenance of that culture. Yet the very different examples of Belgium and Northern Ireland remind us that even the peaceful perpetuation of ethnic or religious rivalries, far from contributing to the maintenance of a peaceful society, may constantly act to frustrate it. In such cases, the existence of the dominant culture is constantly under challenge, but its strength of example ensures the survival of opposition in a form sufficiently effective to keep it constantly on the defensive. The maintenance of separate schools (Ireland) or political parties (Belgium and the Netherlands) as training grounds for the "bearers" of identity is particularly important. The cycle of violence and repression acts permanently to renew the effect of examples instilled by the process of education. The tree of liberty is refreshed constantly by the blood of fresh martyrs, and individuals recruited to the political cause do not, therefore, need a separate identity from that of the group; the roles are already written for them to play.

Obviously, there would be a considerable advantage to a revolutionary movement to be able to recruit to its cause groups of followers already skilled in the art of fighting and so to short-circuit the long process of building up their strength. The recruitment of individuals, both as leaders and supporters, will be considered in detail shortly. As regards groups, however, there does not appear to be much evidence that they come prepackaged to a new cause. Rather, a revolutionary movement tends to draw for its support on politicized groups who then subsequently turn to violence to achieve their ends. Whether they do so or not, of course, depends not only on the existence of such groups with effective leadership, but on two other factors: whether the nature of their political goals are such that violence appears to be a plausible option for achieving them, and whether or not the material facilities (e.g., weapons) can be obtained or made available to them at crucial points in the political action.

Groups which can be recruited *en bloc* to support revolutionary movements may be expected, therefore, to have two characteristics: a preparedness to use force in the pursuit of political objectives, and the material facilities to do so. Two groups present in almost all societies possess both these attributes, the military and the police. Indeed, the nature of the calling of each of these means that, particularly when acting together (as frequently happens) they are most likely to get their way. The special role of the military will be discussed further in Chapter Five. Here it is only necessary to point out that to understand the particular circumstances in which the military, as in Egypt in 1952 and in Peru in 1968, act as a radically transforming social force, it is first necessary to understand the way in which they achieve power, and this requires us inevitably to consider the much larger number of cases in which the military use their capacity for armed intervention in politics to forestall or to arrest the possibility of social revolution.

The existence of a powerful military force in society, if coupled with a draft or selective service system for adult males, has the added effect of spreading military skills more widely within the civilian population. Unfortunately, it is not at all easy to determine how far, if at all, this contributes to the spread of revolution. It is probably true that at most times in most societies, the wide distribution of military skills has acted to promote political violence. Since 1787 in the United States, it has been enshrined in the Second Amendment to the American Constitution, that it should, properly organized, achieve the exact reverse: that the existence of a well-regulated militia force is an essential guarantee of popular liberty.

This view did not originate in the United States. Switzerland is the first country that comes to mind for most people in which the creation of a "citizen army" has acted not only as an effective protection against external attack but also as a barrier to the ambitions of local politicians. Certainly, the history of that country since 1848 would seem to bear that view out. But reference to its earlier history would suggest a modification of that view which in no way supports the views of the American National Rifle Association or those Americans who consider that in arming themselves to the teeth they are helping to keep the communist menace at bay. In the eighteenth century, the sturdy independence of Switzerland made it, not the United States but the Cuba of its day—a place where revolutionaries could find refuge and revolutionary ideas were published and traded in a way that infuriated its larger neighbors. Indeed, without the revolutionary ferment in Switzerland at that time, the onset of the French Revolution of 1789 might well have been delayed, and the dramatic effect of the writings of the Genevan Jean-Jacques Rousseau could scarcely be imagined if he had not had living examples of the things he talked about to back his own philosophical self-assurance.

In any case, the nature of weaponry has changed so much, especially since 1945, that it is now very difficult to see how even the best-trained citizen army could resist the determined use of force by its own government, if for some reason (e.g., defeat in war) that government's capacity for force were to escape from the control of its own citizens. It is not merely the possession of weapons, but the ability to deploy and use them effectively that is at issue, and to restrain the ordinary use of firearms, etc., in crime, modern governments have in recent years acquired a quite extraordinary degree of technical skill. Thus, as a restraint on the spread of weapons, there has been the ability to check for their presence at airports, etc.; to the development of plastic explosives, improved devices for defusing or disposing of bombs and so on.

As is widely recognized, much of the effectiveness of terrorist techniques in promoting the spread of and confidence in revolutionary ideas in the late 1960s and early 1970s stemmed, not from the nature of the acts themselves, but from their role in the "theatre of violence." Liberal democratic societies seemed particularly vulnerable to such challenges because of the way in which the existence of a free press and open access to radio and television enabled terrorists to "orchestrate" their efforts to maximum effect, making use, in fact, of the reactions of uncommitted citizens to put pressure on their governments in a way that the relatively tiny terrorist groups could never in themselves have hoped to do.

In societies with a strong authoritarian tradition, such as Turkey or Guatemala, the ability to take strongly repressive measures unhampered by democratic inhibitions appeared to their governments at one time to be highly effective. Not only could control of the media be used to minimize the theatrical effect of terrorist violence, but governmental counter-terror could proceed unchecked by criticism from within. What was not appreciated was the extent to which the decision of a government to resort to unchecked terror against its own people would, by destroying the internalized norms that check social violence in the individual, create a dangerously unstable situation with an endless potential for the escalation of violence.

The International Dimension

Finally, there is the impact of the international environment. No government has ever succeeded in the past in eliminating entirely all challenges to its authority, nor does the development of technology—despite the extent to which it does offer governments a range of abilities not previously available stop short of national frontiers. Consequently, just as the possibility of the total control of information seemed on the verge of being achieved, the development of the transistor radio, the increase in demand for world travel, and the development of the means of reproducing the printed word, combined to put it once again out of reach.

It is, therefore, with the development of such internalized norms that a society seeking real long-term stability must be concerned, and this, inevitably, means the development of education. Just as, during the Vietnam War, the sight for the first time in the history of warfare of actual battlefield conditions in the homes of ordinary American citizens, was by far the most powerful force in bringing about disillusion with the effectiveness of military action in the international context, so the reporting of the civil war in El Salvador consistently undercut the Reagan administration's persistent assertion that a purely military solution to that conflict was both necessary and desirable (cf. Pearce 1981). On the other hand, the actual presence of such sights in El Salvador itself clearly does not have the same effect on those who are already committed to the victory of one side or the other. There, whatever native inhibitions on killing they may have begun with or been educated in, have long since been overlaid by the conditioning of more recent experiences. It is clearly of crucial importance that a better understanding of the social and psychological mechanisms involved be both developed and imparted to the next generation of citizens, but there can be no great optimism that this will in fact be done.

A great many people are attracted to revolutionary causes but in the case of the great revolutions what really makes them difficult is the presence of an external threat. Perception of an alien threat triggers the mass mobilization of hostility. The alleged aggressor represents all that people regard as being worst in their society. Being outside their society, there are no taboos preventing them from venting their rage. The French aristocrats, for example, were hated, not just because they were aristos, but because they were seen as Austrian sympathizers. The French projected their hostility to the Austrians on to the unfortunate Marie Antoinette, and cut off the aristocrats' heads since they must be foreign spies. The same held true in the Russian treatment of White oppositionists when external intervention also occurred.

The experience of foreign travel seems, paradoxically, to have been important in forming the political perspectives of revolutionary leaders. It acted to liberate them from the constraints and assumptions of their own society, and left them ready to take up the international current of ideas, which included revolutionary ideals and examples. The way in which such ideas were diffused to the mass of potential followers is, however, a much more difficult question to assess. In open societies, such cultural diffusion is normal, and can, as in prerevolutionary France, prepare the way for very radical shifts of ideological perspective. In Austria or in Russia at the same period, the same ideas were indeed known, but confined to a very small section of the ruling elite. They were not widely available to the mass of the population, and the state took good care to ensure that they were not. The introduction of French Revolutionary ideas into Germany and Italy, therefore, was not attended by the same major changes that took place in France, although a generation later they were to produce their own intellectual climate of change which had a very different, nationalist coloration. Application of these findings to current circumstances should suggest to the student of international relations that the widely held view that revolutions can be propagated unchanged across national boundaries is not only likely to be wrong, but is almost certainly the exact converse of the truth; and that the only thing that could make it possible would be the nationalistic response generated by the attempt by an external power to suppress revolutionary feeling by invasion.

CHAPTER FIVE

Aid and Intervention

The mechanism by which revolutions affect other states, or are liable to be affected by them, consists of the way in which they call into question the assumptions of order and stability on which international society is founded. These do not consist simply of an agreement on the formal structure and practices of international diplomacy, and the agents by whom it is carried on, but of the consensus that there is a common interest in maintaining these relations and institutions (Bull and Watson 1984, 1).

As we have already noted, the European states have, in the past four centuries, taken a leading role in setting up a worldwide system of diplomacy. In the present century this has been extended in two ways: on the one hand, its formal structure has been extended to encompass the world system, including the multitude of new states. On the other, it has been extended beyond its original basic concept as an instrument of negotiation between pairs of states into a multilateral system of legal ideals and procedures. Though these fall far short of a workable system of government, such ideas and rules are in general observed by the vast majority of states most of the time. They do so for four main reasons: self-advantage, habit, prestige, and fear of reprisal (cf. Holsti 1967, 412). Custom and habit, therefore, underpin the notion of international society. It is precisely this relationship of custom and habit that is threatened by sudden political changes within individual state actors.

Diplomacy is the conduct of negotiations between states in the international system according to customary practices formulated to assist in securing peaceful agreement. Other writers have offered other definitions, one particularly attractive one still being that of Satow: "Diplomacy is the application of intelligence and tact to the conduct of official relations between the government of independent states, extending sometimes also to their relations with vassal states; or, more briefly still, the conduct of business between states by peaceful means" (Satow 1957, 1).

The official business of doing so is carried on by specially trained officials known generally as "diplomats," and collectively as a state's "diplomatic service."

Diplomacy evolved in a world of monarchical states, and its customs reflect its origins. One ruler could not concede precedence to another. Diplomacy grew up, therefore, on the basis of an equal exchange of representatives, called ambassadors or ministers, between two rulers. Each was regarded as representing his ruler, who as an anointed ruler (Christian or otherwise) was protected from physical harm by religious fear as well as by legal sanction. During his mission, therefore, the envoy was personally immune from arrest or attack, and his house and belongings were exempt from search or confiscation. The beginning of his mission was marked, on arrival, by his formal reception by the head of state, at which he presented the official letters of credence which were the proof of his status and powers, and at the end by a formal leave-taking.

The operation of the entire system depended on the mutual recognition of one another by the states concerned. Once that was achieved, each had an interest in maintaining the links that had been established. From that time onwards the main problems in the extension and maintenance of the system came from states that had undergone revolutionary changes, and who therefore regarded themselves as no longer being bound by the rules of a system to whose growth they had not contributed (Falk 1969). History shows that these problems are not in any way new to the twentieth century, and that some of these earlier experiences have still something to teach us about the nature of diplomacy and of the international system.

First, there is the problem of recognition. A state that changes its form of government has, if it is to continue to deal with other states, first of all to be recognized by them. Until a government is recognized by its peers it can play no formal role. A new government is therefore in an exceptionally vulnerable position to pressure from other states, who can make use of its desire for recognition to try to force it to behave in a way that suits their interests. If it does not, their continued failure to recognize it may well have no significant effect on its internal politics, but it can and does act to reduce its influence in world affairs.

Most states seek recognition, which is not to say that they cannot survive without recognition. But basically a state is handicapped in its international relations by not being admitted into the formal system. To be recognized by other states and to gain admittance into this system, a government has, first, to observe their customs; in other words, to accommodate itself to the existing framework of diplomacy. Thus, for example, G.V. Chicherin, the Soviet People's Commissar for Foreign Affairs from 1918 to 1930, found himself wearing a tailcoat by 1922, so that he could get into international conferences and be dressed like all the others. The United States recognized the USSR in

1933 but withheld recognition from the People's Republic of China from 1949 to 1973. This had no adverse effect on China internally, but it precluded it from a full role in international affairs and by corollary the United States was also able to prevent it from being admitted to the United Nations, where it would otherwise have been able to take up its permanent seat in the Security Council, with the right of veto. However, when the United States did recognize China, it made no effort to support Taiwan, which immediately lost its international status.

Secondly, the incoming government has to recognize the obligations of past governments. There are two ways in which it is likely to give offence. One is by canceling the debts of past governments. The Russian government, in 1917, did that. However, it also violated the trust of the international community in a more serious way, by publishing the secret Czarist archives, including the text of the secret treaties that had been made by Russia during the Great War, describing how the allies were going to carve up the map of Europe, once they had the chance. By doing this, the Bolsheviks struck a political blow but forfeited confidence.

Thirdly, the revolutionary state has to accept the rules of diplomatic relations, embodied since 1961 in the provisions of the Vienna Convention. However, one of the characteristics of a revolutionary state is frequently the rejection of traditional diplomatic methods and techniques, on the grounds that they are "loaded"; that they represent the features of an international order that a revolutionary state opposes. As Spanier puts it, "A revolutionary state—such as the Soviet Union after World War II—is a state at war. It rejects the social and economic structure of the traditional states who dominate the state system because it views this prevailing order as the source of injustice and war" (Spanier 1967). Examples in recent time have been Libya after 1969 and Iran after 1979, to which we could add Venezuela since 1999.

Such states use international agencies not for the resolution of disputes in a peaceful manner, but for propaganda, agitation, and intimidation. Hence, they may, as the communist countries did, make extensive use of insulting epithets and abusive accusations against their political opponents or, as we have already noticed, make use of negotiations as a cover for the more or less surreptitious use of force. In fact, the Iranian Revolutionary Government in 1979–81 rejected the conventions of the diplomatic system entirely, to the extent of abusing the persons of diplomats accredited to them and using them as hostages for demands on foreign governments (Christopher 1985).

These problems arise even before a revolutionary movement succeeds (if it ever does) in seizing power. For nearly a decade from 1967 onwards hostage-taking became routine practice among terrorist movements, with or without revolutionary intent, as a means of publicizing their own cause and often securing large ransom sums for the release of key members of their groups. In these events diplomatic personnel, for a time, became the prime targets, as the individuals most specifically identified with the policies of the governments they served.

This is particularly sad since, whatever its shortcomings, diplomacy is a prime factor in the struggle for peace. Whatever else it may be, diplomacy is not war. War may be the continuation of diplomacy by other means, but it is not just the same thing as diplomacy. Moreover, the existence of a state of war does not put an end to diplomacy, for without diplomacy war cannot be brought to an end. It is one of the most respected principles of international law as well as domestic law that the mere seizure of territory or property by force does not confer a right to it. Only by diplomatic agreement, therefore, can the arrangements be made by which the victors secure their gains or settle their losses.

Diplomatic Immunities

In order for this to happen, as already noted, diplomats have to have protection. Since this protection is supposed to be the same as that enjoyed by the sovereigns they represent, the natural question arises: "How far does a sovereign who has been deposed enjoy the protection of the international system?" In theory, not at all. Neither a sovereign nor a president of a republic who has been overthrown is entitled to any immunities (Satow 1957, 7). But in practice such an individual is usually treated with courtesy by other states, at least for a period of time following his fall, by the unspoken custom of the "trade union of rulers." An important exception was the Shah of Iran, who was denied hospitality by almost all the states which had formerly been his allies. This was wise. When in October 1969 Jimmy Carter reluctantly allowed him to enter the United States to undergo surgery, this was the "provocation" which led the Revolutionary Guard in Tehran to storm the American Embassy and take the staff hostage. The Shah was asked to leave the United States and took refuge for a time in Panama, but was eventually given the hospitality of President Anwar al-Sadat of Egypt, where he died in 1980.

It is clearly a delicate problem for other states as to what to do with exiled rulers. How do they treat them? They are, in fact, technically only private citizens, but usually for diplomatic reasons hosts feel they have to treat them with a certain amount of care in case they might suddenly find themselves back in office the next day, when a public snub might be rather embarrassing. And in Latin America, since the late nineteenth century, politicians generally have been able to avail themselves of a formal international agreement between the American states to respect the diplomatic immunity of the legations or embassies of other countries. This enables fallen politicians to take refuge from revolt (even when of their own making) and pass subsequently into exile in safety, from which they do not infrequently return in triumph at the next turn of Fortune's wheel. Even in Africa, where these rules have not yet generally been accepted, it is certainly not customary to kill rulers who have been overthrown. To shoot four of one's predecessors, as Flight-Lieutenant Jerry Rawlings did in Ghana, is a very bad precedent.

We can now return to the question of immunity for ambassadors. It is the minister for foreign affairs who will normally conduct business with the visiting ambassador. It is his/her responsibility to guarantee the privileges and immunities of ambassadors even in time of civil disturbance. Diplomacy does not easily recognize the existence of a state of civil disturbance and therefore if care is not taken to protect ambassadors and diplomatic personnel generally, this may be taken as evidence by foreign countries that the government is incapable of governing, in which case they are then at liberty to recognize another. And when a civil war or revolution breaks out in a foreign country the representatives of the preexisting government must continue to be treated as being such until the minister is formally notified that that government has been overthrown (Satow 1957, 119, sec. 198). Conversely, in a country where disturbance breaks out the minister there remains responsible for the safety of diplomatic personnel until he himself is actually overthrown. A diplomatic representative in a foreign capital who has been accredited by a government that has been overthrown by force, even in time of war, is still entitled to full immunity until he is safely back in his own country (Satow 1957, 192, sec. 317). Diplomatic immunity applies also in those countries the agent passes through on the way home.

In a civil war, as in Spain between 1936 and 1939, what is the status in international law of the opposition? The answer is: technically, it has no status—a foreign power cannot recognize it diplomatically without automatically breaking off recognition of the existing government. In the case of secession, as in Croatia, for example, recognition of the government of Croatia gave rise immediately to severance of relations by Yugoslavia. Any country may, in theory, at any time, if it wishes, sever diplomatic relations with any other, but it is in fact regarded as a cause of offence to do so.

The status of belligerency to which Satow refers, is a different question. It is open to a government when a country is in a state of civil war, to recognize the opposition party as belligerents. This does not imply diplomatic recognition and it does not entitle them to representation, even if they want it. But it does entitle them to conduct certain kinds of commercial business, particularly buying and selling arms, which they then find extremely convenient. So to recognize a state of belligerency is to recognize the actual existence of a state of war. It is not to pronounce moral judgment, although it tends to be regarded as a sign that perhaps the insurgents have a point. And it is accepted that foreign states may negotiate with belligerents informally, to provide for the safety of their citizens in the territory they control (Oppenheim 1970, I, 693, sec. 362) Similarly, diplomats may have to negotiate with those effectively in power, again unofficially until their government accords recognition and similarly their own government will continue to deal with the diplomatic agent previously accredited to them (Satow 1957, 119, sec. 198).

The mere act of sending out a new ambassador always confers recognition since the ambassador has formally to present their credentials. One cannot, therefore, replace a diplomatic agent under such conditions without formally according recognition to the new regime. There is, however, no fixed method of according recognition to a new government which has assumed office as a result of a revolutionary outbreak. "Any form of notification suffices for the purpose, or any act on the part of a state which is consistent only with such recognition" (Satow 1957, 120, sec. 199). To send a diplomatic note, for example, is consistent only with recognition.

Recognition can, therefore, serve as a bargaining point with new revolutionary governments. Withholding recognition to secure bargaining points is termed *non-recognition*. In 1910, Britain delayed the recognition of the Portuguese Republic until it had called a general election, which gave the majority to the Republicans, and required them to alter their draft Constitution, to permit Anglican worship. In the case of Greece, in 1924, the British government accorded recognition only after the new republic had been approved by a plebiscite. The United States refused to recognize the dictatorship of General Victoriano Huerta in Mexico in 1913 and did not fully accept the government of revolutionary Mexico until the successful conclusion of the Bucareli negotiations in 1923. It is often regarded as being overbearing of large powers to do this but in purely diplomatic terms it is perfectly respectable.

A mere change of ministry does not, however, affect diplomatic recognition. It is a very moot point as to whether it is even necessary to accord recognition to a person who has come to power as a result of a military coup even when he is an executive head of state. For example, in the case of Chile and Ecuador in 1925, and Peru, Argentina and Brazil in 1930, when they had military coups, the British representative was simply instructed to inform the government concerned "that the British Government considered their diplomatic relations between the two countries were in no way affected by the change of government."

In the key case of the Soviet Union in 1924, however, Britain did not use its bargaining power and even recognized the government of the Soviet Union as the "de jure rulers of those territories of the old Russian Empire which recognized their authority." This was surprising, because of the vast difference between *de facto* and *de jure* recognition. *De facto* recognition means only recognizing that the government is effectively in control of the country, and British practice is always to recognize governments when they are effectively in control of their respective countries. In the particular case of the Soviet Union, however, Britain not only recognized the Soviet government as the *de facto* rulers, but also *de jure*. To recognize them *de jure* means that they are believed to have legitimacy and have a right to exist. Recognizing a government *de jure* therefore means that, technically, recognition cannot be withdrawn, unless it commits a really serious offence in the eyes of the international community.

The compliment was not returned and between 1923 and 1989 the Soviet Union expressed its support for many revolutionary movements and in return was suspected in the United States of being behind much of the trouble in their world. However, these fears can now be seen to have been exaggerated. Soviet support was only significant when it was translated into meaningful action, and in fact it seldom was. As with other powers, the Soviets were primarily occupied with their own national interests, and only secondarily with the promotion of revolution (Katz 1990, 9).

Quite often ambassadors have used diplomatic influence against incumbent governments; for example, the United States Ambassador John Puerifoy, in Greece in 1952, and in Guatemala in 1954, and it became something of a habit by the United States in the Caribbean area in the 1980s and 1990s. Ambassadors are allowed to do that; what they are not allowed to do is to promote a military conspiracy against the government to whom they are accredited. In fact, there is no evidence that Puerifoy did this; though in the latter country he did take advantage of a military conspiracy to see that the government that he wanted was put in power. In 1983, the US military attaché in Guatemala was observed, during a military coup, hiding in the pillars of the Presidential Palace talking into a radio. Only very suspicious observers thought that he was directing events.

What is the status of an ambassador of a foreign country who conspires against the country to which he is accredited? The fact is that ambassadors today usually take enormous care to avoid being caught doing this, and therefore there are no recent instances that we can actually prove. It seems customary to entrust these important matters to the Third Secretary's chauffeur who is in fact a colonel in the secret service. The ambassador knows nothing about this and it would be very embarrassing indeed if he did—he takes good care that he does not, just as Ronald Reagan took good care not to know anything about what Oliver North was doing down in the basement of the White House. This is called "plausible deniability."

Diplomatic agents, whether actually engaged in conspiracy or not, can and often are expelled as *persona non grata* to the incumbent regime. No reasons need be given as to why a person is *persona non grata*, and in fact, great care is taken in appointing diplomats to ensure beforehand that they are *personae gratae*. This is done by taking soundings and getting the agreement of the government to whom the diplomat is to be accredited. If the reply is that the government concerned would prefer some other appointment to be made, this advice is always followed for obvious reasons. There is no point in appointing a diplomat who is going to be regarded as undiplomatic. However, it is often done by regimes with revolutionary pretensions.

Revolutionary Diplomacy

Revolutionary governments present a very special problem to other states. A revolution almost certainly heralds a reversal of alliances, and this is very disruptive to the existing order. Furthermore, a revolutionary government will make its first priority to ensure its own survival. Anthony Ascham, the political philosopher, was sent by the Commonwealth of England as ambassador to Madrid. He was a political philosopher who wrote a treatise *Of the Confusions and Revolutions of Governments* (Ascham 1649, repr. 1975), but before he could present his credentials he was murdered by dissident Royalists on May 27, 1650. On behalf of Parliament, John Milton wrote a curt rebuke to Philip IV, and demanded their execution. Despite this, for diplomatic reasons, Spain recognized the Commonwealth government in December. But when relations with Spain soured, and Cromwell saw the opportunity to pick up territory in the Americas, he found a reliable ally in Cardinal Mazarin of France.

Also, when Cromwell took over the reins of office and brought them under his own control, he set up a secret agency for the conduct of foreign policy as well as using official representatives. Unlike later rulers, however, he conducted his foreign policy officially and unofficially through the same man, John Thurloe, the Secretary of State. He was prepared to spend up to

£70,000 annually on obtaining intelligence at foreign courts. Specifically, he would pay up to £1,000 annually to buy good information in Rome, and in fact bought a cardinal for the purpose. It may seem a little improbable that the government of a puritan regime like Cromwell's should have managed to suborn a cardinal but it seems cardinals were going quite cheap in 1650 (Thompson and Padover 1963).

Another aspect of Cromwellian foreign policy, which is also a recurrent feature of revolutionary regimes, was its secrecy. It was so secret that even the Venetian ambassador to Madrid, Sagredo, was unable at first to find out what was going on. The reports of the Venetian Embassy, with all the money that they had at their disposal were second to none, and they had the finest diplomatic and intelligence nets in Europe. They got very upset when in the end they discovered what the English were up to, for they were really descending to thoroughly low tricks. "To discover the affairs of others they do not employ ambassadors, but use spies, as less conspicuous, making use of men of spirit but without rank, unlikely to be noticed," the Venetian complained (Thompson and Padover 1963, 85). Cromwell was, therefore, one of the first to separate the function of intelligence from diplomacy which up to that time had really been one and the same thing.

This is the key to the operation of revolutionary diplomacy, which tends to make use, not of the formal machinery of diplomatic intercourse, but of a separate and distinct net. And in the tremendously status-ridden societies, even—dare one say it—of today, the men of spirit but without rank are the people who are able to pick up the good information. And they are also the people who are able to buy up the information they require or to make the necessary negotiations in delicate parts of the state.

Another great Englishman, if he may be described as such, who was also a revolutionary leader, was William III (1689–1702). William was very short of cash, and he found, contrary to popular belief, that the less cash he had, the better his foreign policy was. Diplomacy was extremely expensive in his day, and it did not bring in very much goodwill either, because one always offended more people than one actually made friends. William set the tone of eighteenth-century diplomacy, which in fact persisted right into the nineteenth century, by using few permanent missions but a great many agents engaged in promoting trade—again a product of a revolutionary situation.

Again, in the time of the French Convention, one finds the sudden reappearance of intelligence and unofficial agents. During 1793 alone, at the height of the Terror, the government spent on spies the sum of 1,300,000 livres (the livre was then worth about 10 pence sterling). They spent this on a centre of espionage in the Ministry of Foreign Affairs, which reported weekly to the ministerial conference and then to the Committee of Public Safety and to the Paris Commune. They paid special attention to foreigners resident in France, who were the subject of great suspicion at all times. They thought they were probably enemies of liberty and engaged in plotting against the regime and none more so than Gouverneur Morris, the minister of the United States, whom they identified as the greatest enemy of liberty because he was not very keen on the public execution of aristocrats. The Convention, however, was again (exactly like the English) not very interested in the effect of their foreign agents. It was considered necessary "to abandon for a time the principles of scrupulousness in dealing with enemies who are unscrupulous, or rather, as ferocious, as ours are" (Thompson and Padover 1963, 184).

Washington's coolness toward the French Revolution was known to the French and in order to try and represent the true feelings of French revolutionary government to the people of the United States, they decided they would send a trusted minister to the United States. Citizen Genêt arrived in Philadelphia in exactly the same spirit as the English revolutionary agents of Cromwell's time, and proceeded to make a series of speeches to the people, inciting them to overthrow President Washington. He was promptly reproved. On the other hand, the Marquis de Chauvelin, sent as French minister to London to persuade Britain to remain neutral, has been unfairly depicted in the works of Baroness Orczy, and was in fact a notable military officer who served in the American Revolution, survived the Terror and went on to serve Napoleon as Intendant-General of Catalonia.

Lastly, we can compare the actions of Russia (from 1922 to 1991 in the Soviet Union). By this time intelligence is by general consent clearly separated from diplomacy. So the official foreign ministry of the Soviet Union, the People's Commissariat of Foreign Affairs, was actually charged with very low-level duties, primarily conducting trade negotiations. The intelligence function was, on the other hand, placed under the same organ as the secret police which they used for internal affairs, though a separate intelligence bureau for the military was established.

Even more important was the setting-up of the Comintern, the Communist International Information Bureau. The Comintern organization was from the beginning an organ of the Soviet government. Its duty was to promote Soviet foreign policy aims abroad by conducting revolutionary movements in other countries (Black and Thornton 1964), and it was appropriately staffed with experts in these activities. Chicherin, the People's Commissar for Foreign Affairs, dealt with trade, conferences, passports, and treaties; in other words, fairly low-level activities. However, like all previous revolutionary regimes, they did use the embassies as a cover for their covert activities, so while the ambassador was busy being nice to the bourgeoisie the chauffeurs were busy subverting them and getting secrets about the atom bomb. The general rule therefore seems to be, the more drastic the change made by revolution in the diplomatic structure, the more likely it is to engage in unconventional diplomacy.

A major revolution of this kind almost always involves a major diplomatic upheaval; for one specific reason it means a reversal of alliances. The revolutionary overthrow of the government means that by definition the new government will not be *persona grata* to those who are already allied to the old government. And a reversal of alliance is therefore necessary and implicates the new government in having to defend its own position in a potentially hostile world. It is bound to be all the more forthright in rejecting the current world order in the most serious of all emergencies, when it is itself seriously menaced and even attacked by counterrevolutionary forces in league with the governments of neighboring states. This was the case in the three historical examples we have just noted: the English, French, and Russian Revolutions. In recent times it has also been notable in the case of Cuba, attacked by the United States in 1961; Angola, where the counter revolutionary movement UNITA was supported by the South African up to and including the deployment of troops; and Nicaragua, where the Reagan administration supported, armed, and financed the counterrevolutionary forces ("contras") operating against it from neighboring Honduras, which slowly eroded the gains of the revolution and ultimately destroyed it (Valenta 1985, Rossett and Vandermeer 1986, Shugart 1987, Spalding 1987, Walker 1987, Gilbert 1988, Gonzalez 1990). In neighboring El Salvador, it was touch-and-go in the early stages of the revolt whether US support would arrive in time, but massive support for the government finally forced a stalemate in the conflict (Shugart 1987, Wickham-Crowley 1989, La Feber 1993).

Types of Intervention

Aid and intervention are both vague terms which require more precise definition. Some writers take the cynical view that aid is what *we* do and intervention is what *they* do. Others make the more specific point that aid refers specifically to material facilities and intervention to the dispatch of personnel. This in turn implies that intervention is one of at least two things: *diplomatic intervention*, in which an ambassador or other diplomatic agent makes a particular move in a specific situation which is designed to affect the internal politics of the country concerned, or *military intervention*, in which a state sends in troops in an effort to change the government or regime of another country.

In the 1980s it became fashionable to use the word "intervention" in an extremely loose way, to cover a third aspect distinguished in the recent literature, *economic intervention*. This is supposed to refer to the processes of economic penetration of a state by foreign companies or by international corporations. But economic intervention is rather an unattractive concept. Although there is no doubt about the existence of economic structures penetrating other states, they do so in a continuous process; it is not something that happens at a specific moment. Yet the word "intervention" implies a process of coming between two contending parties in such a way as to adjust the balance of advantage between them (cf. Little 1975, 6). When we talk about diplomatic or military intervention we do clearly refer to a specific moment in time in which a state intervenes across boundaries of other states in such a way as to change their internal structure.

If we talk about **economic intervention**, therefore, we should by analogy use the term only for a very small category of events, which, paradoxically, we would in practice more often term "aid"; in other words, specific grants of money at a particular moment in time. Generally speaking, most of the economic influence of which the critics have been complaining, will turn out not to be of this character but instead forms part of the normal relationship between states and is as such fairly constant over a period of time. Intervention will, therefore, be treated here as a specific act designed to alter the balance between government and opposition in another state.

Diplomatic intervention is the use of diplomatic personnel or other agents to assist or to prevent specific political changes in a foreign state.

Assuming that the two states have regular diplomatic relations, and that one of them is threatened by a revolutionary outbreak, the other may, on receiving reports of the outbreak, decide to extend an offer of support to the incumbent government. This may well alter the internal balance between government and opposition, but it is legitimate in international law and does not constitute intervention.

If, on the other hand, the decision is made to empower the accredited envoys to enter into relations with the opposition, even if these relations go no further than an exchange of views, this may be regarded as intervention by the government and the offending envoys declared *personae non gratae*. For such purposes, therefore, governments make use in general of unofficial agents whose official character can if necessary be disavowed. A delicate situation then arises if, either by information privately received, or through an analysis of press reports and other public sources of information, the foreign power comes to believe either that its interests will be best served if the government agrees to talk to the opposition or else advises specific concessions. In such circumstances, even an offer of mediation may be regarded as improper diplomatic intervention.

Mediation is a recognized diplomatic activity which consists simply in conveying the views of two parties to one another in such a way so as to further agreement between them. For a foreign power to mediate in a revolutionary situation its mediation must, first of all, be acceptable to both sides, and this is by definition comparatively rarely the case. It may in the first instance therefore be necessary to involve another power in the chain of negotiation. The risk with this, however, is that the contending parties may then come to believe that the other two powers are acting in concert to secure their own ends.

In all cases a special role is played by the United Nations, which has a specific duty to safeguard world peace. Though offers of mediation by the secretary general may often be publicly resented by governments who see them as "official" recognition of a state of belligerency they themselves would prefer to ignore or conceal, in practice they are more readily accepted among Third World states than the mediation of major powers. On the other hand, if the parties are to accept an agreement, they must believe that they are unlikely to get better terms, and it is at this point that unofficial representations from their major allies are of crucial importance.

Technically speaking, advice from another government that it considers the government likely to lose if it does not make concessions is not intervention. A statement to the effect that, if it does not concede, that government will forfeit its support, on the other hand, technically is intervention, and thus the United States Ambassador in Guatemala in 1954 intervened when he advised General Díaz, successor to President Arbenz, that he would not obtain the support of the United States (Gleijeses 1991). The withdrawal of envoys and the severance of diplomatic relations can follow as a public sign of withdrawal of support, as in the case of the Organisation of American States in 1979 at the time of the fall of President Anastasio Somoza Debayle. On that occasion the Government of Costa Rica took the even more controversial step of publicly permitting the formation of a Revolutionary Government on its soil and according it official recognition before Somoza had actually resigned. Under international law such an action could constitute grounds for a declaration of war, for it constitutes public and open aid to an opposition movement, but by that time the Somoza government was no longer able to respond in such a fashion.

Normally, aid afforded to an insurgent movement is clandestine, and channeled through unofficial agents. It can take the form of passively permitting a revolutionary movement to raise funds, organize and prepare for combat on a neighboring state, or of actively fomenting a revolutionary movement, in which case support for that movement may well take the form of armed menaces or actual military intervention.

To begin with, it will be recalled that insurgents have no standing in international law unless they are recognized as belligerents. But access to foreign governments is generally considered desirable by revolutionary movements to buy weapons and to secure diplomatic neutrality or even aid, and hence they will run considerable risks to make such contacts. A classic case was the two Confederate agents named Mason and Slidell who were traveling to Britain on a British vessel, the *Trent*, during the American Civil War when they were intercepted and taken off by the USS *San Jacinto*. On this occasion the Government of the United Kingdom protested at the interference with a British vessel and secured their release, but as unofficial agents Mason and Slidell had no protection in their own right. There was, therefore, no reason in international law why such agents should not be captured, if in fact it is legitimate to do so. In fact, it is quite clear that there are good grounds for a government insisting that other powers do not receive such agents, still less accede to their requests. However, the American captain was not entitled to board a friendly vessel in order to seize them.

The British government was, however, in the wrong in the case of the Confederate agents who bought and fitted out the screw sloop of war, CSS *Alabama,* in Liverpool. She went on to capture and/or burn more than 60 Union merchantmen before she was sunk in an engagement with USS *Kearsarge*.The British government had failed to prevent the *Alabama* from sailing, and subsequently, at arbitration, was held guilty of negligence and had to pay an indemnity of $15m. The cancelled cheque for this amount was framed and hung over the Foreign Secretary's desk. There it can still be seen as a reminder to succeeding foreign secretaries. So the responsibility, therefore, of a state toward an established government of another power is first, *not* to receive the agents and secondly *not* to accede to their demands, particularly where they refer to the supply of arms. So any government receiving agents and any government, still more, permitting them to bear arms, is likely to get itself into trouble.

Despite this, the process is in fact highly institutionalized. In the Chilean Civil War of 1891 the Congressional Party (which eventually won) sent agents both to Europe and to the United States for funds and to buy arms. It is not known, in this particular case, whether there were in fact regular agents in the United Kingdom through which they dealt. But there is no doubt that they dealt with regular agents in the United States, namely the law firm of Hopkins and Hopkins, who were lobbyists of the State Department in Congress. Anyone promoting a revolution in Latin America during the years 1891 to 1920 sent a representative to Hopkins and Hopkins in Washington, who proceeded to intercede with the State Department for them and lobby Congress quite legally and through the usual processes of American government.

After the inception of the Cold War, for the first time since the 1920s it has been possible to play off two or more great powers against each other, in such a way as to maximize the advantages from each—the Bangladeshi secessionists succeeded in getting aid from the United States on the one hand, and their leaders went for medical treatment to the Soviet Union on the other. The local arena, therefore, has been expanded into a worldwide one, and the role of the dominant power has been complicated by the intrusion of other powers.

It is, however, rather doubtful whether foreign aid is as important a factor as often thought. First, no coups, and very few revolutionary movements construed in the broadest possible sense, continue long enough to involve foreign intervention—diplomatic or otherwise (Rosenau 1964, 19; see also David 1987). Secondly, the recognition of new governments today, therefore, tends to be primarily a question of recogniszng faits accomplis. In this situation, unofficial agents do not appear to perform much of a role, and recommendations for recognition are made by regular diplomatic personnel, who would otherwise be out of a job.

Unofficial agents are also used by governments, where a government finds itself confronted with an insurgent movement in a country with which it feels, for the safety of its nationals and otherwise, it needs to deal. This is perfectly legitimate in terms of international law—but only if the agents are unofficial and engage only in discussion. Agreement with insurgent parties cannot be binding because they have no standing in international law. In rare cases governments send unofficial agents to insurgents in their own country; in other words, they open negotiations with an existing revolutionary movement in order to establish some kind of peace. This, however, is very seldom and only normally happens when the incumbent government has been defeated and wishes to yield gracefully. In practice, we are concerned rather more often with the sending of unofficial agents from governments to foreign insurgent movements which, as noted above, is a dangerous thing to do, as it is liable to be misconstrued.

It is hard to distinguish here between the three major categories of individuals operating in this situation. First, it can be assumed that most great powers were interested in the insurgent movement in the neighboring country and will ensure that they have on the scene spies or informants, agents whose job it is to simply find out what is going on. The problem of sending such agents is that they tend to become committed to one or other side and to start actually trying to influence the situation, such as by establishing unofficial contact with a view to ultimate recognition.

If they do this, they move into the second category, that of *unofficial diplomatist*. Unofficial diplomatists are those that engage in diplomacy without having official status. This is most frequently, in practice, carried out by regular members of the diplomatic, or possibly the consular, corps; as for example, in the case of Sir Robert Bruce Lockhart who, as Consul, was in Moscow in 1917-18 and therefore was in the right place at the right moment when in fact the diplomats were still in Petrograd, and too far away to be able to tell what was going on (Bruce Lockhart 1950). In such a case, an agent on the spot may be empowered to engage in negotiations which otherwise would not come within his sphere of competence. Alternatively, ordinary citizens may be sent or in rare cases assume an unofficial diplomatic task.

Occasionally, there may be a third category of unofficial agents, the *agents provocateurs*, who try to cause trouble for a government which is considered to be dangerous or hostile, either by inciting an existing revolutionary movement or by attempting to stir up a revolutionary movement that is not yet in being.

Some kind of influence by one or other of these means is probably inevitable today. The days of slow communications and relatively sealed frontiers are now at an end. People can move with great speed, and large categories of people, such as tourists, relief personnel, communications personnel, are now in continual transit in almost all the countries of the world. It is no longer as easy to seal a frontier and to keep things under wraps as it once was. Even the People's Republic of China is now seeking to increase its tourist trade. As Soviet penetration of the US Central Intelligence Agency shows, it is a relatively easy matter in a democratic society to introduce or recruit a foreign agent and to maintain communications with him, though it is unlikely that, given the existence of a reasonably competent police force, that agent can engage in such high-level activities.

Outside all but the most developed countries, however, the government is not in effective control of a great deal of its national territory and things are very different. It is in such areas that opportunities arise which mean that the great powers no longer necessarily have to engage in overt military intervention in order to achieve their objectives. In the uncertain twilight zone between diplomatic activity and subversion there are numerous possibilities for a government that is not too scrupulous about the means it uses to secure its ends.

K.J. Holsti (1967) claims that in the period 1900–50, in 200 revolutions, intervention occurred in half that number and more than one intervention in a quarter. Intervention included sending diplomatic notes or making military threats, infiltrating foreign voluntary organizations, sponsoring strikes and riots, creating political scandals, attempting a *coup détat*, or, on their own or an ally's territory, organizing, training, and arming a group of foreign dissidents and then sending them home to conduct guerrilla warfare against a "friendly" government. While it is undoubtedly true that multiple interventions are common, and not simply a product of the period of the Cold War, some caution is needed about these figures. Taking the narrower criterion of aid actually afforded during the active period of the revolutionary incident, the author found that in 364 incidents between 1901–60 aid was afforded to the government in 24 instances and to the opposition in 76 (Calvert 1970b, 219). Subsequent research has shown, however, that aid of this kind appears to be particularly significant in the population of successful incidents (Brier and Calvert 1975, Brier 1982). Above all, it was strongly correlated with proximity to one or other of the superpowers, a fact that speaks for itself.

Military Intervention

The role of military intervention itself, however, is still a rather obscure one—for two reasons. To begin with, the use of foreign troops is often not practicable. Intervention, for example, of the United States in the Dominican Republic in 1965, where a very large amount of force could be brought to bear by a very large country on a relatively small situation, was feasible. So too was the Soviet intervention in Czechoslovakia in 1968. But it is not to be deduced from this that the United States government, for example, could land troops in Chile or Brazil, or the Russian government in France or Britain. Secondly, it is only realistic to say that the capacity to intervene indirectly is limited. Any attempt to use an overt military threat, for example, in the case of the Soviet Union to influence a change of government in Turkey, or in the case of the United States in Venezuela, one of the medium rank powers would probably create such a backlash of hostility, both in the country concerned and in the neighboring countries, that it would be totally counterproductive.

The threat of direct military intervention, therefore, has been very much downgraded since 1945, compared with the fear of clandestine conspiracy or guerrilla warfare. There is no doubt that a considerable number of insurgent movements in being at any given moment receive a good deal of foreign support. Whether these come into the category of intervention or aid is a nice question. As they are in fact constant, it is probably difficult to describe them accurately as intervention, even today. The last of Holsti's categories, the organization, training, and arming of a group of foreign dissidents and sending them home to conduct guerrilla warfare or subversion certainly is intervention. American examples are the Bay of Pigs expedition to Cuba (1961) and the *contras* in Honduras; a Soviet example is the training, through the North Korean training agency, of the various guerrilla agents who have been sent to Central America. Lesser powers can find such methods both convenient and cheap, as witness the late President Nkrumah's training ground in Ghana for freedom fighters to liberate the African continent, because this too had a certain limited role at this particular period of history.

It is true that we know most about the activities of the great powers, and we are inclined nowadays to pin the label of intervention specifically on the great powers. But caution is needed here. Both great and lesser powers practice clandestine activities, though not necessarily subversion. But it is not so easy to avoid the challenge of subversion—it is a very flexible concept. All countries like to be liked by their neighbors and if those neighbors involve, or have within their national boundaries, substantial minority groups who appeal to their fellows to join them, then this comes very definitely within the category of subversion. For example, the appeal to the Northern Irish of those of their compatriots who press their views, that they should become part of a unified Ireland, is one that, if it came from a great power to a little one, would be regarded as being subversion. In the case of a little power to a great power it is not traditional to regard it as subversion, and yet it is in fact indistinguishable. And the same kind of comment applies to a vast number of other situations, and also to situations in which the powers are reasonably equal in size.

The limitations on the nature of subversive appeals to neighboring countries are fairly easily delineated. First, there is the fortunate *scarcity of target groups.* Owing to the period after the First World War, in which people endeavored as far as possible to redraw the map of the world, to keep international minorities at a minimum as far as possible, there are relatively few significant national minorities in countries other than African ones, where the boundaries, being both colonial and artificial, are still unforged. The target groups need to be of a certain size before they can actually or potentially prove to be a danger to a neighboring state or limit its potential for action. If they are very small indeed, they may be a running sore to some government but they are not likely to be of very great significance. In fact, it is interesting to see how in the case of a country, the size of Britain, the action in Northern Ireland can in fact be contained and can be regarded as being of relatively small significance in terms of overall national politics. Even in a close election like the General Election of February 1974, Northern Ireland was only marginally significant, though it became more so in the last days of the Major government.

The *apathy of the target group* is the second limitation. In Spain ETA continue to be active and from time to time plant bombs to prove that they are. But the response of the majority of the Basque population suggests that they are not actively interested, as long as their regional government continues to function and to treat them with moderate fairness.

Poor communications are a third factor. In many parts of the world, national minorities are so concerned with staying alive and so far from any of the centers of population concentration, that their insurgency has little effect. An example is the Nagas in India. The Nagas are, of course, a secessionist movement, and not the product of external subversion, but in fact Nagaland is so small and so peripheral as far as India is concerned that the conflict has been almost completely contained, while the neighboring states are too remote to assist them. This is clearly also the case with at least some of the numerous minorities in Burma (Myanmar).

Lastly, there is the *weakness of the claimant state*. Many states that in fact affect their neighbors through their appeals to shared minorities are not themselves very strong. Tunisia and Algeria function in this respect in Morocco. Morocco does the same for Mauritania and the Spanish Sahara; Ghana does for Nigeria and Togo for the Ivory Coast and Niger; Egypt for Yemen, South Yemen and Israel (Zartman 1966). Extend this pattern throughout the world and consider in fact just how many states have been medium-size irritants to their neighbors, without necessarily being able to secure a decisive shift of power in their favor.

Such problems are the stuff of international relations. Here we are interested in the revolutionary dimension, the possibility of stirring up informal dissension or appeal to minorities as a means to secure state objectives. Holsti (1967) identifies five specific factors determining the outcome of intervention in modern conditions.

First—and it would be natural for an American to stress this first perhaps—we live in an age in which it is more or less universally accepted that great powers have a certain obligation toward the welfare of smaller ones. There are, therefore, programs of economic and military aid in being all the time, in most parts of the world, which implies a degree of political interest in how those funds are spent. States accepting foreign aid *necessarily* accept a degree of derogation from their national sovereignty, if there can indeed still be said to be such a thing.

Secondly, it is a fact that in many of the extreme cases of actual military intervention, the intervention is in fact requested. In other words, where there is a great power with sufficient capacity to be called into play in an internal situation, then it is quite easy for it, as with the Soviet Union in Afghanistan in 1979, to arrange to be called in to intervene on behalf of the incumbent. And this is—given the present nature of international law—a perfectly legitimate action.

Thirdly, ideological affiliations transcend state boundaries. We do not live only in the era of the national minority, we also live in an era of political strife. Such ideas create common interests across boundaries. Fourthly, many governments today come to power through the use of force and therefore they quite naturally tend to use force in securing their further objectives. Having used force to gain power, they use it to secure any other objectives which they may have in mind (Calvert 1976).

And last, but not least, there was the Cold War and its accompanying nuclear stalemate. The existence of the nuclear stalemate predisposed countries to seek a balance of advantage within the international system by use of subversion (cf. Herz 1959). This incentive is undoubtedly less than it was, but it has not wholly gone away. Meanwhile, dangerous new polarities have emerged, between Pakistan and India, and Iran and Israel.

Levels of Intervention

We can therefore identify six levels of intervention. First, there is *diplomatic intervention* in the internal affairs of a state, where a country deliberately uses diplomatic weight in order to try to secure a governmental outcome which is favorable to it. An example which is frequently cited is that of the United States ambassador in Greece, Ambassador Puerifoy in 1952. But this is a poor example for many reasons because Greece fell clearly, according to the famous terms of the bargain at Yalta between Churchill and Roosevelt, on the one hand, and Stalin on the other, within the Western sphere of influence and therefore was recognized as such. What we tend to forget, however, is that there are other examples which were much less happy than this. For example, at the end of the war the incumbent American ambassador in Argentina, Spruille Braden, took a dislike to Perón and arranged the publication of a blue book on national subversion in Latin

America during the war, in which it was made quite clear that Perón was regarded in Washington as pro-Nazi. Then all Perón had to do was campaign on the slogan "Perón or Braden" and the result was, of course needless to say, a landslide for Perón. However, these lessons have not been learnt. US opposition to the reelection of President Ahmadinejad in Iran in 2009 was quite plain and no doubt did much to ensure the massive majority he was said to have received. Of course, widespread electoral fraud undoubtedly helped.

The State Department very nearly repeated the same mistake in the case of Vargas in Brazil. They were strongly urged by their resident ambassador in Rio to issue a public statement calling for the democratization of Brazil at the end of the war, and they actually issued such a statement and then hurriedly realized that it was going to produce almost exactly the opposite effect to the one they intended, so they very sensibly did not continue with it and the result was in fact, before the election itself, the institution of a civilian republican government. So diplomatic experience makes uncertain precedent. It is undoubtedly the lowest level of intervention and one which is commonplace *in favour of* an existing government. It is relatively rare to use diplomatic intervention *against* an incumbent government if only because it is not likely to work.

Secondly, it is possible to use *clandestine political action*, that is, where a power may make use of internal forces in order to try and overturn an incumbent government. Such actions have included bribery, the planting of rumors or stories, propaganda, agitation and even, on rare occasions, political assassination.

Thirdly, a state may use *demonstrations of force*. The Lebanon landings in 1958 were not merely an attempt by the United States to forestall the communization of the Lebanon itself, they were also intended to serve notice on the Soviet Union that any attempt to intervene in the internal affairs of Lebanon by subversion or otherwise would be resisted by the United States, and by derivation, to strengthen the position of the United States generally in the Middle East. The deployment of a US fleet off the Dominican Republic in 1961 was made for a different reason, to serve notice on the surviving members of the Trujillo family that the United States required their removal from Dominican politics. This they did, but not before one of them had personally machine-gunned to death the men responsible for the assassination of his late father, the former president of the country (Diederich 1978). US intervention in Grenada in 1983, or in Panama in 1989, was intended to serve notice that the United States would not hesitate to use force to protect its interests in Central America (Tiwathia 1987).

Subversion may be used to make a country less capable of resisting an internal as well as an external attack. The Nazi putsch in Czechoslovakia in 1938 found key Nazi sympathizers in all key positions. Similarly, the Soviet putsch in 1948 found communists already installed where they could ensure that the takeover went without interruption. The activities of the American CIA in Iran in 1952 in creating the climate for the fall of Mossadegh and the return to power of the Shah would also fall into this category (Wise and Ross 1964), as did the "destabilization" of Grenada before the military coup that deposed Maurice Bishop (Searle 1983, Ambursley and Dunkerley 1984, O'Shaughnessy 1984).

Subversion does not necessarily imply the existence of a state of unconventional warfare, although it may well act either as a prelude or as an accompaniment to it. Nor should it be assumed that all such occurrences are subversive in origin. Following the Cuban Revolution in 1959, quite a number of guerrilla movements appeared in imitation of the Cubans, notably in Colombia, Venezuela, Guatemala, and Peru (Gott 1970, cf. Debray 1969). The only campaign that developed out of an expedition planned and outfitted from Cuba for the purpose, however, was the unsuccessful expedition of Che Guevara to Bolivia in 1966–7. On the other hand, a power with sufficient resources to spare may achieve much more considerable results by actively extending aid to indigenous movements, such as that of the Sandinistas in Nicaragua, who received aid from Costa Rica, Panama, and Cuba. The United States later complained that the FMLN in El Salvador was receiving aid from Cuba via Nicaragua, but we now know that they had already planted counterrevolutionary forces in Honduras to strike down into northern Nicaragua (McMichael and Paulus 1983).

Lastly, as we have seen, a power may choose to intervene militarily with its own forces in a revolutionary situation, though the risks of doing so are considerable and the rewards of success unlikely to justify the risks. It cannot be stressed too often that one of the most dangerous things a great power can do is to intervene militarily in a revolutionary situation. If the revolutionary government is not effectively crushed, opposition to it immediately becomes treason and may be punished as such; in any case, the almost inevitable result is the radicalization of the revolutionary government and the destruction of the political moderates.

Humanitarian Intervention

After 1989, the situation in former Yugoslavia led to revival of interest among the Western states in so-called humanitarian intervention (Walzer 2002).

The premise behind this is that, in some circumstances, states should be prepared to use a judicious amount of force either to try to end a civil conflict or at least to minimize the resulting casualties. Of course, this is contrary to the basic assumptions of international law that internal conflict is not a matter for international concern. Walzer notes, using the example of "Operation Just Cause" in Panama in 1989, that it may also be immoral because unjust (Walzer 1992, preface). Under the provisions of Chapter VII of the Charter, the United Nations may authorize intervention if a conflict is so serious that it constitutes a "threat to international peace and security." But the notion of humanitarian intervention owes more to a basic human feeling that it is morally wrong to allow a conflict to continue without trying to do something about it. It is significant that such casualties are predominantly civilian and disproportionately of women and children. In the end there were several cases during the 1990s, not all of them encouraging, and by the end of the decade many felt that the concept was unrealistic and some even argued that the weakness of the world community actually had resulted in the perpetuation of civil war (Hironaka 2005).

External intervention with humanitarian motives can, however, also be very dangerous for those intervening, and this was demonstrated most sharply in 1983 when US forces which had been sent into Somalia to try to maintain peace, were attacked, slaughtered, and their bodies dragged through the streets of Mogadishu. However, in the different conditions of the 1990s, in 1992 a Unified Task Force was sent back into Somalia, though it was not very successful. In 1994, US troops sent to try to restore order in Haiti were successfully prevented from landing until the Clinton administration had reached an agreement with the Haitian military forces as to the limits of their powers. The United Nations also provided peacekeepers for the United Nations Assistance Mission for Rwanda (UNAMIR) in 1993–96 and for the United Nations Transitional Administration in East Timor (UNTAET) in 1999. In the first case, following the assassination of President Habyarimana in April 1994, over 800,000 Tutsis were murdered by their Hutu neighbors while UN forces were powerless to act under the inadequate mandate they had been given. The fact that this was one of only two major acts of genocide since 1945 did nothing for the theory of humanitarian intervention. The latter case, in which forces from Australia and New Zealand, as well as other countries, helped maintain order following the withdrawal of Indonesian forces and the independence of Timor Leste in 2002, was a success.

Meanwhile, war broke out in the former Yugoslav state of Bosnia and Herzegovina, in which three different ethnic groups maintained an uneasy coalition for several months after the secession of Croatia. Then on one hand the Serbs (October 1991) and on the other the Croats (in the following months) set up their own distinct governments in Bosnia and Herzegovina with pretensions to rule the whole. The result was that when Bosnia and Herzegovina voted to leave Yugoslavia, the Serbs, in particular, were already prepared to take it over, and fighting broke out around Sarajevo in April 1992. The Croats took advantage of the fighting to try to expand their own borders, though this was seldom admitted. It was Croatian forces who shelled and largely destroyed Mostar, including the celebrated Bridge. Hence, the conflict went on for three years, during which Sarajevo was for months under siege from Serbian forces on the surrounding hills, under the eyes of world press and television. The Serbs, who regarded the conflict as a civil war rather than a war of aggression by Serbia and Croatia, meanwhile embarked on a systematic program of "ethnic cleansing" in which a systematic pattern of rounding up Bosniak civilians and interning them was accompanied by the beating and killing of men of military age and the systematic rape of women, often with the express aim of forcing them to bear Serbian children.

In April 1993, UN peacekeepers were sent in, but lacking the backing of force, were unable to do anything effective. Worse, after trying to create a so-called safe area for civilians at Srebrenica, 400 Dutch troops of the United Nations stood by and failed to intervene to stop a Serbian massacre between 13 and 22 July 1995 of more than 8,000 Bosnian males, many of them no more than boys. In the meantime, tens of thousands of Bosniak civilians had been driven out. Belatedly, in September 1995 a NATO bombing campaign, Operation Deliberate Force, was launched against the army of Republika Srpska. This succeeded in bringing the contending parties to the conference table, but not until more than 100,000 lives had been lost. A ceasefire was agreed in Paris on July 22, 1995, and a week later peace negotiations in Dayton, Ohio, resulted in a definitive settlement (Cigar 1995, Rieff 1996).

The Bosnian case illustrates very clearly how picking sides in a civil war is immensely difficult for foreign observers and the effects may be very different from those intended. The Bosniaks began the war at a considerable disadvantage because of the UN Resolution imposing an embargo on the supply of arms to former Yugoslavia. Well intentioned though this may have been, it had no effect on the Serbs, who inherited the arms of the JNA, and very little on the Croats, whose long seacoast made it easy for them to smuggle in weapons and supplies. The complex ethnicity of the area led some to be prepared to accept the results of aggression and accept the breakup of Bosnia. However, though the Bosniaks constituted the most significant Muslim minority in Europe, and during the conflict were almost invariably, if unhelpfully, referred to in press and television as "Bosnian Muslims," it should be remembered that in the end both Europe and the United States were prepared to back their claim to independence against that of their nominally Christian opponents.

The Serbs regarded the autonomous province of Kosovo, despite its substantial Albanian minority, historically and emotionally as a part of Serbia, and when the Kosovars showed that they too wanted independence, President Slobodan Milosevic sent Serbian forces into the territory. To redress the balance, NATO launched air strikes against Yugoslav (Serbian) targets, both military and civilian. Over the 3 months, the bombing lasted, from March to June 1999, however, some 850,000 refugees fled from Kosovo as Serbian security forces and paramilitaries systematically chased Albanians out of their homes in a program of "ethnic cleansing." Finally, UN mediation resulted in a ceasefire and NATO provided a Kosovo Force (KFOR) to maintain civil order.

Neither of the two major examples of armed intervention since 2001, in Afghanistan and Iraq, had a humanitarian purpose. The purpose of the invasion of Afghanistan was to neutralize Osama bin Laden and overthrow the Taliban government which had given him hospitality, and the invasion of Iraq was in theory to prevent Saddam Hussein acquiring and/or deploying weapons of mass destruction. Both well illustrate that the biggest problem of intervention is bringing it to a satisfactory end.

CHAPTER SIX

Counterinsurgency

Counterinsurgency is perhaps the most neutral term available for the various techniques and theories that relate to the prevention and suppression of armed insurgencies, but it is not wholly neutral. Most of the people who are interested in counterinsurgency are military strategists, and military and civilian agents of incumbent governments, whose duties are to maintain some sort of strategic order. Counterinsurgency has, therefore, come to mean a form of strategy which is mainly military and within the military context, one designed to fight irregular, especially guerrilla, war. Though much of the literature reflects the US belief that in the Cold War period the Soviet Union was behind each and every example of insurgency in the world (Shultz, Ra'anan, Pfaltzgraf, Olson, and Lukes 1988), it is interesting to note that before 1989 conversations had already begun between the two superpowers with a view to concerting a common policy against Third World insurrections (Marks and Beliaev 1991).

For an insurgency to succeed, there are, however, two preconditions that are so obvious that their importance is often neglected. Most people in most countries believe that the best chance of avoiding insurgency altogether lies in having good government; but then people differ considerably on what they class as a good government. Boris Yeltsin's administration in Russia was regarded in the West—at least at first—as "democratic" and therefore good; the constitution on which its rested, however, was a recipe for authoritarian rule and the government itself was both weak and accident prone. Western governments were quite prepared to do business with Ceaucescu's Romania, simply because it was not the Soviet Union. Secondly, it is generally agreed by experts that effective counterinsurgency must involve political action by civilians as well as military action by soldiers. In fact, there is no clear distinguishing line between the two. Soldiers have to operate in a political context and civilians for their own safety have to operate in a military one, and as a result of this a good deal of confusion has grown up.

For there is in fact a very wide range of political situations in which insurgency occurs, or may occur, depending on the nature of the arena chosen (urban or rural) and the status of the territory in which it occurs (a province, a dependent territory, a protectorate or a friendly state), as well as on the political order of the state that is combating the insurgency (liberal democracy, authoritarian government, or dictatorship).

The term counterinsurgency has come to be used since 1945 specifically to designate a struggle against rural movements in a colonial or quasi-colonial situation. Not surprisingly, the views, both of civilians and military advisers, tend still to be particularly strongly colored by those experiences. These influences are, therefore, predominantly reflected in the available literature. This literature, too, is the product of writers in liberal democratic states in which domestic public opinion has proved to be one of the major targets of insurgent action. Again, the literature reflects this. There are 3 main types: (1) books on how insurgencies have been successfully countered, usually concentrating on the military aspects of the struggle, aimed at the general reader; (2) books for specialists on the same subject; and (3) books seeking to show that works in the first two categories are wrong. Of this last category, as we shall see, a consistent theme has been the debasement, as their authors see it, of the principles of the liberal democratic state when confronted with an armed insurgency. The most extreme form of this is the thesis that repeated or prolonged involvement in counterinsurgency creates an irresistible tendency to use military necessity as an excuse for the government to disregard others and abuse the exceptional powers it has assumed, as, for example, in the case of the Nixon administration and Vietnam.

Mention of the Nixon administration, however, should alert us to the fact that this literature is very much the product of a period and of one country, the United States, when its chief foreign policymakers (Nixon and Kissinger) began to carry to extremes the assumption that they might safely do anything that did not arouse too great a public outcry. This assumption was, as P.E. Haley has shown (Haley 1982), something that had grown up earlier in the post-1945 period but had not previously been put to the test. Its failure was inevitable, given the structure of the American constitutional system, as soon as it was challenged by any substantial body of public opinion, and, in the event, the generation of such a body of public opinion was strongly encouraged by the feeling of deceit and betrayal that the "politics of acquiescence" had hitherto not encountered.

The United States is, however, a most unusual country even by the standards of liberal democracies, and in the postwar period had only confronted insurgencies in the Philippines and Indo-China, before the advent of the Reagan administration led to its increasing involvement in Central America. In the same period, there also occurred the campaigns of Portugal in Angola,

Mozambique, Guinea, and Cabo Verde; the Netherlands in Indonesia and Dutch New Guinea (Irian Jaya); France in Indo-China, Tunisia, Morocco, and Algeria; and the United Kingdom in Greece, Palestine, Kenya, Cyprus, Malaya, Borneo, South Yemen, and Northern Ireland. So there are plenty of examples to go on, and it is specifically these sorts of examples that we need to compare with the United States experience. In the literature that has grown up around these examples emphasis is still on the military rather than the civilian combating of these insurgent movements. The only point of considerable difference between the countries is, of course, the economic resources available. The United States had enormous resources compared with the other states mentioned and despite all mistakes which it made, which were numerous, was able to sustain a lengthy war in Vietnam (1965–75). This succeeded in achieving essentially what it set out to do, namely the countering of communist insurgency in the southern part of Vietnam. It did not succeed in conquering North Vietnam, nor did it even succeed in turning back the communists and North Vietnamese forces already entrenched in South Vietnam. Ironically, it appears that big countries may find it much more difficult than smaller ones, to win a war against a much smaller opponent (Mack 1975).

Britain, during the period 1946–67, was often very stretched. On the other hand, Portugal, a very small country in comparison, sustained an even longer campaign than that of the United States. This casts doubt on the theory that a very large force is proportionately necessary to counter insurgency by military means. The example generally given is that there were 15 times as many Commonwealth troops in Malaya as there were guerrillas. It took 6,500 hours for an individual soldier on patrol to even see one guerrilla, let alone actually shoot him. The belief therefore grew up that it was not possible to counter insurgency by military means alone, unless the balance of forces is quite disproportionate to the goals to be achieved.

This was extended by certain left-wing writers into the theory that it is not possible to counter insurgency at all, consistent with Marxist views about the logic of history and the irreversibility of socialist revolutions. But this is not quite true, as the examples of Palestine, Cyprus, and Malaya make quite clear. It is possible; the question for the government is, is one willing to take the consequences of doing so? If the government is not "good" enough to avert insurgency altogether, it is probably true that the best chance of its suppressing an insurgent movement lies in that period of its development which corresponds to Mao's stages one and two; in other words, at the point at which the insurgency is moving from preparation to action; being transformed from being clandestine into being overt. The next best chance comes at the stage at which the rebels try to transform the guerrilla movement campaign or sporadic terrorist acts into a regular military movement committed to destroy the government.

Mao, on the one hand, and, for example, the British writer Sir Robert Thompson (Thompson 1970), on the other, agree on this point; that the point of initial operations is that at which insurgencies are most vulnerable. Once an insurgent movement is already in being, and is larger than a certain size, the government will have to put up a very disproportionate amount of effort and stand a relatively small chance of being able to reduce it. Hence, alertness to the possible emergence of such movements is crucial. Countries such as Cuba with a strong intelligence capability and networks informing the government have proved very resistant to insurgent action.

Another factor that is very important to remember is that just because the number of guerrillas in a rural situation, or a number of urban terrorists, in a situation such as Cyprus or Northern Ireland, is very small, it does not mean that the government can ignore them. It is probable that the activists actually engaged on the part of the Provisional IRA in Northern Ireland, were at most times as few as 200 and perhaps less. In such cases, it is extremely difficult to eradicate an insurgent movement completely, as their small numbers make concealment easier, but for as long as there is even a small number of people left—too small to easily be caught, but too large to be negligible—then it is very difficult to persuade civilians that the movement is at an end. The government has many resources at its disposal. In the earlier stages of the conflict it can offer very handsome rewards to those who surrender or who are prepared to come to an agreement. It can offer them, as in Venezuela and, less successfully in Colombia, the opportunity to transform themselves into a normal political party (Ellner 1988). At the time of writing (2009) it is being suggested that this will be a key part of the US strategy to extricate itself from Afghanistan, though the fiasco of the 2009 elections suggests that by far the best course would be to withdraw at once.

Finally, like the insurgents, the government will seek to use the prospect of negotiations as a bargaining strategy to disrupt the unity of its opponents and to offer a chance to regroup its forces. It may even be prepared to take a risk, at a certain stage, as for example did the government in Malaysia (1960), of simply declaring the insurgency to be at an end. However, insurgent movements also use the prospect of negotiations to gain or retrieve ground at the expense of the government. The Tamil Tigers in Sri Lanka were accused of taking advantage of the ceasefire negotiated by the Norwegians in 2002 both to regroup and rearm. The circumstances in which the ceasefire finally broke down in 2008 remain disputed, but there is no doubt that this perception led to the election of Mahinda Rajapaksa as president and a government in Colombo who believed that it could defeat the Tigers by military means. As events proved, they were correct, though as predicted the cost in civilian lives has been high.

Planning for Counterinsurgency

The first and most important lesson of counterinsurgency is the importance of maintaining the primacy of civilian government. A government confronted with a domestic emergency should make the minimum possible use of emergency powers, since resorting to them gives the opposition a powerful propaganda card, by suggesting at least that the government is badly shaken and at worst that it is becoming dictatorial and ignoring the principles of justice. Thus, the decision in Northern Ireland by the government of Brian Faulkner to introduce internment immediately destroyed the minimal political consensus that was required if a political settlement based on the integral unity of Northern Ireland was to be maintained. After that, direct rule from Westminster, for the Parliament at which the citizens of Northern Ireland at least have a vote, was the only solution that in practice (though not in theory, for of course direct rule was never accepted as legitimate by Nationalists) was accepted as the best available in the circumstances.

In the case of insurgency in a colonial territory, best results have been achieved where, as in Malaya, the colonial government has had the option open to it of handing over power in the medium term to an elected civilian government that can command substantial popular support, and has been prepared to embrace this opportunity. Where, as with the Smith regime in Rhodesia, the need to accept such a transfer is accepted too late, the probability is that the more extreme factions in the insurgent movement will have gained so much ground that to all intents and purposes it will have succeeded in its original purpose.

In the case of an insurgency in a friendly state, however, the situation is very much more difficult. In South Vietnam and Cambodia, as earlier in South Korea, the United States found itself bound by the concept of its obligations to give military support to a government with only tenuous claims to constitutional legitimacy or popular support. Vietnamese peasants subjected to military government rightly felt that a victory for that government would mean the surrender of the lands expropriated by them in the Delta region of the Mekong (Sansom 1970). There at least the concept of constitutionality had already virtually disappeared. In the case of Cambodia, however, the military coup that displaced Prince Sihanouk and established the short-lived Khmer Republic destroyed the only traditional authority that had been able to mediate between the army on the one hand and the communists on the other, supported by the force of nationalism which the Prince personified. The result was the disastrous power-vacuum when United States forces were withdrawn, which was filled by a highly radicalized Khmer Rouge bent on revenge and determined to eradicate all trace of its predecessors.

Counterinsurgency forces operating in a friendly state are always liable to be regarded by the local inhabitants as antinational, if not indeed as an occupying force, as the Russians were in Afghanistan. After all, British forces were so regarded by French peasants during the First World War, and United States forces similarly by the West Germans after 1950. In Iraq the Americans in particular have continued to be regarded as an occupying force. The situation is then complicated by the possibility, encountered almost from the beginning in El Salvador, that attempts to encourage the government to adopt more democratic practices will be used by the government itself as a pretext for nationalistic resistance, which its members often naively believe will bring them genuine political popularity. But the Salvadoran Alianza Renovadora (ARENA) was an extreme case. A government can simply disregard such pressure from its allies; it does not have to oppose it publicly unless it chooses, because it knows that its allies, once committed to battle, have little alternative in their own domestic environment but to accomplish their mission. Even if a civilian government does pay attention to the advice it is given, moreover, it is likely that, as in the Salvadoran case again, it will find that it is unable to count on the obedience of its own military commanders, to whom the fact of the insurgency makes it virtually subject. Later disclosures about the close relationship between the CIA and Batallion 316 of the Honduran Army made clear how far both armed forces and intelligence agencies are prepared to go in defense of their own position (Cohn and Thompson 1995).

The next important thing for a successful counterinsurgency campaign is to understand the mind of the opposition. It is here that the literature of counterinsurgency is most seriously deficient, and at worst highly tendentious, supporting an extreme right-wing interpretation of postwar events in which little or no room is left for the possibility that the rebels might have a point or two on their side (cf. Crozier 1960; Osanka 1962; Paret and Shy 1962; Thayer 1963; Pustay 1965; Taber 1965). The best accounts (e.g., Thompson 1970) of postwar insurgency, therefore, need the added corrective of studies by academic observers or other writers more detached from events, as with Anthony Short's excellent analysis of the Malayan Emergency (Short 1974). What is clear from all these and the other available sources is that specialists in counterinsurgency still conceive of their task in military terms, with the

inevitable corollary that success depends on certain kinds of military preconditions being met. Provided, we remember that these are not the only conditions, and hence that their absence does not necessarily imply defeat for the
incumbent government, we can note the principal points that emerge.

1. *Planning.* Planning is the most essential prerequisite of a successful
   counterinsurgency campaign and its absence has led to more serious
   trouble than any other omission. A government confronted for the first
   time with the threat of an armed insurgency tends to give a panic response.
   The immediate imposition of emergency regulations, and the dispatch
   of troops in an unprepared state, who, if heavily armed, are all too likely
   to loose off ammunition in all directions, is the first serious mistake
   in alienating a civilian population and driving recruits into the hands of
   the insurgents. The heavy-handed Russian response to insurgency in
   Chechenya is an example. The first response to an armed threat should
   be through the police and not the armed forces, and the very minimum
   additional force should be brought to bear on the situation so as to avoid
   the psychological consequences of an apparent defeat in a public confrontation. If armed forces are to be deployed, vital strategic links and
   communications must first be clearly established, and the aim of the
   intervention closely defined.

   The essential links that are necessary are (as applicable) those between the
army and the police, the army and other military forces, and between the
government and the provincial authorities that may report incidents and
require military support at short notice. All such action must be refused unless
it fits in with the overall strategic plan. To do otherwise is to risk forces being
pinned down in static defensive positions and the loss of the overall initiative.
Alternatively, rivalry between the services, or between the services and the
police, may grow to such an extent that effective combined operations become
impossible. The key, therefore, is to maintain the supremacy of the civil power,
to which military operations must remain subordinate. At the national level,
this is achieved through a civilian "war cabinet" and at provincial level through
civilian and military commissioners working very closely with one another
but with primacy always to the former.

2. *Intelligence.* Successful planning depends on good intelligence. At the
   outset of an insurgency, if the government has indeed been taken by
   surprise, intelligence is obviously deficient and will have to be rectified.
   Again, there is no substitute for careful preparation and the use of time to

develop the necessary, structures. As noted above, it will be the aim of the insurgent to deny all knowledge of his activities to the government, while obtaining the fullest knowledge of the government's activities, and it will be the objective of the government to reverse this state of affairs.

The insurgent, however, starts with the advantage of secrecy and surprise, and may well have made the disruption of intelligence networks by sabotage or diversion part of his original strategic plan. In the government's favor is its unique characteristic of legitimacy. It therefore has the "right" to use force against the insurgent, whether the insurgent likes it or not, and enjoys in most cases a good deal of residual support from normal law-abiding citizens. The government's aim must therefore be to achieve total information about the insurgent and deny information about its own actions.

In practice, this is relatively difficult since it is large and therefore its movements are evident. But it is also extremely rare, in fact, for insurgents to have a great deal of information. It is clear that in the anticolonial struggles their local knowledge was limited as long as security was maintained and forces did not become overconfident. The only time that an urban terrorist movement has enjoyed the great knowledge theoretically possible to it was the Tupamaro movement in Uruguay, where it appears that the government and revolutionary personnel were often identical than could be imagined, the government elite being riddled with insurgent sympathizers (Labrousse 1970).

3. *Training.* It is obviously important to train counterinsurgency personnel in the appropriate techniques. Many of the techniques for which armies are normally trained, like using machine guns or bazookas, firing artillery, driving tanks, or exploding nuclear weapons, have the effect of blasting a whole street or neighborhood out of existence. To do this seems perfectly normal in conventional war, but in counterinsurgency the effects on the government's public image of competence is fatal. Troops, therefore, have to be trained for special purposes, and the more so since governments have to make use of the recruits available. Many countries, as cannot too often be remembered, are dependent for their supply of other ranks (enlisted men) on conscription. Some senior officers and politicians have always liked the idea of conscription as it means more personnel to command. Conversely, it means less security. Raw troops can be trained more easily because they are raw, but they have to be renewed at frequent intervals just when they have achieved proficiency in the necessary skills. Moreover, conscript troops bring with them an ever-present risk of disaffection. This is much less likely in a

colonial situation but particularly dangerous in a domestic one, where the custom is to rotate troops from one province to another to avoid the fraternizsation that may make them a particular risk.

Just as we have seen guerrillas, in particular, rely on a kind of "militia" to relieve their scarce combat forces of unnecessary burdens, so too must the government establish such forces to relieve its cadres of specially trained counterinsurgency forces. Needless to say, it is no less important that these militia forces be well trained. The nearer they can approximate to a police role rather than a military one, the better. The point that must be stressed is that this must be the case from the beginning of the campaign. If a government is unable to persuade its people to defend it, no amount of foreign troops are likely to be successful in doing so. The "Vietnamization" of the American presence in Indo-China came much too late, and indeed was a mere political excuse for the Nixon administration to withdraw from an untenable position. It followed a series of unsuccessful attempts to adopt models of strategy that were either inadequate or not properly applied (Shafer 1988a, b). Had the huge build-up of American forces in 1965 been resisted, and had the aid begun under President Kennedy quietly extended, the subsequent history of events would have been very different. It is more than probable that a South Vietnamese government would still survive, and it is almost certain that if this had been the case, then Cambodia and Laos would have been able to retain their existing neutralist governments.

4. *Technology.* Note has already been made of the disadvantages of technology as applied to the use of arms. This, however, is at least an old problem. Ever since the first caveman, whoever he was, found he could throw a rock at his neighbor and kill him without having to engage in hand-to-hand combat, governments have preferred to use technology rather than sacrificing men. The problem is that technology no longer does this; though the lives sacrificed are different lives, they are also more numerous and the effects more indiscriminate. Part of the reason, however, has less to do with arms as such than the general advance of technology in other fields. In Vietnam, for example, the Americans found that their aircraft actually flew too fast. This did not matter when approaching an industrial target that could be sighted and destroyed by radar; insurgents, however, were hard to detect without the use of the human eye. Special aircraft thus had to be built or adapted to act as "spotters," as, later, was the Argentine *Pucará* during the period of the "dirty war" (1976–9).

In the meantime, however, permanent problems were created for the Vietnam campaign as a whole. Much wasted effort went into trying to pretend that people were not being hit more or less at random. Bombing of jungle trails was almost completely futile, but it terrified civilians. Defoliants poisoned them and blighted their crops, for which compensation, if offered, always came too late. Worst of all was napalm, used precisely because of its ability to destroy all life within range. The horror of seeing people who had been burned to death by napalm—or worse, badly burned but not dead— was so appalling that it destroyed confidence in any government that made use of it, and Ho Chi Minh frequently evoked images of burning flesh in his speeches and writings. Hence, in countering rural insurgency in Vietnam, the reliance on technology was strongly counterproductive.

On the other hand, there have been certain ways in which technology has helped governments rather than insurgents in towns. Towns are the natural habitat of governments, and it is very hard to challenge their use of authority successfully on their own terrain. The use of shield, helmets, water cannon, nonlethal gases, rubber or plastic "bullets" (baton rounds), trained sniffer dogs, and bomb-disposal teams have enabled governments to meet the insurgent challenge in towns and to demonstrate their competence to do so, without killing their own citizens. The speeding-up of communications helps too, since it enables governments to deploy their police and military forces much more quickly. Thus, a gathering crowd can be met with an effective counterinsurgency response before the enthusiasm of its members has reached the pitch of being prepared to take on a superior force with inadequate preparation. Again, the ability to do so, however, depends always on the superior training of the forces involved, and casualties must always be avoided, even at the cost of casualties among the security forces, if the government is to retain its essential claim to legitimacy.

The Doctrine of Counterinsurgency

The history of counterinsurgency in the twentieth century has shown a natural tendency to develop in parallel with developments in the concept of insurgency itself. In the first period after 1945 down to the mid-1960s, the main theatre of insurgency was the countryside. Accordingly, the literature reflects in this period an overwhelming concern with the guerrilla and how to fight him (sic).

Guerrilla warfare, as a development of partisan warfare, was well understood to be dependent on an infrastructure of civilian support for motivation, the supply of food and other material resources, and the provision of disguise.

In the very special circumstances of multiracial Malaya, physical separation in the form of a resettlement program was highly effective in cutting off the supply of food and making effective disguise almost impossible. What made it relatively easy to achieve, however, was the fact that in the divided community, the majority had a strong reason to accept it, and the creation of the so-called white areas gave a practical demonstration of the effectiveness of the technique.

In Malaya, therefore, psychological warfare was aimed primarily at the small number of active terrorists, with the aim of encouraging them to surrender. The combined effects of isolation, fear, and hunger led many to do so, once they knew that they could do so in safety. As far as the civilian population was concerned, the most effective psychological stimulus was the truth; that the country was moving steadily toward independence under a multiracial government and that the number of insurgents, never great, was steadily declining.

In Algeria, on the other hand, the French found themselves in a very different position. A small minority in the Muslim majority, the French, were not willing to move toward independence and were confronted with a substantial difficulty in maintaining their support among the civilian population as neighboring states moved toward, and eventually achieved, independence. In the first instance they had borrowed from their wartime experience the notion of *la guerre psychologique* (psychological warfare) in the style of Chakotin, involving large-scale propaganda in 1930s style. With this precedent in Indo-China, United States forces used loud hailers, leaflets, radio broadcasts, and comics, and indeed anything that seemed to serve the purpose, to put over the message that they were helping to defend freedom in Vietnam, and so drive a wedge between the civilians and the guerrillas. As already noted, however, the overpowering effect of their tactics and firepower destroyed the goodwill that they were at such pains to create, and the massacre at My Lai was only the culmination of this process of alienation, much of which was both unintentional and unintended (Miller and Aya 1971). The creation of "strategic hamlets" did not succeed in driving a wedge between the guerrillas and their supporters because the two could not be distinguished. Instead, it offered a series of hostages to fortune and facilitated the selective assassination of rural political leaders who were willing to take orders from the government.

Faced with such pressure and such uncertainties, it appears that the Americans did at times, as the French had before them, succumb to the temptation to employ what the French had earlier euphemistically, but entirely misleadingly, termed *l'action psychologique*, more properly termed counterterror. No army can ever be immune from the temptation to use counterterror, particularly after a particularly bloody terrorist attack launched with all the advantages of surprise and rejection of the customary usages of regular warfare. But it has repeatedly been demonstrated to be a disastrous course if not checked. It is natural for guerrillas to believe that they will be tortured and killed if they fall into the hands of the government. It is understandable if terrorists caught in the act of planting bombs and suchlike are manhandled by police or security forces, and there is much evidence from conventional war that prisoners are quite frequently shot to avoid the trouble of bringing them in. But the large-scale use of force to try to coerce a civilian population into accepting an unpopular government or regime is bound to confirm the certainty that both these things will happen, and so do exactly what its proponents seek to avoid, create a bond between active insurgents and civilians (Rubin 1989).

It was the objective of creating a school of counterinsurgency methods that President Kennedy set himself when he came to power, and there can be no doubt that in the early 1960s, especially in Latin America, its trainees were highly successful. As W.W. Rostow put it in a speech at Fort Bragg in 1961: "My point is that we are up against a form of warfare which is powerful and effective only when we do not put our minds clearly to work on how to deal with it" (Osanka 1962). With the additional advantage of such training, the Bolivian army proved easily capable of rounding up Che Guevara's expedition in 1967; his subsequent death was, however, the most dramatic evidence, if that were needed, that the successful forces did not know when to stop. President Fujimori dealt a near fatal blow to the hopes of Peruvian insurgents when he ordered its captured leader to be exhibited in a steel cage as if he were a dangerous animal.

In the second stage, after 1967, counterinsurgency was to evolve into the "justification" for what was later known in the 1970s and 1980s as the "national security state." The "national security state" was typically a Latin American (or Middle Eastern) military government obsessed with the overall objective of permanently eliminating foreign "subversion" by the imprisonment, torture, and execution of political opponents, many of whom had no connection with any form of insurgent activity. Fuelled by inter-service rivalry, such military establishments built up vast "intelligence" organizations whose functions had little enough to do with real intelligence, that is, the gathering and evaluation of information. These were in fact secret police under another name. Argentina and Brazil in the late 1960s, Guatemala after 1967, and Chile and Uruguay after 1973, evolved into "national security states," and in Argentina and Brazil heads of "intelligence" organizations were to be found even in the Presidency of the Republic. With the outbreak of armed conflict in Peru in 1980, it was not long before its armed forces, too, followed the same path (McClintock 1984, Palmer 1992).

Several factors were responsible for this change. To begin with, the number of trained personnel, always small, was swallowed up in the indigenous tradition of military government and repression, and their training dissipated. Secondly, the arena of conflict had, after the kidnapping of US Ambassador Gordon Mein in Guatemala in 1967, visibly shifted away from the countryside to the big cities where the majority of the population of Latin Americans lived. The student revolt in Europe and North America had its counterparts there, and, as with the Tupamaros, the unpredictable and spontaneous nature of what were often foolhardy gestures on their part aroused unreasoning primitive panic in police and soldiers, who responded by firing on crowds and rounding up suspects wholesale. In the mid-1970s many of these suspects then simply "disappeared," as in Chile, or were "transferred," in Argentina in both cases, to hastily dug graves or to the sea, or, to demonstrate their point, as became commonplace in Guatemala and El Salvador in the 1980s, to refuse tips, gullies and, where available, the mouths of volcanoes.

The developed powers of Europe and North America found very soon that the threats with which they too appeared to be confronted were in fact very easily tackled, though not without some minor risks. It was an irony that the development of the "national security state" coincided with the growth of expertise in the technology and practice of countering urban terrorism which proved more than adequate to achieve its purpose without the use of counterterror (cf. Oppenheimer 1970).

Basic to the maintenance of urban control was the existence of well-trained police forces. Equipped with modern weapons and gadgetry, such forces proved easily able to counter mass demonstrations. Speedy, radio-equipped cars and even helicopters enabled them to deploy with great success against individual terrorists, and improved methods both of bomb disposal and of forensic investigation enabled them to check the impact of urban terrorism and to run to earth at least some of its users without having to resort to methods endangering civilians to any additional extent (Clutterbuck 1973).

Two new uses for political violence that at first appeared even more alarming to government and the general public also responded to careful and considered responses in which violence was at best wholly avoided and at worst kept to the very minimum. These were the kidnapping of ambassadors and other distinguished figures and the hijacking of aircraft.

Kidnapping was designed to secure a number of aims; to raise money through ransom, to destroy the credibility of governments that "failed" to "prevent" it, and to secure the release of prisoners both to strengthen the cause and to demonstrate their ability to safeguard their members. It was best countered by a firm refusal to make concessions. This procedure obviously had its risks for the hostages, the taking of whom western governments, notably West Germany, found it difficult to tolerate, but once the procedure was used, the government in question was rarely troubled the same way again. Brazil, on the other hand, which did make concessions, found that further demands followed.

Hijacking was even more embarrassing, since the hostages, being civilians, could not be regarded as having consented to the risks of their position. The introduction of metal detectors at airports and the agreement of governments not to receive hijackers under the International Convention on Air Piracy (1971) proved, however, in the end to be highly effective.

The worst casualties of this period occurred where international rather than internal conflict was the prime cause. The death of the Israeli athletes at Munich resulted from faulty police technique, as did the disastrous aftermath of the abortive Egyptian attempt to prove at Larnaca airport, Cyprus, that they could be as effective in a lightning counterstrike against a terrorist hijacking as the Israelis themselves had been at Entebbe airport, Uganda. Even in the latter, the effect of the strike was somewhat spoilt by the murder in hospital of the only hostage not freed, Mrs. Dora Bloch, who was killed, moreover, not by the terrorists, but by the forces of General Amin that were supposed to be protecting her.

In fact, the very range and effectiveness of the responses of Western governments to these two apparently very new and threatening developments are the surest sign that the development of the "national security state" was, in terms of its ostensible purpose, quite unnecessary. It was to disappear again slowly after 1979, as the internal contradiction of military rule in developing countries began to become too great to be managed, but not before it had cast guilt by association on the governments not only of the United States, but of lesser powers such as the United Kingdom which had sold the "national security states" arms and extended to them credits which they used in the control of their own citizens. Moreover, two of these states, Somoza's Nicaragua and Shah Reza Pahlevi's Iran, succumbed to the very revolutions that the elaborate structure of secret police and repressive forces was designed to avert.

It is a matter for particular regret that the initiative that did most to offset these harmful associations for the United States, President Carter's stand on human rights, was not only abandoned by the incoming Reagan administration, but explicitly reversed. It is hard to think of any more serious blunder that they might have perpetrated. To reverse such a policy, once adopted, was not by any means the same thing as failing to adopt it in the first place. Had its disregard for moral obligations not been made so clear, the Reagan administration might have found it easier to defend itself when the Iran-Contra scandal broke.

The Iranian Revolution

It has already been suggested that the wrong kind of response to an insurgency may well succeed in precipitating, rather than averting, a revolution. Only a year before the Iranian Revolution it was generally accepted outside Iran, even by leading experts on the area, that the Shah's regime was stable. Yet it was the so-called White Revolution, launched by the Shah in the 1960s to modernize Iran that was the first step toward his downfall, as was the fact that the secret police, Savak, which was the ultimate guarantor of his regime, was so brutal that it consolidated the political opposition rather than neutralizing it.

The beneficiary was the unlikely figure of Ayatollah Ruhollah Musavi Khomeini. Born of a poor family in provincial Khomein in 1902, he began his theological studies at the age of 6 (as one does) and gained a substantial reputation as an Islamic jurist, leading ultimately following the death of Ayatollah Seyyed Husayn Borujerdi in 1962 to his appointment as a Grand Ayatollah. He was now the senior Shi'a cleric in Iran. It was the tradition in Iran that clerics did not intervene in politics. However, there were those who held that they should, and even before his elevation Khomeini was the most conspicuous of those who argued in favor of the Shi'a doctrine of the *velayat-e faquih*, that Islamic jurists should exercise guardianship over the state. So it was Khomeini who emerged as an outspoken critic of the Shah's secularization policies, which like other conservative Iranians he conveniently blamed on the influence of the United States. He was banished to Turkey from where he called not only for the fall of the Shah but his replacement by an Islamic regime. Meanwhile, the Shah had become increasingly unpopular. Public demonstrations broke out in January 1978 and escalated in the latter part of the year. Abandoned by almost all his supporters, in January 1979, the Shah left the country. Khomeini, who had been forced to retreat to France, played relatively little part in this.

> Yet when he returned to Iran from exile on the first day of February 1979, it was to the greatest welcome in history, with millions of Iranians flooding on to the streets, sobbing and roaring with joy. The Shah was gone, toppled by months of street protests provoked by soaring inflation and economic chaos and what followed was the last of the great revolutions, comparable with the French and Russian in narrative drama, ideological passion, human cost and international consequences.

(Dominic Sandbrook, "As powerful in death as in life," *The Observer,* Sunday, February 15, 2009)

Khomeini immediately chose his own nominee, Mehdi Barzagan, claiming that in doing so he was exercising the guardianship of the Prophet himself. Within days, with his assent, rebel soldiers and guerrillas destroyed the remnants of the armed forces of the old regime. The immediate beneficiaries were the Revolutionary Guard formed by Khomeini in April from a large number of young men, loosely organized and undisciplined, whose immediate task was to round up suspected supporters of the Shah. Leading generals and civil servants were summarily tried and shot or hanged, and many more lesser figures were to follow. With the support of the Guard, Khomeini was able to replace the draft constitution for a conventional republic with one in which, though elections would still be held, the persons elected would be subordinate to himself as leader of the Islamic Revolution. In November, the Revolutionary Guard, in search of new prey, stormed the US Embassy and seized 52 hostages, whom they held in captivity for well over a year. An immediate casualty was Barzagan who was ordered by Khomeini to release the hostages but was of course quite unable to do so.

In neighboring Iraq, its dictator Saddam Hussein concluded that if he were to attack Iran, he would have the support of the United States and be able to achieve a valuable victory. His secularist regime was supported by the United States, but after 2 years its initial gains had been reversed and in the end the war was to drag on for 8 years with huge losses on both sides. Instead, it proved an ideal pretext for the mullahs to use the theme of national unity and the victory of Islam to root out any hint of democratic accountability. When Khomeini died, he should have been succeeded as leader of the Revolution by the only eligible candidate, Grand Ayatollah Hossein Montazeri. Since he had been a critic of the numerous executions carried out under Khomeini, however, and had called for the end of his unaccountable rule, liberalization, and the restoration of political parties, before he died Khomeini altered the constitution so that his successor no longer had to have the scholarly credentials his doctrine required. That this was completely contrary to the doctrinal basis of the regime he seems to have considered as of secondary importance.

The Crisis of Communism and the Collapse of the Soviet Union

It is widely believed, especially in the United States, that the collapse of communism in the Soviet Union was the result of resolute opposition by the West to its expansionist tendencies. Conservative leaders, notably Ronald

Reagan in the United States and Margaret Thatcher in the United Kingdom, were credited with having forced the Soviet government into bankruptcy by having forced it to try to keep up with the West in expenditure of nuclear and conventional weapons. However popular this interpretation, it took insufficient account of the fact that, though Soviet military expenditure in the early 1980s exceeded 25 percent of GDP, many regimes (e.g., South Korea) have been able to maintain very high military expenditures for years. What made the collapse of the Soviet Empire in Eastern Europe possible was that Mikhail Gorbachev was not prepared to sacrifice lives to maintain it. What he was interested in doing was correcting the fundamental weakness of the Soviet economy in meeting the needs of its own people. Although covering a huge land area, more than twice of that of any other country, the Soviet Union was in fact relatively poor—Richard Perle among others described it as "Upper Volta with rockets" (Anderson 2007; see also *The Economist*, April 9, 1988, unattributed). It had huge energy and mineral resources, but it used them very inefficiently and its northerly latitudes meant that its agriculture would have been very unproductive, even if it had not been for the setback of coerced collectivization under Stalin. Reform was long overdue and might have come much earlier had it not been for Hitler, who turned support for the regime into a patriotic duty, on which it was able to trade for the next three decades.

The final crisis of the regime was triggered by the decision by Leonid Brezhnev in December 1979 to send troops into Afghanistan in support of a pro-Soviet government there. Although that country had been very unstable, both before and since the fall of the monarchy, it became a threat to the Soviet Union only when President Muhammad Zia ul-Haq of Pakistan supported an anti-Soviet mujahideen. But it was not possible to disguise the fact that the troops had not really been invited (the "government" that invited them had actually been in Czechoslovakia at the time), and open intervention committed the Soviet government to a protracted war which it could not win and which alienated other Asian states. And it was this rather than the nuclear arms race with the Reagan administration that imposed strains on the Soviet military establishment that it was not well fitted to meet.

The death of Leonid Brezhnev in 1983 offered the chance of change. However, instead there followed a brief period of uncertainty during which matters got worse, under two leaders both of whom were terminally ill even before they took office. It was not until March 1985 that the relatively youthful Mikhail Gorbachev was elected general secretary of the Communist Party of the Soviet Union at the age of 54. In 1986, he officially launched a new period of openness (*glasnost*) and reform (*perestroika*) which was intended to bring about much-needed changes enabling the acceleration (*uskoreniye*) of economic development. In 1988, a further impetus to change was given by the Law on Co-operatives which accepted for the first time the limits of the command economy to meet the needs of the people. Prominent among the "New Thinking" in foreign affairs were his initiatives to reduce nuclear weapons, but owing to Western suspicions these took a long time to achieve and in the meanwhile the Afghan war continued, further draining state resources.

Accompanying cuts in state expenditure meant, however, that the Soviet Union was no longer able, even if it wanted to, intervene to suppress the rising demand for change in the Soviet empire in Eastern Europe. The flashpoint came on December 9, 1979 in Berlin, when civil unrest in East Germany led to its government reluctantly agreeing to allow its citizens to cross to the West. Within days the Wall that had divided Berlin since 1961 had been demolished and on October 3, 1990 Germany was officially reunified. Within months the Soviet empire in Eastern Europe had fallen apart. What few had predicted, on either side, however, was that the Soviet Union itself would then fall apart, beginning with the Baltic States annexed by Stalin in 1940.

Counterinsurgency played a very minor role in this process. Only in Romania did the regime offer any serious resistance to the processes of change, and the outcome was a popular, urban insurrection culminating in the seizure and summary execution of the Ceausescus.

The "Third Wave" of Democratization

The French Revolution, both directly and indirectly, initiated a period of democratization in Europe, which spread to other parts of the world, notably Latin America. It was Samuel P. Huntington who suggested that this was the first of three waves of democratization, punctuated by relatively short periods of movement back toward authoritarian government. It has been cogently argued that his first wave was really three, making in all five waves to date, but the term "third wave" of democratization has stuck. This began in 1974, with the restoration of democratic government in Portugal and Greece, and was followed in Latin America by the fall of the Cold War dictatorships which had been established by the armed forces in Brazil, Chile, and Argentina, and imitated in other neighboring countries in South and Central America (Shin 1994). Similar forces led to the fall of the Shah in Iran, though this was not to have a democratic outcome. In fact, the Middle East remained, throughout the period, the principal stronghold of authoritarianism.

The disintegration of the Soviet empire in Eastern Europe led to the establishment of democratic government in a wide arc stretching from Poland to Bulgaria, in what Gorbachev had already termed "our common European home" in a speech in Czechoslovakia in April 1987 (Svec 1988). George Bush was later to appropriate this term and claim credit for it in his slogan "Europe Whole and Free," but it was because it owed its origin to indigenous forces for change rather than US intervention that it was to be successful (Ash 1990).

The subsequent collapse of the Soviet Union itself was not to have such a positive outcome (Sebestyen 2009). Among the former Union Republics only the Baltic States were to achieve both independence and democracy, as they were the only one that had had any previous experience of true representative government. A general problem was that Western style democracy was widely, and in the United States and right-wing circles deliberately identified with capitalism. But generations of Soviet children had been brought up to believe that capitalism was a conspiracy of small groups of criminals against the people in general. So when they set to work to establish capitalism, that seems to have been precisely what they created (Lane 2000–1, Clarke 2006).

The collapse of the Soviet Union was swiftly followed by the collapse of Yugoslavia. Created in the aftermath of the Great War, this ambitious union of six South Slav nations had never functioned very effectively, but from 1943 until his death in 1980, it was held together by the charismatic leadership of Josip Broz Tito, and (following his break with Stalin) the hostility of the Soviet Union. As there was no agreement on who should succeed Tito, arrangements were made for him to be succeeded by a collective leadership. Toward the end of the 1980s, Prime Minister Ante Marcovic led an unsuccessful attempt to move away from the command economy but the country began to fall apart before this could be completed. This was the result of the rise to power within the collective presidency of the Serbian Slobodan Miloševic. His success in gaining control of the autonomous province of Kosovo was greeted with hostility by its large population of ethnic Albanians, who could do very little at that stage about it, but it also alarmed both the non-Serb majorities of the Western states of Slovenia and Croatia, whose representatives soon seceded from the League of Communists of Yugoslavia. In their new multiparty systems, however, the nationalists came to the fore, and after a referendum in each, Slovenia and Croatia declared their independence in June 1991.

Though for the time being they were persuaded to work for a peaceful solution, the precedent alarmed the Serbs, who controlled most of former Yugoslavia and with it the Yugoslav National Army (JNA). A half-hearted attempt to seize control of Slovenia was resisted and the JNA withdrew after only 10 days, leaving Slovenia independent. Macedonia, too, was able to secede in September, when US peacekeepers were sent to prevent conflict. But it was a different question in Croatia, where the Serbs were able to build up an effective local resistance among ethnic Serbs. Hence, when Croatia finally did secede in October, much of it was soon occupied by the JNA and its capital, Sarajevo, placed under siege. German support meant that it was soon recognized both by the European Union (EU) and the United Nations, though this was not successful in averting what proved to be 4 years of civil war, characterized by the widespread displacement of populations brought about by deliberate "ethnic cleansing." At the end of it, in 1995, the Croats, with Western support, were able to regain control over their territory. In the final days of the war more than 120,000 Serbs left the country and few have chosen to go back. By the time "9/11" happened, policymakers in Washington, London, and elsewhere should have been well aware that it is much easier to start a protracted conflict than to end one (Heiberg, O'Leary and Tirman 2007).

The Impact of "9/11"

At 8:46 a.m. EDT on the morning of September 11, 2001, a commercial jet airliner crashed into one of the twin towers of the World Trade Center in New York City. It became clear that it was a deliberate act when a few minutes later a second airliner crashed into the other tower. Thousands of gallons of burning aviation spirit cascaded into both towers, fatally weakening their steel frames, and within 2 hours both had collapsed. A third building, World Trade Center 7, was also so weakened by its proximity to the fire that it collapsed later in the day. Meanwhile a third airliner had been crashed into the outer ring of the Pentagon and a fourth, believed to be bound for the Capitol building in Washington, DC, crashed in a field in Pennsylvania after its passengers tried to regain control of it. There were no survivors from any of the aircraft and in all 2,993 people died, including the hijackers.

The coordinated attack was planned by Khalid Sheikh Mohammed, a member of the shadowy organization al-Qaeda, led by a renegade Saudi, Osama bin Laden (known for short in the United States as UBL). In 1979, bin Laden had traveled to Afghanistan where, with the backing of the United States, he helped organize Arab volunteers (mujahideen) to fight against the Soviet invaders. When they withdrew in 1989, he and his organization, Maktab al-Khidamat, turned their attention to pro-Western Arab governments and to his former allies. Increasingly radicalized, notably by the influence of his second-in-command, Ayman el-Zawahiri. In 1996 he denounced the presence of US troops in Saudi Arabia, where they had been since the Gulf War of 1991 (Freedman and Karsh 1993), and 2 years later, citing also US support for Israel, he issued a fatwa calling for a holy war (jihad) on the United States. At the same time, the first proposals were made for what was to become the attack on the World Trade Center. Within hours of the attacks, the US National Security Agency had intercepted communications which confirmed the involvement of al-Qaeda, and the luggage of Mohammed Atta, one of the hijackers, which had been delayed on a connecting flight, revealed abundant details of all the participants. Though at the time bin Laden denied any connection with the attack, eventually in 2004, in the run-up to the American presidential election, he was to admit that al-Qaeda was involved in the attacks and claim that he personally had directed the 19 hijackers. Khalid Sheikh Mohammed was arrested in Pakistan in March 2003 and confessed to his role in the matter. Unfortunately, his confession is worthless as it was secured after he had been intensively tortured both by the Pakistanis and by the Americans.

For the attack was to lead to a remarkable chain of events which within a few short months was to destroy the prospects of peace which a new Christian millennium had seemed to offer. The immediate response of the Bush administration was to suspend all commercial flights within the airspace of the United States, while urgent attempts were made to determine the extent and nature of the intelligence failure, which had made the attack possible. Meanwhile all members of the bin Ladin family were permitted to return home. Then in a speech to Congress on September 21, 2001, about 4 days after the country's airspace had been reopened to commercial flights, President Bush proclaimed a "war on terror." "Our war on terror begins with al-Qaeda," he said, "but it does not end there. It will not end until every terrorist group of global reach has been found, stopped and defeated" (Isikoff and Hosenball 2009). This was soon to be hijacked by interests both within the United States and abroad, interested in paying off old scores.

The principal instrument of the war within the United States was the USA PATRIOT Act, pushed through Congress by large majorities of both parties and signed by the president on October 26, 2001. The absurdly forced acronym stands for *Uniting and Strengthening America by Providing Appropriate Tools Required to Intercept and Obstruct Terrorism*, and the Act was Public Law 107–56 of 2001. It expanded the definition of terrorism to such an extent that it drove a coach and horses through most of the civic rights enshrined in the Constitution of the United States.

Since bin Laden was known to be based in Afghanistan, and to enjoy the protection of its Islamic fundamentalist regime, known as the Taliban, the obvious move was to bring pressure to bear on the Taliban to hand him over. Ironically, the Taliban ("students"), were an offshoot of the mujahideen supported by the United States against the former Soviet Union. Made up primarily of young Pashtun Sunnis from both Afghanistan and Pakistan, led by Mullah Mohammed Omar, the Taliban captured Kandahar in 1994 and, with the support of the Pakistani Intelligence Agency (PIA), successfully overran most of the country and captured Kabul in 1996 (Griffin 2001).Their government, recognized only by Pakistan, Saudi Arabia, and the United Arab Emirates, was characterized by an extreme interpretation of Sharia law. Men were required to wear beards and cover their heads. Women had to be completely covered in public by the burqa or be beaten with long sticks. They were not allowed to work, to take part in sports, to be educated in any-thing other than Islamic theology, and were married off at the earliest possible age, often by force. Television, computers, and all forms of music were banned and images, including photographs and dolls, were prohibited. Thieves had their hands cut off, adulterers were stoned to death, and rape (except within marriage) and murder punished by death. Obedience to the moral code was ensured by the religious police, an innovation for Afghanistan, apparently copied from Saudi Arabia (Waldman 2001; Maley 1998).

US influence had successfully driven al-Qaeda out of Somalia. However, with the protection of Mullah Omar and the Taliban they were not only able to move to Afghanistan and regroup in the mountains of Khost, but to establish a network of camps and safe houses where their mainly Arab instruc-tors had been able to train impressionable young volunteers for global jihad (Shay 2002). These volunteers were not usually Afghani. A few were Arabs from the Middle East, as were most of their instructors. But a substantial number came from the West, having been radicalized to hate and to betray the countries that had given them and their families hospitality.

The Bush Doctrine, as it later became known, held that the United States should not distinguish between terrorist organizations and the nations or states that harbored them. The UN Security Council had passed two resolu-tions, 1267 in 1999 and 1333 in 2000, authorizing limited sanctions against Afghanistan for failing to hand over bin Laden for trial in connection with the bombings of two US embassies in Africa in 1998. In a speech to a joint session of Congress on September 20, 2001, President Bush publicly issued an ultima-tum to the Taliban to surrender al-Qaeda leaders to the US government and close all terrorist training camps. The Afghan government responded that the US government had not shown them that there was any connection between bin Laden and 9/11 and that in any case he was a guest in their country, protected by traditional rules of hospitality. Subsequently they did offer to try him themselves, in an Islamic court. But by that time preparations were well advanced for the US-led Operation Enduring Freedom (OEF), intended to capture bin Laden, break up his organization and bring about the fall of the Taliban government—indeed there is evidence that something of the sort had been planned long before 9/11 provided the pretext. Subsequently the UN Security Council authorized an International Security Assistance Force (ISAF) to secure control of Kabul, and in 2003 NATO assumed responsibility for this, although its troops would for the first time be acting out of area.

The combined effect of these two operations was to bring down the Taliban government. More specifically, they were able to provide protection behind which Afghan factions hostile to the Taliban forming the so-called Northern Alliance were able to occupy Kabul and make way for a provisional government. After 6 months their representatives met in a grand council or *loya jirga* which chose Hamid Karzai, a Pashtun from Kandahar, as president. In due course, elections were held which confirmed him in office, although by that time it was already clear that his writ hardly ran outside the capital itself. In effect, therefore, the United States and its allies had sponsored a revolution. But OEF forces in the South, primarily American with some British support, failed to capture bin Laden, and both he and, it is thought, a majority of his supporters were able to escape across the porous border into the tribal areas of Pakistan, where, in the course of time, there was a substantial growth of Islamicist groups holding very similar views.

The successful overthrow of the Taliban did not prevent three major atrocities, for which, in varying degrees, al-Qaeda was to claim credit.

On October 12, 2002 two bombs, one carried by a suicide bomber and another a car bomb, detonated on the Indonesian island of Bali in the vicinity of a nightclub in Kuta popular with foreign tourists. They killed 202 people, the majority (152) young foreigners, and injured more than 200. The attack was carried out by members of a local Islamist group, Jemaah Islamiyah, several of whom, including the movement's leader Abu Bakar Bashir, were later convicted in connection with the crime, including three sentenced to death. Bali is the one part of Indonesia which is not predominantly Muslim and whose Hindu inhabitants were unprepared for the attack.

In the Madrid train bombing on March 11, 2004, suicide bombers traveling on trains converging on Atocha station in the morning rush hour simultaneously detonated ten explosive devices, killing 191 and injuring over 1,800. The carnage would have been even worse but for the fortunate fact that one of the trains was running late, although up to three other improvised explosive devices did not go off and were rendered safe. The Madrid bombings were blamed by the incumbent government on the Basque separatist group ETA, and when it was found that this was not true, the Spanish electorate 3 days later gave a massive vote to their opponents, who immediately withdrew Spanish troops from Iraq. Those responsible belonged to a Moroccan Islamist group, 21 of whom were later convicted on various charges, though 4 were released on appeal. However, when on 3 April Spanish police raided a flat in the Madrid suburb of Leganes in an attempt to arrest two of the prime suspects, the two brothers and five other men set off an explosion in the apartment killing themselves and one police officer. One of the dead was Serhane ben Abdelmajid Fakhet, "The Tunisian," whom police believe was the ringleader of the bombings.

In the London bombings of July 7, 2005, a series of coordinated suicide attacks on the Underground and on a crowded bus killed 56, including the bombers, and injured more than 700 (BBC News, Saturday, July 9, 2005). The four bombers, two of whom left suicide videotapes, were all British and had been living in Leeds where they were said to have attracted no more than cursory interest from the authorities. Their attacks were coordinated by the oldest of them, 30-year-old Mohammad Sidique Khan, who had been in Pakistan and was said to have trained there. While still in a state of high alert, 24 hours after the bombing, armed police shot and killed a harmless Brazilian who had been wrongly identified as a suspect.

Iraq—War or Civil War?

The war in Afghanistan was still in progress when the Bush administration turned its attention to Iraq. The Baathist regime of Saddam Hussein was a secular regime and had no sympathy with the Islamists, but it had survived its defeat by the US-led coalition in the first Gulf War, which was authorized by the United Nations only to drive its troops out of Kuwait. Ironically, the only representatives of al-Qaeda in the country seem to have been in the one area that Saddam Hussein did not control, in the "no-fly" zone adjoining Iran. However, this did not protect him from the imperial ambitions of some of Bush's closest advisers. The pretext they advanced for attacking Iraq was that Saddam Hussein was manufacturing weapons of mass destruction; an allegation which, if true, would lay him open to attack on the grounds that he constituted a threat to world peace—unlike, of course, the governments of the existing nuclear powers.

Originally, there was no Iraqi insurgency. The US-led coalition attack on Iraq went well from a military point of view. Saddam Hussein's government collapsed and US forces, meeting very little resistance, advanced far beyond the limits of what would otherwise have been thought safe, and got away with it. This was later to be a problem when Shi'a insurgents were able to impede imports into the Southern port of Basra, but this area had been left to the British and they could be blamed for everything that went on there. Responsibility for public order elsewhere by default fell to the United States. The problem was that the United States was not prepared for military government, and infighting in Washington ensured that any information that the US government did have about Iraq (and specifically the views of the State Department, the only agency really well qualified to give advice) was ignored. Nor were any weapons of mass destruction found.

An early casualty was any idea that Iraq should be returned to self-government. Instead, in short order a series of serious mistakes were made.

It was assumed that none of the existing agencies of government (except for the Oil Ministry) was of any importance. The result was that unguarded building after building was looted or set on fire and virtually all the working records of government lost. Meanwhile the provisional military government was set up in one of Saddam Hussein's former palaces, in the Green Zone, a compound walled off from any contact with reality, while the US military dumped a major airbase on the historic archaeological site of Babylon and allowed the National Museum to be looted and pillaged.

At least there had been a clear prior decision to disband Saddam Hussein's Revolutionary Guard as soon as victory had been achieved. However, when it was discovered that virtually all the members of the regular army had gone home, leaving their barracks to be looted, instead of recalling them, the decision was taken in the "Emerald City," the so-called Green Zone, summarily to disband the Army. Hence, it was soon found that any regular troops who might have been prepared to serve the new Iraq felt insulted and many of them joined the insurgency which was already brewing (Chandrasekaran 2007, 43–7).

The police had also fled, and the few who were willing to return soon though better of it when they found they were heavily outgunned by the armed criminal syndicates that had sprung up in their absence. Asked for over 5,000 police to restore order, President Bush sent only one. He was a product of the NYPD and already celebrated for his bravery following "9/11." But his solution to the police problem was simply to choose an Iraqi colleague and leave him to choose whoever he liked. He then left for the United States, with no intention of returning (Chandrasekaran 2007, 92–101).

The first provisional military governor, retired General Jay Garner, had at least been chosen because of his knowledge of Iraq. But he was not shown any of the detailed plans made for the future and within a month he was fired, and replaced by a civilian recommended by US Vice President Dick Cheney. This was L. Paul (Jerry) Bremer III, a diplomat with no previous experience of the country. As head of the new Coalition Provisional Administration (CPA) he interpreted his post as a grant of authority to exercise viceregal powers. The most urgent problems that faced him was getting the power stations running again and repairing the national grid, as for all the rest of the country outside the Green Zone a reasonably reliable electricity supply was something that they had enjoyed under Saddam Hussein. Unfortunately, this was not a problem that could be solved by simply issuing orders. Under Saddam, the main power station had in fact been neglected and it was only possible to generate about two-thirds of the amount needed by running what was left of the generators into the ground.

Because of the insurgency, it proved impossible to do anything like enough work to restore the oil industry, as some had hoped, for the restoration of the rest of the economy.

Before the war, most manufacturing enterprises had been state owned. If their records had not been destroyed in the first orgy of looting they would undoubtedly have shown that very few of them had ever made anything like a profit. Yet the free-market ideologues sent over by the US administration had a simple solution to the task of getting them back into production, namely wholesale privatization. The problem was that few of them could be shown to have a value, so investors were interested only in government contracts and without investment, there was no money to keep the employees in work and prevent them joining the ranks of the disaffected. Money that could have been used to help restore Iraq's infrastructure was wasted in the costs of administration and inadequate control of expenditure. It was estimated that one US firm alone, Halliburton, had been awarded $19.3 billion in single-source contracts (Stiglitz and Bilmes 2008, 11–15).

Meanwhile, there was pressure from Washington to form an Iraqi government to which the coalition could hand over authority. The problem was that democratic elections would undoubtedly result in a substantial majority for the Shi'a, but their spiritual leader, Grand Ayatollah Sayyid Ali al-Husayni al-Sistani, was adamant that nothing else was acceptable. The situation was not helped that in his eagerness to meet Washington's demand for a quick answer, Jerry Bremer chose to hold the elections under the US-style system of single member constituencies. So the elections held in January 2005, which were largely boycotted by Sunni Iraqis, produced a government dominated by Kurds and Shi'a, headed by the Kurd Jalal Talibani, as president, and a Shi'a, Nouri al-Maliki, his party's second choice, as prime minister.

The new government took over from the CPSA in May, but was very unstable from the outset. In fact, by September 2005 an undeclared war was in full swing between the Shi'ite majority and the Sunni minority who had held power under Saddam. The steady loss of life, estimated at between 50 and a 100 dead a day, was punctuated by various spectacular reprisals, reaching a low point with the Sunni bombing of the golden-domed Al-Askari Mosque in Samarra on February 22, 2006, which devastated a site held particularly holy by Shi'ites. The United States was caught in a dilemma, foreseeing serious consequences if it were seen to lean too much toward either side (Patten 2007). Meanwhile the Iraqi government, with its weak armed forces and inadequately organized police, was quite unable to cope with the problem of identifying and neutralizing the insurgents.

Withdrawal

US forces, therefore, remained deployed and a gradual improvement did take place. British forces were withdrawn from Basra in September 2007 to a base outside the city (*New York Times*, September 3, 2007). At the beginning of 2008, however, an upsurge in violence ended hope of further troop withdrawals for the time being and it was not until June 2009 that US troops were also withdrawn from the cities, but not from the country, in preparation for the forthcoming election. From then on however, although the overall level of violence fell compared with 2008, bombers successfully targeted the finance and foreign ministries in August and other ministries in late October, responsibility being claimed by Islamic State in Iraq, a Sunni group affiliated to al-Qaeda (Tisdall 2009). Meanwhile, Iraqi politicians, as might have been predicted, again failed to agree on an electoral system, and with the prospect that elections might be delayed, the withdrawal of US forces looked as far away as ever.

As long as a country relies on foreign forces to maintain security, there will always be a debate as to whether those forces are the cause of insurgency or necessary to its solution. In a sense of course both are true. Certainly with hindsight, the ideal—and perhaps the only—moment to withdraw from Afghanistan came early on, after the fall of the Taliban and the choice of a new government by the *loya jirga*, the accepted Afghan way of doing things. The attempt in 2009 to hold a US-style election there has foundered on President Karzai's belief in his own importance leading to widespread ballot rigging and the potential fiasco of a second round held in wintertime. The presence of NATO forces in Afghanistan has undoubtedly been an important factor in the destabilization of neighboring Pakistan, a reminder of the importance in counterinsurgency as in all else of the law of unintended consequences.

Bibliography

Adorno, T.W., Frenkel Brunswik, Else, Levinson, Daniel J., and Sanford, R. Nevitt (1964), *The Authoritarian Personality*, New York, John Wiley.

Ambursley, Fitzroy and Dunkerley, James (1984), *Grenada – Whose Freedom?*, London, Latin American Bureau.

Anderson (2007), *The Economist*, April 9, 1988.

Anderson, Perry (2007), *London Review of Books*, 29, No. 2, January 25, 2007.

Anon, "Lebanon: The Terrible Tally of Death", *Time*, Monday, March 23, 1992 (online, accessed September 26, 2009).

Arendt, Hannah (1969), "Reflections on Violence", reprinted from *New York Review of Books*, February 27, 1969. online: www.cooperativeindividualism.org/arendt-hanna_reflections-on-violence.html accessed January 4, 2010.

Arjomand, S.A. (1988), *The Turban for the Crown: the Islamic Revolution in Iran*, New York, Oxford University Press.

Armstrong, David (1993), *Revolution and World Order: the Revolutionary State in International Society*, Oxford, Clarendon Press.

Arnell, Lars and Nygren, Birgitta (1980), *The Developing Countries and the World Economic Order*, London, Frances Pinter and Methuen.

Ascham, Anthony (1649), *Of the Confusions and Revolutions of Governments, 1649. A Facsimile Reproduction* (sic), New York, Delmar, Scholars Facsimiles and Reprints, 1975.

Ash, Timothy Garton (1990), *The Magic Lantern: The Revolution of '89 Witnessed in Warsaw, Budapest, Berlin, and Prague*, Random House. Paperback reprint Vintage Books, USA, 1993.

Babbington, Anthony (1991), *Military Intervention in Britain; From the Gordon Riots to the Gibraltar Incident*, London, Routledge.

BBC News, Wednesday, December 24, 2008.

BBC News, "Honduran leader forced into exile", Sunday, June 28, 2009.

Bell, J. Bowyer (1976), *On Revolt; Strategies of National Liberation*, Cambridge, MA, Harvard University Press.

Beloff, Nora and Bruno (1997), *Yugoslavia: An Avoidable War*, London, New European Publications.

Billington, James H. (1980), *Fire in the Minds of Men; Origins of the Revolutionary Faith*, New York, Basic Books.

Black, Cyril E. and Thornton, Thomas P. (1964), *Communism and Revolution, the Strategic Uses of Political Violence*, Princeton, NJ, Princeton University Press.

Bourne, Richard (2008), *Lula of Brazil: the Story so far*, London, Zed Books.

Brier, Alan (1982), "Revolution as a form of political succession", unpublished paper for Planning Session on Political Succession, ECPR Joint Sessions of Workshops, Freiburg, 1982.

Brier, Alan and Calvert, Peter (1975), "Revolution in the 1960s", *Political Studies*, 32, No. 1, March 1975, pp. 1–11.

Brinton, Crane (1952), *The Anatomy of Revolution*, New York, Vintage Books.

Bruce Lockhart, Robert (1950), *Memoirs of a British Agent: Being an Account of the Author's Early Life in many Lands and of his Official Mission to Moscow in 1918*, Harmondsworth, Penguin Books.

Bull, Hedley and Watson, A. eds (1984), *The Expansion of International Society*, Oxford, Oxford University Press.

Burnett, John S. (2003), *Dangerous Waters, Modern Piracy and Terror on the High Seas*, New York, Dutton, Plume.

Calvert, Peter (1967), "Revolution, the Politics of Violence", *Political Studies*, 15, No. 1, February 1967, p. 1.

Calvert, Peter (1970a), *Revolution* (Key Concepts in Political Science), London, Pall Mall and Macmillan.

Calvert, Peter (1970b), *A Study of Revolution*, Oxford, Clarendon Press.

Calvert, Peter (1976), "On attaining sovereignty", in Anthony Smith (ed.), *Nationalist Movements*, London, Macmillan, pp. 134–49.

Calvert, Peter (1982), *The Falklands Crisis: the Rights and the Wrongs*, London, Frances Pinter.

Calvert, Peter (1986), "Terror and the theory of revolution", in Noel O'Sullivan (ed.), *Terrorism, Ideology and Revolution; the Origins of Modern Political Violence*, Brighton, Wheatsheaf, pp. 27–45.

Calvert, Peter (2008), "Challenges to security in central America and the Caribbean", in Peter Calvert (ed.), *The Central American Security System: North-South or East-West?* Cambridge, Cambridge University Press, pp. 45–59.

Cammack, Paul (1989), "Bringing the state back in?" *British Journal of Political Science*, 19, No. 2, April 1989, pp. 261–90.

Canetti, Elias (1973), *Crowds and Power*, Harmondsworth, Penguin Books.

Cardoso, Fernando Henrique and Faletto, Enzo (1979), *Dependency and Development in Latin America*, Berkeley, CA, University of California Press.

Carr, Raymond (1966), *Spain 1808–1939*, Oxford, Clarendon Press.

Chakotin, Serge (1940), *The Rape of the Masses: the Psychology of Totalitarian Political Propaganda*, London, Routledge.

Chalk, Peter (1998), *Contemporary Maritime Piracy in Southeast Asia*, Studies in Conflict & Terrorism, January–March 1998, Vol. 21, Issue 1, p. 87, 26p, 1 chart; (AN 286864).eResource.

Chan, Stephen and Williams, Andrew J., eds. (1994), *Renegade States: the Evolution of Revolutionary Foreign Policy*, Manchester, Manchester University Press.

Chandrasekaran, Rajiv (2007), *Imperial Life in the Emerald City: Inside Baghdad's Green Zone*, London, Bloomsbury.

Christopher, Warren, et al. (1985), *American Hostages in Iran: the Conduct of a Crisis*, New Haven, CT, Yale University Press.

Cigar, Norman (1995), *Genocide in Bosnia: The Politics of Ethnic Cleansing*, CollegeStation, TX, Texas A&M University Press.

Clarke, Simon (2006), *The Development of Capitalism in Russia*, London, Routledge.

Clutterbuck, Richard (1973), *Protest and the Urban Guerilla*, London, Cassell.

Cohn, Gary and Thompson, Ginger (1995), "When a wave of torture and murder staggered a small US ally, truth was a casualty", *The Baltimore Sun*, June 11, 1995, accessed October 23, 2009.

Colburn, Forrest D. (1994), *The Vogue of Revolution in Poor Countries*, Princeton, NJ, Princeton University Press.

Collier, Paul and Hoeffler, Anke (2001), "Greed and Grievance in Civil War", World Bank Working Paper, *Oxford Economic Papers*, 56, No. 4, 2004, pp. 563–95.

Collier, Paul, Hoeffler, Anke, and Sambanis, Nicholas (2005), "The Collier-Hoeffler Model of Civil War Onset and the Case Study Project Research Design", in Collier, Paul and Sambanis, Nicholas (eds.), *Understanding Civil Wars: Evidence and Analysis*, Volume 1: Africa, The World Bank, 2005, p. 13.

Craig, Michael (1996), unpublished Ph.D. dissertation, University of Keele.

Cramer, Christopher (2006), *Civil War Is Not a Stupid Thing: Accounting for Violence in Developing Countries*, London : Hurst & Co.

Crozier, Brian (1960), *The Rebels: A Study of Post-War Insurrections*. London, Chatto & Windus.

Dahrendorf, Ralf (1961), "Über einige Probleme der sociologistischen Theorie der Revolution", *Archives Europeennes de Sociologie*, 2, No. 1, 1961, 153.

David, Steven R. (1987), *Third World coups d'état and international security*, Baltimore, MD, Johns Hopkins University Press.

Davies, James C. (1962), "Toward a Theory of Revolution", *American Sociological Review*, 43, No. 1, February 1962, pp. 5–19.

Dawisha, A.I. (1980), *Syria and the Lebanese Crisis*, Basingstoke, Palgrave Macmillan.

Debray, Regis (1965), "Latin America the Long March", *New Left Review*, 33, September–October 1965, p. 17.

Debray, Regis (1969), *Revolution in the Revolution?*, London, Penguin Books.

DeFronzo, James (2007), *Revolutions and Revolutionary Movements*, Boulder, CO, Westview Press, 3rd edn.

Desai, Raj and Eckstein, Harry (1990), "Insurgency: the Transformation of Peasant Rebellion", *World Politics*, 42, No. 4, July, pp. 441–66.

Diederich, Bernard (1978), *Trujillo the Death of the Goat*, London, Bodley Head.

Drummond, S.H. (1979), "British Involvement in Indonesia, 1945–1950", unpublished Ph.D. dissertation, University of Southampton.

Dunn, John (1989), *Modern Revolutions: an Introduction to the Analysis of a Political Phenomenon*, Cambridge, Cambridge University Press, 2nd edn.

Durgan, Andrew (2007), *The Spanish Civil War*, Basingstoke; New York: Palgrave Macmillan, 2007.

Durkheim, Émile (1965), *The Division of Labor in Society*, trs. George Simpson, New York, The Free Press.

Eckstein, Harry (ed.) (1964), *Internal War*, New York, The Free Press.

Eisenstadt, S.N. (1978), *Revolution and the Transformation of Societies*, New York, The Free Press.

Ellner, Steve (1988), *Venezuela's Movimiento al Socialismo: from Guerrilla Defeat to Innovative Politics*, Durham, NC, Duke University Press.

English, Richard (2009), *Terrorism: How to Respond*, Oxford, Oxford University Press.

Erikson, Erik (1968), *Identity: Youth and Crisis*, New York, W.W. Norton.

Eysenck, H.J. (1963), *The Psychology of Politics*, London, Routledge.

Falk, R.A. (1969), "World revolution and international order", in C.J. Friedrich (ed.), *Revolution*, New York, pp. 154–76.

Fals Borda, Orlando (1965), "Violence and the break-up of tradition in Colombia", in Claudio Veliz (ed.), *Obstacles to Change in Latin America*, New York, Oxford University Press.

Farhi, Farideh (1988), "State Disintegration and Urban-Based Revolutionary Crisis: A Comparative Analysis of Iran and Nicaragua", *Comparative Political Studies*, 21, No. 2, July, pp. 231–56.

Fearon, James and Laitin, David (2003), "Ethnicity, Insurgency, and Civil War", *American Political Science Review*, 97, pp. 75–90.

Feinberg, Richard E. (1983), *The Intemperate Zone; The Third World Challenge to U.S Foreign Policy*, New York, W.W. Norton.

Feit, Edward (1973), *Armed Bureaucrats*, Boston, MA, Houghton Mifflin.

Finer, Samuel E. (1962), *The Man on Horseback*, London, Pall Mall.

Foran, John and Goodwin, Jeff (1993), "Revolutionary Outcomes in Iran and Nicaragua: Coalition Fragmentation, War, and the Limits of Social Transformation", *Theory and Society*, 22, No. 2, April, pp. 209–74.

Foran, John (ed.) (1997), *Theorizing Revolutions*, London, Routledge.

Foran, John (2005), *Taking Power: On the Origins of Third World Revolutions*, Cambridge, Cambridge University Press.

Frank, André Gunder (1969), *Latin America; Underdevelopment or Revolution*, New York, Monthly Review Press.

Frank, André Gunder (1978), *Dependent Accumulation and Underdevelopment*, London, Macmillan.

Frankel, Joseph (1979), *International Relations in a Changing World*, Oxford, Oxford University Press.

Freedman, Lawrence and Karsh, Efraim (1993), *The Gulf Conflict*, London, Faber & Faber.

Freeman, Michael (1983), "Revolution as a Subject of Science", in Noel O'Sullivan (ed.), *Revolutionary Theory and Political Reality*, Brighton, Wheatsheaf, pp. 23–40.

Fromm, Erich (1960), *The Fear of Freedom*, London, Routledge.

Gamson, William A. (1975), *The Strategy of Social Protest*, Homewood, IL, The Dorsey Press.

García Márquez, Gabriel (1978), *One Hundred Years of Solitude*, London, Pan Books.

Giap, Vo Nguyen (1965), *People's War, People's Army*, New York, Praeger.

Gibb, C.A. (ed.) (1969), *Leadership*, Harmondsworth, Penguin Books.

Gilbert, D. (1988), *Sandinistas: the Party and the Revolution*, New York, Basin Blackwell.

Gleijeses, Piero (1991), *Shattered Hope: the Guatemalan Revolution and the United States, 1944–1954*, Princeton, NJ, Princeton University Press.

Goldenberg, Boris (1965), *The Cuban Revolution and Latin America* London, Allen & Unwin.

Goldstone, Jack A. (1980), "Theories of Revolution: the Third Generation", *World Politics*, 32, No. 3, pp. 425–53.

Goldstone, Jack A. (1991), Revolution and Rebellion in the Early Modern World, Berkeley, CA, University of California Press.

González, Luis J. and Sanchez Salazar, Gustavo A. (1969), *The Great Rebel; Che Guevara in Bolivia*, New York, Grove Press.

Gonzalez, Mike (1990), *Nicaragua: What Went Wrong?* London, Bookmarks Publications.

Goodspeed, D.J. (1962), *The Conspirators; A Study of the Coup d État*, London, Macmillan.

Goodwin, Jeff and Skocpol, Theda (1989), "Explaining Revolutions in the Contemporary Third World", *Politics and Society*, 17, No. 4, December, pp. 489–509.

Goodwin, Jeff (2008), *No Other Way Out: States and Revolutionary Movements, 1945–1991*, Cambridge, Cambridge University Press, Cambridge Studies in Comparative Politics.

Gott, Richard (1970), *Guerrilla Movements in Latin America*, London, Nelson.

Greene, Thomas H. (1990), *Comparative Revolutionary Movements: Search for Theiry and Justice*, Englewood Cliffs, NJ, Prentice-Hall, 3rd edn.

Griffin, Michael (2001), *Reaping the Whirlwind; the Taliban Movement in Afghanistan*, London, Pluto Press.

Gross, Feliks (1958), *The Seizure of Political Power in a Century of Revolutions*, New York, Philosophical Library.

Guevara, Ernesto Che (1967), *Guerrilla Warfare*, New York and London, Monthly Review Press.

Guevara, Ernesto Che (1968a), *The Complete Bolivian Diaries of Che Guevara and Other Captured Documents*, ed. and intro. Daniel James, New York, Stein & Day.

Guevara, Ernesto Che (1968b), *Reminiscences of the Cuban Revolutionary War*, trs. Victoria Ortiz, London, Allen & Unwin and Monthly Review Press.

Gurr, Ted Robert (1970), *Why Men Rebel*, Princeton, NJ, Princeton University Press.

Haas, Ernst B. (1965), *Beyond the Nation State: Functionalism and International Organization*, Stanford, CA, Stanford University Press.

Haley, P.E. (1982), *Congress and the Fall of South Vietnam and Cambodia*, New Jersey, Fairleigh Dickinson University Press.

Hall, J.A. and Ikenberry, G.J. (1989), *The State*, Milton Keynes, Open University Press.

Hall, Stuart and Jefferson, Tony (eds.) (1977), *Resistance Through Rituals; Youth Subcultures in Postwar Britain*, London, Hutchinson.

Halliday, Fred (1979), *Iran: Dictatorship and Development*, Harmondsworth, Penguin.

Halliday, Fred (1999), *Revolution and World Politics; The Rise of the Sixth Great Power*, Basingstoke, Macmillan, 1999.

Halliday, Fred (2006), "Why Do Revolutions Happen?", in: Swain, Harriet (ed.), *The Big Questions in History*, London, Vintage, pp. 71–84.

Harris, Richard L. (1970), *Death of a Revolutionary; Che Guevara's Last Mission*, New York, W.W. Norton.

Hatto, Arthur (1949), "Revolution: an Enquiry into the Usefulness of an Historical Term", *Mind*, 58, October, p. 495.

Heiberg, Marianne, O'Leary, Brendan, and Tirman, John (2007), *Terror, Insurgency, and the State: Ending Protracted Conflicts*, Philadelphia, PA, University of Pennsylvania Press.

Held, David (1989), *Political Theory and the Modern State*, Cambridge, Polity Press.

Henderson, Errol A. and Singer, J. David (2000), "Civil War in the Post-Colonial World, 1946–92", *The Journal of Peace Research*, May 2000, pp. 275–99.

Herz, J. (1959), *International Politics in the Nuclear Age*, New York, Columbia University Press.

Hibbert, Christopher (1958), *King Mob: the Story of Lord George Gordon and the Riots of 1780*, London, Longmans.

Hironaka, Ann (2005), *Neverending Wars: The International Community, Weak States, and the Perpetuation of Civil War*, Cambridge, MA, Harvard University Press, p. 3.

Hobsbawm, E.J. (1972), *Bandits*, Harmondsworth, Penguin Books.

Hobson, John Atkinson (1968), *Imperialism: a Study*, London, Allen & Unwin.

Hoffer, Eric (1951), *The True Believer, Thoughts on the Nature of Mass Movements*, New York, Harper.

Holsti, K.J. (1967), *International Politics, a Framework for Analysis*, Englewood Cliffs, NJ, Prentice-Hall.

Howson, Gerald (1998), *Arms for Spain: the Untold Story of the Spanish Civil War*, New York, St Martin's Press.

Huntington, Samuel P. (1968), *Political Order in Changing Societies*, New Haven, CT, Yale University Press.

Hyams, Edward (1975), *Terrorists and Terrorism*, London, Dent.

Isikoff, Michael and Hosenball, Mark (2009), "War on Words: Why Obama May Be Abandoning Bush's Favorite Phrase", *Newsweek*, February 4, 2009, accessed October 19, 2009.

Israel Academy of Sciences and Humanities (1984), *Totalitarian Democracy and After*, Jerusalem, The Hebrew University.

James, William (1907), *Pragmatism*, London Longmans.

Johnson, Chalmers (1964), *Revolution and the Social System*, Stanford, CA, The Hoover Institution on War, Revolution and Peace.

Johnson, Haynes (1965), *The Bay of Pigs: the Invasion of Cuba by Brigade 2506*, London, Hutchinson.

Jung, Carl Gustav (1933), *Psychology of the Unconscious: a Study of the Transformations and Symbolisms of the Libido*, London, Kegan Paul.

Kaldor, Mary (2001), *New and Old Wars. Organized Violence in a Global Era*, Cambridge, Cambridge University Press.

Kalyvas, Stathis (2001), "'New' and 'Old' Civil Wars: A Valid Distinction?", *World Politics*, 54, No. 1, 2001, pp. 99–118.

Kalyvas, Stathis (2006), *The Logic of Violence in Civil War*, Cambridge, Cambridge University Press, Cambridge Studies in Comparative Politics.

Kant, Immanuel (2007), *Perpetual Peace*, London, Filiquarian Publishing.

Katz, Mark N. (ed.) (1990), *The USSR and Marxist Revolutions in the Third World*, Cambridge, Woodrow Wilson Center for Scholar and Cambridge University Press.

Katz, Mark (ed.) (2000), *Revolution: International Dimensions*, Moscow, CQ Press.

Kirkham, James F., Levy, Sheldon G., and Crotty, William (1970), *Assassination and Political Violence*, New York, New York Times Books.

Kissane, Bill (2007), *The Politics of the Irish Civil War*, Oxford, Oxford University Press.

Klaits, Joseph and Haltzel, Michael H. (eds.) (1994), *The Global Ramifications of the French Revolution*, Cambridge, Cambridge University Press.

Kumar, Krishan (1992), "The Revolutions of 1989: Socialism, Capitalism, and Democracy", *Theory and Society*, 21, No. 3, June, pp. 309–56.

Labrousse, Alain (1970), *The Tupamaros*, Harmondsworth, Penguin Books.

La Feber, Walter (1993), *Inevitable Revolutions: the United States in Central America*, New York, W.W. Norton, 2nd edn.

Lane, David (2000–1), "What Kind of Capitalism for Russia? A Comparative Analysis", *Communist and Post-Communist Studies*, 33, No. 4, December 2000, pp. 485–504 and volume 34, No. 1, March 2001, pp. 129–31.

Lasswell, Harold D. (1960), *Psychopathology and Politics*, New York, Viking Press.

Leiden, Carl and Schmitt, Karl M. (1968), *The Politics of Violence; Revolution in the Modern World*, Englewood Cliffs, NJ, Prentice-Hall.

Lenin, Vladimir Ilyich (1967), *Selected Works*, Moscow, Foreign Languages Publishing House, 3 vols.

Lewin, K., Lippitt, R., and White, R. (1939), "Patterns of Aggressive Behaviour in Experimentally-Created 'Social Climates'", *Journal of Social Psychology*, 10, pp. 271–99.

Little, Richard (1975), *Intervention; External Involvement in Civil Wars*, London, Martin Robertson.

Lorenz, Konrad (1966), *On Aggression*, London, Methuen.

Luttwak, Edward (1968), *Coup d'État, a Practical Handbook*, London, Allen Lane, The Penguin Press.

McClelland, J.S. (1989), *The Crowd and the Mob: from Plato to Canetti*, London, Unwin Hyman.

McClintock, Cynthia (1984), "Why Peasants Rebel: the Case of Peru's Sendero Luminoso", *World Politics*, 37, October 1984, pp. 48–84.

McDonald, Joan (1965), *Rousseau and the French Revolution, 1762–1791*, London, University of London, The Athlone Press.

McMichael, R. Daniel and Paulus, John D. (eds.) (1983), *Western Hemisphere Stability – the Latin American Connection*, Pittsburgh, World Affairs Council of Pittsburgh 19th World Affairs Forum.

Machiavelli, Niccolo (1950), *The Prince and The Discourses*, New York, Random House.

Mack, Andrew (1975), "Why Big Nations Lose Small Wars: the Politics of Asymmetric Conflict", *World Politics*, 27, No. 2, January 1975, pp. 175–200.

Maisonnave, Fabiano (2009), "Manuel Zelaya Undergoes Strange Siege Inside Brazilian Embassy", *The Guardian*, Monday, October 26, 2009.

Malaparte, Curzio (1932), *Coup d'Etat the Technique of Revolution*, trs. Sylvia Saunders, New York, E.P. Dutton.

Maley, William (1998), *Fundamentalism Reborn? Afghanistan and the Taliban*, London: C. Hurst & Co.

Marighela, Carlos (1971), *For the Liberation of Brazil*, Harmondsworth, Penguin Books.

Marks, John and Beliaev, Igor (eds.) (1991), *Common Ground on Terrorism: Soviet-American Cooperation against the Politics of Terror*, New York: W.W. Norton.

Martí, Jose (1968), *The America of José Martí: Selected Writings*, trs. Juan de Onis, New York, Funk & Wagnalls.

Martin, Everett Dean (1920), *The Behavior of Crowds; a Psychological Study*, New York and London, Putnam.

Marx, Karl and Engels, Frederick (1962), *Selected Works*, Moscow, Foreign Languages Publishing House, 2 vols.

Meisel, James (1965), *Pareto and Mosca*, Englewood Cliffs, NJ, Prentice-Hall.

Mercier Vega, Luis (1969), *Guerrillas in Latin America; the Techniques of the Counter-State*, London, Pall Mall.

Meusel, Alfred, "Revolution and Counter-Revolution", *Encyclopedia of the Social Sciences*, 13, New York, Macmillan, 1934, pp. 367–76.

Michels, Robert (1959), *Political Parties: a Sociological Study of the Oligarchical Tendencies of Modern Democracy*, New York, Dover Publications.

Miller, Norman and Aya, Roderick (eds.) (1971), *National Liberation: Revolution in the Third World*, New York, The Free Press.

Minogue, Kenneth (1969), *Nationalism*, London, Methuen.

Moore, Barrington, Jr. (1969), *Social Origins of Dictatorship and Democracy; Lord and Peasant in the Making of the Modern World*, London, Peregrine Books.

Morris, Desmond (1969), *The Naked Ape*, New York, Dell.

Nasution, Abdul Haris (1965), *Fundamentals of Guerrilla Warfare*, facsimile edn., intro. Otto Heilbrunner, New York, Praeger.

Neuberg, A. (1970), *Armed Insurrection*, London, NLB.

Nkrumah, Kwame (1965), *Neocolonialism, the Last State of Imperialism*, New York, International Publishers.

O'Ballance Edgar (1998), *Civil War in Lebanon, 1975–92*, Basingstoke, Palgrave Macmilllan.

O'Donnell, Guillermo (1988), *Bureaucratic Authoritarianism: Argentina, 1966–1973, in Comparative Perspective*, Berkeley and Los Angeles, CA, University of California Press.

O'Kane, Rosemary (1991), *The Revolutionary Reign of Terror*, London, Edward Elgar.

Omissi, David E. (1990), "British Air Power and Colonial Control in Iraq, 1920–1925", (1990), reprinted by Global Policy Forum. online: www.globalpolicy.org/component/content/article/169/36386.html accessed October 8, 2009.

Oppenheimer, Martin (1970), *Urban Guerrilla*, Harmondsworth, Penguin Books.

Osanka, Franklin Mark (ed.) (1962), *Modern Guerrilla Warfare: Fighting Communist Guerrilla Movements 1941-1961*, New York, The Free Press.

O'Shaughnessy, Hugh (1984), *Grenada: Revolution, Invasion and Aftermath*, London, Sherer Books with *The Observer*.

Palmer, David Scott (1992), *Shining Path of Peru*, London, Hurst and Co.

Paret, Peter and Shy, John W. (1962), *Guerrillas in the 1960s*, New York, Praeger, rev. edn.

Patten, David A. (2007), "Is Iraq in a Civil War?", *Middle East Quarterly*, 14, No. 3, Summer 2007, pp. 27–32.

Pearce, Jenny (1981), *Under the Eagle: U.S. Intervention in Central America*, London, Latin American Bureau.

Pettee, George Sylvester (1938), *The Process of Revolution*, New York, Harper & Brothers.

Picard, Elizabeth (2002), *Lebanon: A Shattered Country: Myths and Realities of the Wars in Lebanon*, rev. edn.

Pustay, John W. (1965), *Counterinsurgency Warfare*, New York, The Free Press.

Putney, Snell and Putney, Gail J. (1964), *The Adjusted American; Normal Neuroses in the Individual and Society*, New York, Harper & Row.

Rabe, Stephen G. (1988), *Eisenhower and Latin America: the Foreign Policy of Anticommunism*, Chapel Hill, NC, University of North Carolina Press.

Ramazani, R.K. (1986), *Revolutionary Iran: Challenge and Response in the Middle East*, Baltimore, MD, The Johns Hopkins University Press.

Rieff, David (1996), *Slaughterhouse: Bosnia and the Failure of the West*, New York, Simon and Schuster.

Richardson, Lewis (1960), *Statistics of Deadly Quarrels*, London, Stevens & Sons.

Rosenau, James (ed.) (1964), *International Aspects of Civil Strife*, Princeton, NJ, Princeton University Press.

Rossett, P. and Vandermeer, J. (eds.) (1986), *Nicaragua: Unfinished Revolution*, New York, Grove Press.

Royal Engineers Museum (2009). Online: www.remuseum.org.uk/corpshistory/rem_corps_part8.htm#equip accessed October 8, 2009.

Rubin, Barry (ed.) (1989), *The Politics of Terrorism: Terror as a State and Revolutionary Strategy*, Washington, DC, Johns Hopkins Foreign Policy Institute, School of Advanced International Studies.

Rudé, George (1964), *The Crowd in History: A Study of Popular Disturbances in France and England 1730-1848*, New York, John Wiley.

Russett, Bruce M. (1964), *World Handbook of Political and Social Indicators*, New Haven, CT, Yale University Press.

Sandbrook, Dominic (2009), "As powerful in death as in life", *The Observer*, Sunday, February 15, 2009.

Sansom, Robert L. (1970), *The Economics of Insurgency in the Mekong Delta of Vietnam*, Cambridge, MA, The MIT Press.

Satow, Sir Ernest (1957), *A Guide to Diplomatic Practice*, London, Longmans.

Schram, Stuart R. (ed.) (1963), *The Political Thought of Mao Tse-tung*, New York, Praeger.

Scurr, Ruth (2006), *Fatal Purity: Robespierre and the French Revolution*, London, Metropolitan Books.

Searle, Chris (1983), *Grenada, the Struggle against Destabilization*, London, Writers and Readers.

Sebestyen, Victor (2009), *Revolution 1989: The Fall of the Soviet Empire*. London, Weidenfeld & Nicolson.

Seton-Watson, Hugh (1977), *Nations and States: an Inquiry into the Origins of Nations and the Politics of Nationalism*, London, Methuen.

Shafer, D. Michael (1988a), *Deadly Paradigms: the Failure of U.S. Counterinsurgency Policy*, Princeton, NJ, Princeton University Press.

Shafer, D. Michael (1988b), "The unlearned lessons of counterinsurgency", *Political Science Quarterly*, 103, No. 1, pp. 57–80.

Shay, Shaul (2002), *The Endless Jihad: the Mujahidin, the Taliban and Bin Laden*. Herzliya, Israel: International Policy Institute for Counter-Terrorism.

Shin, Doll Chull (1994), "On the Third Wave of Democratization: a Synthesis and Evaluation of Recent Theory and Research", *World Politics*, 47, October, pp. 135–70.

Short, Anthony (1974), *The Communist Insurrection in Malaya 1948–1960*, London, Frederick Miller.

Shugart, Matthew Soberg (1987), "States, Revolutionary Conflict and Democracy: El Salvador and Nicaragua in Comparative Perspective", *Government and Opposition*, 22, No. 1, pp. 13–32.

Shultz, Richard H., Ra'anan, Uri, Pfaltzgraff, Robert A., Jr., Olson, William J., and Lukes, Igor (1988), *Guerrilla Warfare and Counter-Insurgency: U.S. Soviet Policy in the Third World*, Lexington, MA, Lexington Books.

Skocpol, Theda (1979), *States and Social Revolutions: a Comparative Analysis of France, Russia and China*, Cambridge, Cambridge University Press.

Skocpol, Theda (1982), "Rentier state and Shi'ia Islam in the Iranian Revolution", *Theory and Society*, 11, pp. 265–83.

Skocpol, Theda (1985), "Bringing the State Back in: Strategies of Analysis in Current Research", in Evans, P.B., Rueschmeyer, D., and Skocpol, T. (eds.), *Bringing the State Back in*, New York, Cambridge University Press, pp. 3–43.

Smelser, Neil J. (1962), *Theory of Collective Behavior*, London, Routledge.

Smith, Anthony D. (ed.) (1976), *Nationalist Movements*, London, Macmillan.

Smith, Dennis (1983), *Barrington Moore: Violence, Morality and Political Change*, London, Macmillan.

Sorel, Georges (1950), *Reflection on Violence*, trs. T. E. Hulme and J. Roth, intro. Edward A. Shils, Glencoe, IL, The Free Press.

Sorokin, Pitrim Aleksandrovitch (1937), *Social and Cultural Dynamics III; Fluctuation of Social Relationships, War and Revolution*, New York, American Book Company.

Spalding, R.J. (ed.) (1987), *The Political Economy of Revolutionary Nicaragua*, Boston, MA, Allen & Unwin Hyman.

Stanford Central America Action Network (1983), *Revolution in Central America*, Boulder, CO, Westview Press.

Stevens, Evelyn P. (1974), *Protest and Response in Mexico*, Cambridge, MA, The MIT Press.

Stiglitz, Joseph and Bilmes, Linda (2008), *The Three Trillion Dollar War; the True Cost of the Iraq Conflict*, London, Allen Lane.

Stone, Lawrence (1966), "Theories of Revolution", *World Politics*, 18, No. 2, January, pp. 159–76.

Sunday Times Insight Team (1975), *Insight on Portugal; the Year of the Captains*, London, Andre Deutsch.

Svec, Milan (1988), "The Prague Spring 20 Years Later", *Foreign Affairs*, 66, No. 5, Summer 1988, pp. 980–1001.

Taber, Robert (1965), *The War of the Flea: a Study of Guerrilla Warfare Theory and Practise*, New York, Lyle & Stuart.

Talmon, Jacob L. (1961), *The Origins of Totalitarian Democracy*, London, Mercury Books.

Thayer, Charles W. (1963), *Guerrilla*, London, Michael Joseph.

Thompson, James W. and Padover, Saul K. (1963), *Secret Diplomacy, Espionage and Cryptography 1500-1815*, New York, Ungar.

Thompson, Robert (1970), *Revolutionary War in World Strategy 1945–1969*, New York, Taplinger.

Tiger, Lionel (1969), *Men in Groups*, London, Nelson.

Tilly, Charles (1985), "War Making and State Making as Organised Crime", in Evans, P.B., Rueschmeyer, D., and Skocpol, T. (eds.), *Bringing the State Back in*, New York, Cambridge University Press, pp. 169–91.

Tisdall, Simon (2009), "Iraq's Last Chapter Is Still Not Written", *The Guardian*, Tuesday, October 27, 2009.

Tiwathia, Vijay (1987), *The Grenada War: Anatomy of a Low-Intensity Conflict*, New Delhi, Lancer International.

Trotsky, Leon (1966), *History of the Russian Revolution to Brest-Litovsk*, London, Gollancz.

Trotter, William Finlayson (1953), *Instincts of the Herd in Peace and War*, London, Oxford University Press.

'Truong Chinh', pseud. of Dang Xuan Khu (1963), *Primer for Revolt, the Communist Takeover in Viet-Nam: A Facsmile Edition of The August Revolution and The Resistance will Win*, intro. and notes by Bernard B. Fall, New York, Praeger.

Turner, J.C. (1991), *Social Influence*, Milton Keynes, Open University Press.

United States, Department of the Army (1990), Field Manual 100–20, *Military Operations in Low Intensity Conflict*, Washington, DC.

United States Institute of Peace (2002), *The Ethics of Armed Humanitarian Intervention*, Washington, DC, USIP, August 2002.

Vagts, Alfred (1959), *A History of Militarism, Civilian and Military*, London, Hollis & Carter.

Valenta, J. and V. (1985), "Sandinistas in Power", *Problems of Communism*, September–October, pp. 1–28.

Waldman, Amy (2001), "A Nation Challenged: the Law: No TV, No chess, No kites; Taliban's Code, from A to Z", *The New York Times*, Thursday, November 22, 2001, accessed October 13, 2009.

Walker, Thomas W. (ed.) (1987), *Reagan versus the Sandinistas: the Undeclared War on Nicaragua*, Boulder, CO, Westview.

Wallensteen, Peter and Sollenberg, Margareta (1995), "After the Cold War: Emerging Patterns of Armed Conflict 1989–94", *Journal of Peace Research*, 32, No. 3, August, pp. 345–60.

Walt, S.M. (1992), "Revolution and War", *World Politics*, 44, No. 3, April, pp. 321–68.

Walzer, Michael (1992), *Just and Unjust Wars. A Moral Argument with Historical Illustrations*, New York, Basic Books, 2nd edn.

Walzer, Michael (2002), "The Argument about Humanitarian Intervention", *Dissent*, Winter 2002, pp. 29–39, reproduced in polylog: Forum for Intercultural Philosophy 5 (2004). Online: www.them.polylog.org/5/awm-en.htm accessed October 19, 2009.

Weinstein, Jeremy M. (2006), *Inside Rebellion: the Politics of Insurgent Violence*. Cambridge, Cambridge University Press, Cambridge Studies in Comparative Politics.

Wickham-Crowley, Timothy P. (1989), "Understanding Failed Revolution in El Salvador: A Comparative Analysis of Regime Types and Social Structures", *Politics and Society*, 17, No. 4, December, pp. 511–37.

Wilkie, James W., and Wilkie, Edna (1970), *The Mexican Revolution: Federal Expenditure and Social Change since 1910*, Berkeley, CA, University of California Press.

Wilkinson, Paul (1974), *Political Terrorism*, London, Macmillan.

Wilkinson, Paul (1978), *Terrorism and the Liberal State*, London, Macmillan.

Wise, David and Ross, Thomas B. (1964), *The Invisible Government*, New York, Random House.

Wolf, Eric (1970), *Peasant Wars of the Twentieth Century*, New York, Harper & Row.

Wolfenstein, E. Victor (1967), *The Revolutionary Personality: Lenin, Trotsky, Gandhi*, Princeton, NJ, Princeton University Press.

Wolfgang, M. and Ferracuti, F. (1964), *The Subculture of Violence*, London, Tavistock Press.

Wright, Quincy (1965), *A Study of War*, Chicago, IL, University of Chicago Press, 2nd edn.

Yablonsky, Lewis (1962), *The Violent Gang*, New York, Macmillan.

Zartman, I. William (1966), *International Relations in the New Africa*, Englewood Cliffs, NJ, Prentice-Hall.

INDEX